The New Learning Commons Where
Learners Win!

Reinventing School Libraries and Computer Labs

2nd Edition

For further connections to this book, please visit:
https://sites.google.com/site/schoollearningcommons/

David V. Loertscher
Carol Koechlin
Sandi Zwaan
Esther Rosenfeld

Learning Commons Press
an Imprint of: Hi Willow Research & Publishing
2011

Content current through Oct. 10, 2011

A digital collaborative or Book2Clud edition is available to the owner of this book. See
details after the table of contents.
The code for the Book2Cloud edition is: LC2011

Learning Commons Press is an imprint of:
Hi Willow Research and Publishing
312 South 1000 East
Salt Lake City UT 84102

Distributed by:
LMC Source
P.O. Box 131266
Spring TX 77393
800-873-3043
lmcsourcesales@gmail.com
http://lmcsource.com

ISBN: 1-933170-67-0

In Appreciation

We express appreciation to the many colleagues and students throughout the years who
have helped shape the ideas in this book.

Contents

Introduction: Let the Journey Begin iv

Chapter 1: The Learning Commons: A Justification 1

Chapter 2: The Learning Commons: A Tour 11

Chapter 3: Knowledge Building and the Learning Commons 25

Chapter 4: Learning Literacies and the Learning Commons 53

Chapter 5: Technology and the Learning Commons 77

Chapter 6: Collaboration and the Learning Commons 107

Chapter 7: Personal Learning Environments in the Learning Commons 125

Chapter 8: Building the Learning Commons as a Client Side Organization ... 139

Chapter 9: School Improvement and the Learning Commons 161

Chapter 10: Connections with People and Ideas and the Learning Commons ... 183

Chapter 11: Everyone Wins in the Learning Commons 217

Appendix 227

Glossary 233

Index 245

About the Authors 248

Introduction to the Book2Cloud Edition of this Book

For the first time, this book is being issued in a Book2Cloud edition. The purpose of a digital collaborative edition, known as a Book2Cloud edition of a book, is to promote a conversation among individuals or groups with the authors of the various chapters in a book. Unlike a static ebook, the objective is to extend ideas, build deeper understanding, and build collaborative intelligence.

Conversations and Additions

In the Book2Cloud edition, each chapter of the book has its own separate page. There are two ways to interact with the text:

1. Read the entire book on the first page and add comments at the very bottom. The advantage is that all the links are hot so that you can go to the many documents, blogs, videos, etc. instantly.
2. Click on the editable version of each chapter in the upper right ribbon where you are encouraged to add comments or lists or materials in the original text, thus creating your own or your group's chapter. You can add comments, copy passages into your own personal notes, and add information (please use a different color), attach documents, add general comments at the bottom for discussion, ask questions of the authors or what your group thinks, add links to even better or more current materials, correct URLs, and any number of interactive things.

Public Edition

When you have purchased the printed book, you have the opportunity to collaborate with others in not only reading the original text, but enhancing the text with additional titles, links, discussion, attachments, and anything else that might enhance the text. To edit the site, you will need to request permission. When you do so, give the permission code as proof of purchase. This is found on the verso of the title page of the book. If you are having trouble accessing the book, email davidlibrarian@gmail.com for assistance.

Professional Development and Classroom Editions

Your group or class can have your own private space where you are discussing and adding materials to the digital version of the text.

The instructor should notify reader.david@gmail.com that you intend to have a group and wish to have your own private edition. Your site will be created with you as owner so you can add your students who have purchased the book to your "class."

Group discounts to the book are available. Call the 800 number or email lmcsourcesales@gmail.com for information.

The Learning Commons Introduction
Let the Journey Begin

Chapter 1

The Learning Commons
A Justification

How do we best help today's learners?
http://www1.teachertube.com/viewVideo.php?video_id=12272&title=A_Vision_of
_K_12_Students_Today
Some schools sport professionally staffed state-of-the-art libraries that serve as
centers of inquiry where students master technology and develop information
literacy skills. Other schools languish with industrial age facilities designed for
20th century learning, or worse yet, they have no libraries at all.

Not Your Grandmother's Library! http://www.learningandleading-
digital.com/learning_leading/20110304?pg=18#pg18

School libraries became commonplace in schools during the 1960s when the United States
was worried about competing with the USSR in the space race and when an article in
Redbook magazine reported that Americans spent more on dog food than on library
books. Computer labs in schools developed much later as Apples and PCs became
affordable.

The advent of the Internet and of ubiquitous portable computing devices such as smart
phones and tablets has stimulated a great deal of rethinking about how everyone works,
learns, and communicates. Certainly, the science fiction writers of yesteryear were on
target in their predictions as we now see our computers becoming extensions of
ourselves. However, there is a disconnect between the personal use of technologies and
most educational practice. Why should we, in the world of academia, try to exist without
the technologies that are prominent in the world at large?

The current duel between two major business models also gives us the incentive to
rethink school organization. The Microsoft Model and the Google model, two very
different philosophies of doing business, are quite familiar to us in various aspects of our
consumer behavior. In the following illustration, the underlying principles of the two
business models are compared in the context of education.

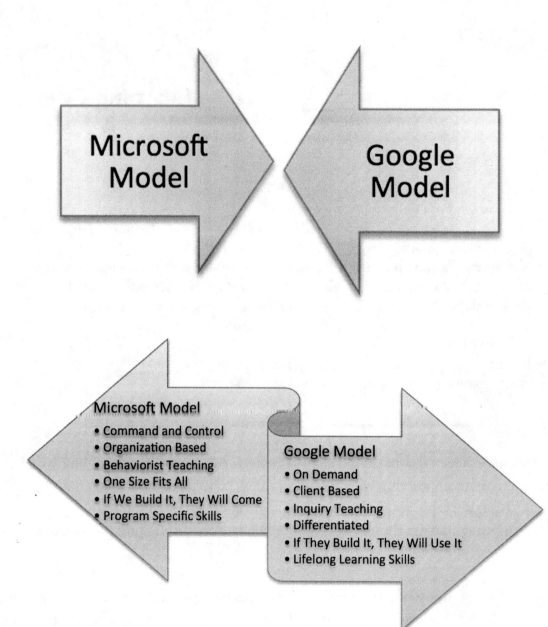

The music industry is a good example of the clash of the two models. For half a century, major labels dominated the recording industry and controlled what albums were put on the market. In today's market, the customer is saying, "I want what I want, where and when I want it." Many musical groups have bypassed the traditional model and have turned directly to the consumer. These groups try to "go viral" by using YouTube giveaways of their music. The "If we build it" company markets packages of software that we are expected to use on their terms. The "If *they* build it" company supplies us with a set of tools and we are allowed to creatively build our own information systems. This is the major difference between "If we build it, they will come," and, "If *they* build it, they will use it." The argument for the "If we build it" model is that structure and organization coupled with a service orientation is really what is needed. The argument against the "If *they* build it" model is that it is fragmented, is messy, lacks uniformity, and transfers control to the novice.

Both the school library and the computer lab have been designed on the "If we build it" model with the command and control idea as their structure. Stereotypically, librarians have been viewed as "keepers of the books" and tech directors as dictators of their networks. While our service-oriented library and computer professionals ensure that their systems work efficiently under their direction, there are major leaks in the dam. Classroom teachers, unsatisfied with the limited availability of print, build their own classroom book collections and other teachers begin using Web 2.0 tools that bypass the school's central networks. Students bypass both libraries and computer labs by going directly to the Internet since it is always there and always returns an answer to any query. The answer may be an inferior one, but convenience usually wins. Since both the school library and the computer lab consume resources, financial exigencies have caused many to question whether schools need these two services at all.

New Learning Models
Schools must develop new relevant learning models in response to students who expect to learn in new ways using the technologies they use ubiquitously outside of school. The Learning Commons is a real world whole school approach to creating such a new collaborative learning model for students and teachers.
Koechlin, Rosenfeld, and Loertscher (2010, 2)

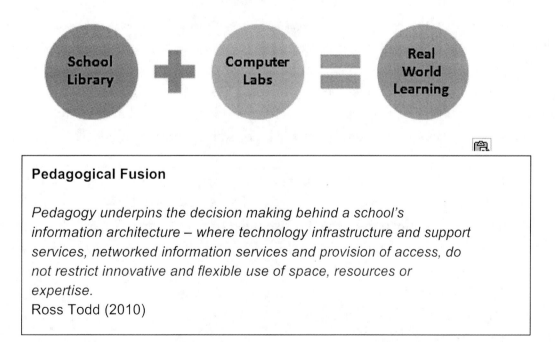

Pedagogical Fusion

Pedagogy underpins the decision making behind a school's information architecture – where technology infrastructure and support services, networked information services and provision of access, do not restrict innovative and flexible use of space, resources or expertise.
Ross Todd (2010)

Moving Toward a Client-Side Learning Commons

We argue that information, resources, computer access, and instruction in the information world and the tech world are still essential components of a quality education. We argue that moving libraries and computer labs toward the client-side, or "If they build it" model, is inevitable. Our clients, both teachers and students, increasingly demonstrate that they are not only comfortable in an "If *they* build it" model information world, but stop using our services when alternatives are friendlier. It is quite possible to clamp down on the customer by insisting that they use our systems, but we are generally accessible only during the school day and sometimes because of various scheduling practices, by appointment only. Consumers generally select a new store if the current one doesn't have what they want or need or is not open when they have time to come.

> **Discussion Point** Do Librarians really listen to the needs of their patrons?
> http://www.youtube.com/watch?v=W3ZHPJT2Kp4

A move to client-side information systems is often stalled because of fear and suspicion about users: "If you let them on the Internet, they will instantly stray away from their purpose and possibly encounter predators." Thus, systems are filtered heavily in response not only to those fears, but also because of federal laws and the threat of lawsuits.

We argue that school administrative and instructional information systems are quite different. Administrative computing needs to be locked down against hackers who might cause all kinds of mischief with schedules, grades, or budgets. Instructional computing, however, is quite another matter, since it is in place to facilitate learning. The trend in Web 2.0 applications is toward very safe collaborative digital areas where groups of learners can thrive. However, these are not necessarily served out from school district computer networks. While providing these safe collaborative digital areas may cause temporary panic for those who want "control," a re-examination is currently in order.

We posit that both adults and young people need to learn to build their own information spaces and to learn to be responsible for their actions in those spaces. Since our clients are under our influence only part of the day, we need to help them learn and help them to create rules of behavior both in the real world and in the digital world. It would seem wise to teach them how to cross the digital freeway safely because we cannot always be there to help and guide them across. Users with some degree of computer ability already know how to get around the most stringent of controls. It is a myth that Web 2.0 tools and spaces are automatically dangerous.

The flip side of traditional practice in education is to consider the users and then figure out how the organization can fill their needs and wants. When this concept is applied to traditional school libraries and computer labs we witness the emergence of the Learning Commons. The following chart documents a few examples of transformational practices.

"Client-Side" Education Versus the Traditional Model

Responsive to Users		Controlled by Educators
Information available on any device anywhere 24/7/365	vs	Information available when the library or lab is open
Acquire the books kids want to read	vs	Acquire the books adults think the children need to be reading
Internet filters set up on "dimmer switches" that can be adjusted in relation to user and level of responsibility	vs	Tightly controlled "one level fits all" filters
Totally movable furniture for instant re-configuration	vs	Heavy stationary furniture
Allow students to check out as many books as they can be responsible for	vs	Allow students to check out only two books
Flexible scheduling	vs	Fixed timetable
Just-in-time coaching and mentoring	vs	After school assistance
Focus on knowledge and understanding	vs	Teach to the test
Collaborative action-research based teaching	vs	Isolated classroom teaching
Learning to learn as we teach content	vs	Teaching content

Going client-side is a habit of mind. It is a conscious effort to think of the needs of the customer first rather than of the needs of the organization. Making the shift is not as complicated as one might think. It need not always require years of planning and astronomical budgets as first anticipated. As planners shift from a command and control organization, they will find greater potential for creativity and problem solving. Initial fears and blocks are often overcome easily as success builds.

One of the major changes is the inclusion of clients in the planning, implementing, and evaluation of the changes made. Clients have to help us build it so they will use it. If they have a stake in it, they will care and be more responsible.

What is the parent's role? Going client side requires that parents understand clearly what is going on and understand that they are expected to participate in the new system. Consent forms acknowledge that responsibility is a privilege and everyone is involved, supportive, nurturing, and participating in this extension of educational opportunities. Everyone means school administrators, teacher technologists, teacher librarians, classroom teachers, parents, and, most importantly, the students themselves.

Learners Win!

Soaring dropout rates, bored students, and students who choose not to access the computer or library services of the school all contribute to the creation of a chasm between the digital habits of students and the traditional nature of schooling. Schools must respond to the clients they serve. It is not just a problem with educators being perceived by students as being out-of-touch. This generation of adults must boost the prospects of the next generation by providing them with opportunities to learn, grow, excel, and compete globally. It is time learners won, and it is time for us as educators to stop being ignored as irrelevant.

Everyone Wins!

It is time that Googlers accept teacher librarians and teacher technologists as the school's information and technology coaches. It is time that learners see the school's technology specialists as enablers rather than as permeable brick walls. As we, the adults, rethink and reinvent we trust that the best pieces from our former library and computer lab will find a place in the new milieu and boost the new whole-school learning atmosphere.

The benefits of the Learning Commons to the entire school community and to teaching and learning will be explored in each of the subsequent chapters. It is worth noting before we begin our journey that the hard work of school improvement is more readily attainable by creating a Learning Commons space and culture. Funding, resourcing, implementing, and tracking of programs can radiate from one common space. At any time, administration can measure the pulse of improvement in one spot rather than chasing down initiatives all over the school.

It's time to reinvent so that everyone wins.

> *Rather than being victimized by our program structures, we should be creating new types of learning environments for a new time and for various types of teaching and learning. Not to do so is a declaration not to learn.*
> Heidi Hayes Jacobs (2010, 79)

> *It is illogical to imagine an information age school without a fully functioning library serving as the information centre. Guided Inquiry calls for rethinking the function of the school library and the librarian role in transforming K-12 education to meet the demands of the 21st century.*
> Kuhlthau, Maniotes, and Caspari (2007, 50)

BRIGHT Ideas to Build On - More reasons to reconsider reinventing school libraries and computer labs

- These college students have definite ideas about change: http://www1.teachertube.com/viewVideo.php?video_id=1184&title=Digital _Students___Analog_Schools
- Listen to the kids' opinions: http://www.youtube.com/watch?v=bIRG0UJ0jWE
- Teens sing about their Commons: http://www.youtube.com/watch?v=4z4Z717yD08
- Kim Cofino's analysis of learners today http://www.slideshare.net/mscofino/the-21st-century-learner
- Justification for technology as a tool at: http://www.youtube.com/watch?v=_VnHdqpE4RM
- An example of new mindbending technologies http://www.fluency21.com/blogpost.cfm?blogID=2107&utm_source=Com

mitted+Sardine+Blog+Update&utm_campaign=2129ef4829-
RSS_EMAIL_CAMPAIGN&utm_medium=emai
- Alan November interviews the principal of Cushing Academy:
  http://novemberlearning.com/category/podcasts/
- Five myths about the information age: http://chronicle.com/article/5-
  Myths-About-the-Information/127105/
- Finally, enjoy with us this takeoff on the popular Old Spice commercial:
  http://www.youtube.com/watch?v=2ArIj236UHs&feature=related

Another Bright Idea

Dream School

I have been dreaming lately, dreaming about starting a school, a place where kids can ask questions and follow their passions. A place where caring adults create the conditions where deep learning can thrive and are willing to get out of the way and let it happen. A place where we value what all learners have to offer teachers and students.
This school is a blended place with inquiry occurring both online and face to face. A school, like a lab school, where others could see self-directed learning in action.
Sheryl Nussbaum-Beach (2011)

Read right to the end of her blog and don't miss the video of a school that has embraced a client side approach and the students who have been empowered by it.

Over to You Discuss with your group or the authors:

- In the book: *Inside Steve's Brain*, we get a picture of how Steve Jobs saved Apple. What business model did he use and how could we reinvent using some of his ideas?

- What behaviors are you seeing in learners that encourage us to rethink current practice?

- What do the kids at your school say about the need to reinvent education?

- How is the move toward open-source applications encouraging rethinking?

- What is crowd sourcing? Could it help us rethink? Clue: Read the book: *We Are Smarter Than Me: How to Unleash the Power of Crowds in your Business.*

- What about *The World is Flat?*, or, *Wikinomics*, or, Daniel Pink's *A Whole New Mind*?

References

- Hayes Jacobs, Heidi. 2010. *Curriculum 21: Essential Education for a Changing World.* Alexandria, VA: Association for Supervision & Curriculum Development.

- Koechlin, Carol, Esther Rosenfeld, and David V. Loertscher. 2010. *Building a Learning Commons: A Guide for School Administrators and Learning Leadership Teams.* Salt Lake City, UT: Hi Willow Research and Publishing.

- Kuhlthau, Carol, Leslie K. Maniotes, and Ann K. Caspari. 2007. *Guided Inquiry: Learning in the 21st Century.* Westport, CT: Libraries Unlimited.

- Nussbaum-Beach, Sheryl. 2011. *Dream School.* http://www.21stcenturycollaborative.com/2011/04/dream-school/

- Todd, Ross J. 2010. *Keynote Presentation at New England School Library Association Leadership Conference.* http://neschoollibraries.org/leadership-conference/ http://neschoollibraries.files.wordpress.com/2010/01/2010-01-15-rosstodd.pdf

Resources

Foundational Ideas

- Foley, Mary Jo. 2008. *Microsoft 2.0: How Microsoft Plans to Stay Relevant in the Post-Gates Era.* Hoboken, NJ: John Wiley & Sons.

- Vise, David and Mark Malseed. 2006. *The Google Story: Inside the Hottest Business, Media, and Technology Success of Our Time.* Brooklyn, NY: Delta Publishing Group.

Other Resources

- Bellanca, James and Ron Brandt, eds. 2010. *21st Century Skills: Rethinking How Students Learn.* Bloomington, IN: Solution Tree.

- Chorost, Michael. 2010. *World Wide Mind: The Coming Integration of Humanity, Machines, and the Internet.* New York: Free Press.

- Darling-Hammond, Linda. 2010. *The Flat World and Education: How America's Commitment to Equity Will Determine Our Future.* New York: Teachers College Press.

- Friedman, Thomas. 2007. *The World Is Flat. 3.0: A Brief History of the Twenty-First Century.* New York: Picador.

- Fullan, Michael. 2010. *All Systems Go: The Change Imperative for Whole System Reform.* Thousand Oaks, CA: Corwin Press.

- Hayes Jacobs, Heidi. 2010. *Education for a Changing World.* Alexandria, VA: Association for Supervision & Curriculum Development.

- Interview with Heidi Hayes Jacobs
  http://video.ascd.org/services/player/bcpid55275595001?bctid=61455698001

- Kahney, Leander. 2008. *Inside Steve's Brain.* New York: Penguin Group.

- Libert, Barry and Jon Spector. 2007. *We Are Smarter Than Me: How to Unleash the Power of Crowds in Your Business.* Upper Saddle River, NJ: Pearson Prentice Hall.

- Pink, Daniel. 2006. *A Whole New Mind: Why Right-Brainers Will Rule the Future.* New York: Riverhead Books (Penguin Group).

- Tapscott, Don and Anthony D. Williams. 2010. *Wikinomics: How Mass Collaboration Changes Everything.* New York: Portfolio Books (Penguin Group).

Chapter 2

The Learning Commons
A Tour

Why do students need a Learning Commons?
Ross Todd suggests that the Learning Commons will "turn on the lights of learning". Be inspired by his dedication speech at the formal opening of Chelmsford HS Learning Commons.
http://www.youtube.com/watch?v=6764xxwQNMM&feature=results_main&playnext=1&list=PLDD3DECB5AEA

Now watch the early journeys of a school embracing a Learning Commons.
http://www.youtube.com/watch?v=EpwhQYafNp4&feature=related

———————————— ❋ ————————————

As we enter the Learning Commons, our first impression differs greatly from the first impression on entering a traditional library or computer lab. Immediately, we notice a completely flexible learning space where neither computers nor books get in the way. If we were to come back in an hour, we might see a completely different configuration of individuals and groups of youth, adults, or both, busily working, consulting and collaborating. The buzz in the air is both purposeful and casual and it is a mix of learners, both adult and student, engaged in a wide variety of activities.

Upon further examination, we discover that two major functions are being accommodated simultaneously in the Commons. The first is the Open Commons, and the second is the Experimental Learning Center. Each is controlled by its own calendar of events but coexists in a busy real place while also extending into virtual space. The faculty, in consultation with the learners, creates a powerful learning environment through a combination of innovation, learning tools and learning science. Thus, it is a micro R&D center of testing, experimentation, and exhibition connected to a larger network of educational research and practice.

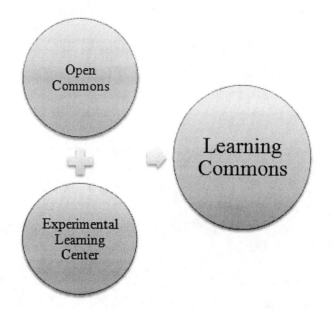

The Open Commons

Constructed around client-based principles, the Open Commons is a service center planned by both the youth and the adults, drawn there by its inviting and collaborative atmosphere. Obviously equipped with wireless access, both students and adults are using personal digital devices as individuals, small groups, or as large groups. Students stream in and out of the Open Commons during the day and are virtual visitors at night as they take advantage of the vast array of information sources, various service centers, production capabilities, and communication possibilities.

In one area, we notice an expert bar staffed by students and adults who are consulting with individuals or small groups needing assistance with software and hardware. In another area is the mentor bar where adults—faculty, staff, and volunteers—are providing individual group guidance on projects, assignments or just personal advice and encouragement. At any given time we notice that beyond the support staff and volunteers, learning specialists are also coaching.

It is easily apparent that the Open Commons is an extension of the various classrooms of the school. It is a place where everyone works and collaborates in a collegial social environment, and is a place everyone owns. The space runs on its own calendar to avoid chaos and overcrowding. Students have been major players in the creation of policies and behavior guidelines that make the environment inviting and conducive to learning. These same policies exist not only in the physical space of the Commons but also into its virtual equivalent. These emphasize a welcome and purposeful enticement rather than a practice of exclusion.

Instead of a single person in charge, one notices the various specialists of the school coming and going as they consult with individuals, small groups, and whole classes as they co-teach alongside the classroom teachers. The following illustration shows that the various classrooms of the building are intertwined with the various specialists in the Learning Commons.

A Learning Commons is a flexible and responsive approach to helping schools focus on learning collaboratively.....Within a Learning Commons, new relationships are formed between learners, new technologies are realized and utilized, and both students and educators prepare for the future as they learn new ways to learn.
Ontario Library Association (2010)

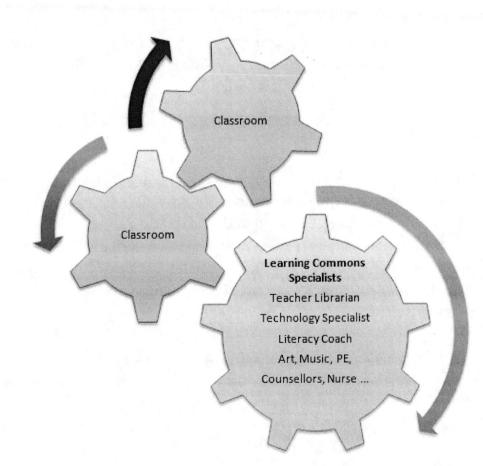

The list of activities co-existing simultaneously, is long and might include:

- A group of students gathering print and digital resources for a temporary classroom collection on a topic of study.
- A student team editing their own documentary on homeless persons in the school's neighborhood.
- A student technology expert seeking advice to work out connection problems to networks in the classroom.
- A classroom teacher and the music teacher who are helping learners compose original music for podcasts of their own stories.
- A class working with their teacher and teacher librarian to select both biased and unbiased resources on a controversial topic to be analyzed by the group.
- A single student linked into an online experimental study being done in the rain forest of Brazil.
- A small group of students having a brown bag lunch as they discuss the latest book in a fantasy novel series.
- Students in one corner receiving instruction from an artist in residence.
- Students in a conference room practicing for their poetry reading scheduled for the next day in the Commons during lunch, and slated to be videotaped to upload to the community performance digital site.

The Experimental Learning Center

Constructed around teacher-centered principles, the Experimental Learning Center hosts professional development, experimentation, and exhibition of exemplary teaching and learning experiences in the school. Centered in this space, that no one owns but everybody owns, is the laboratory for testing new curriculum initiatives, experimental technologies, collaborative strategies, and cross grade-level or cross-curricular initiatives. The Experimental Learning Center is the heart of professional development and school improvement initiatives

Governed by its own calendar, it draws upon the expertise of school, district, and outside experts and learner representatives who coach, do action research, and test new ideas for implementation throughout the school as a whole. Administrators walk through regularly to monitor initiatives and provide guidance and encouragement. This is the center of the school's professional learning community, focusing on instructional improvements that deserve full implementation based on pilot testing.

The Experimental Learning Center is crucial to the orientation of new faculty members. Here, they can consult the various subject specialists, teacher technologists, teacher librarians, coaches, counsellors, and any other specialists serving in the school. Here, the Learning Leadership Team may arrange job-embedded staff development opportunities with outside experts. Here, other faculty may develop new technological skills, classroom management strategies, safety training, or perhaps refresher courses on legal responsibilities.

School-wide initiatives, projects, or grant writing happen in the Experimental Learning Center as the faculty pulls together in a purposeful agenda for change and improvement. Issues across grade levels and disciplines (such as literacy programs) are planned, carried out, and evaluated. It is the learning laboratory of the school; a center of creativity, and innovation. Specific activities that might be happening at any given time in the Experimental Learning Center might include:

- Demonstration Lessons to model the teaching of student questioning skills to promote critical thinking across the curriculum.
- The district/board technical director (teacher technologist) meeting with the student tech team to teach them about new network procedures so that they can teach the protocols to the entire school.
- Writers of a new course conferring with the teacher librarian to select resources to address the needs of all students.
- Teacher representatives meeting with a consultant via video conference to plan an in-service day for the next month.
- The superintendent of school facilities discussing potential new policies with a class that has been studying vending machine usage across the district.
- Students writing in a blog environment are monitored and assessed for skill development, growth and fluency by the Literacy Learning Team and the classroom teachers.

The Virtual Learning Commons

Running simultaneously, 24/7/365 is the school's Learning Commons built by the students, teachers, learning specialists, and administrators with the two learning specialists, the teacher librarian and the teacher technologist as enablers and shadow leaders.

Like the physical space, the virtual space is constructed in two major configurations that constitute what the directors of technology might call instructional computing. This is quite different in nature from the administrative computing space where access is tightly controlled.

The Virtual Open Commons

The virtual space supporting the Open Commons is a very busy connection of projects, resources, tutorials, advice, repositories, as well as a tool source, assignment center, and a project production collaboration center. While there is a recognizable front page, this virtual space is a collection of links, sources, and projects being developed by learners, teachers, and learning specialists simultaneously. It may have originally been the library home page, but now it is constructed by the users who support each other in the overall learning community. Rules of behavior are supported and enforced by everyone. Various safeguards are in place to make the community functional and open to those who are working within its confines, including parents, partnering groups, schools, and anyone else who has a reason to be there.

Here, one might observe:
- Learners taking tutorials on how to cite various information sources in their productions and writings.
- Small groups in a class building a knowledge base on a topic they are studying.
- A team of learners uploading tutorial videos they have created which demonstrate to the faculty and students how to upload their own materials to the school's digital showcase.
- Learners taking online courses that could not be offered at their school.
- Teacher librarians preparing personal tip sheets that connect to teachers' assignments and uploading them to automatically appear on the home page of each student in a particular course.
- Virtual discussions of the latest award winning books in preparation for virtual voting in the state readers' choice awards program.
- A list constructed by a student club of best sources about bullying where they are asking for recommendations from others before they construct a school-wide policy.
- Areas where parents can collaborate as experts on various learning projects when they cannot be present in person.

The Virtual Experimental Learning Center

As the place where professional development, experimentation, professional learning communities, and learning initiatives are centered, this virtual space is communication central for the learning improvement in the school. Announcements, calendars, and progress reports, plus the tools needed to support the Experimental Learning Center are located in the Center. This center provides the virtual glue that makes collaboration and school improvement work. It is constructed by the various leadership teams of the school—the administration, the faculty, and even district personnel—under the leadership of the teacher librarian and the teacher technologist.

At any given time, one might encounter:
- A group of teachers and learning specialists constructing a collaborative learning project, carrying it out, performing collaborative assessments, and reflecting on successes and challenges for the future.
- Administrators providing the first glimpses of a new statewide initiative that will be discussed with the Learning Leadership Team.
- Teacher librarians uploading a list of professional resources to a virtual chat space where the professional learning community can access them for an upcoming discussion.
- Schedules for an experimental classroom learning strategy that the entire faculty is invited to observe and reflect on as it progresses.
- The calendar of the Experimental Learning Center where all the learning specialists of the school can be invited and scheduled for collaborative development of learning activities by any faculty member.
- Announcements of local, state, and national conferences and professional learning opportunities.
- Grant opportunities for individuals, groups, and the school as a whole.
- Connections to major research, documents, forums, and other opportunities relevant to the focus of the individual school.
- Access to various assessment data sources of student performance.

When the virtual and real spaces are combined, then the total Learning Commons appears:

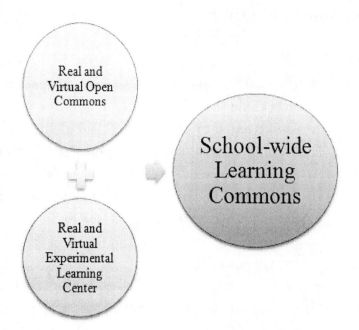

Digging Deeper

Checkup – Ask the Learners

If a visitor to the school were to randomly select a table during lunch and ask students about the role the Learning Commons plays in their school life, how would students respond? What sort of information would the students share? Perhaps they would share something along these lines:

- **Environment** – A comfortable place where they can work, relax, learn, create or do.
- **Access** – A convenient, 24/7, source of materials, information, and advice they trust and can contribute to.
- **Assistance** – They can comfortably obtain help from both adults and fellow students.
- **Personal Contributions** – They can voice opinions and give advice to assist in decisions about the construction of the Learning Commons. They have made contributions and feel some sense of ownership.
- **Experimentation** – They try new things, test technology or software, develop special projects, and see the adults doing the same.
- **Technology** – This is where you go to access and use hot new technologies and programs/software. The Learning Commons is the source of their connection to the digital world, and it is the center for discussion about that world and how they control it to their advantage.

- **Activities and Exhibitions** – They describe a variety of activities they have participated in or have seen happening and know that many student productions are a part of the digital museum of the school.
- **A sense that adults coach and mentor them when they need help and that staff inquire about how they learn as well as what they know.**
- **It is a caring, supportive, place to learn without angst and pressure.**

In other words, the various learners recognize that the Learning Commons is a client-side organization where they have some say in what goes on and they are contributing as well as receiving as a user. They may not understand the impact that the Learning Commons is having on teaching and learning throughout the school, but they should recognize that they are engaged as they inquire, use, contribute, work and create.

Digging Even Deeper

Checkup – Ask the Teachers

Likewise, if a visitor to the school were to enter the teachers' lounge and interview random teachers about the Learning Commons, what sense of its value would be expressed? Perhaps teachers would offer something along these lines:

- **Environment** – a part of their classroom – an extension of both work and learning activities; a model of environmental sustainability.
- **Access** – The source 24/7 of materials, information, and advice they trust and contribute to. That they can send individuals, small groups, and schedule the entire class there as needed.
- **Assistance** – A place where they obtain help from both adults and students who are sharing their expertise.
- **Personal contribution** – They can voice opinions and give advice to assist in decisions about Learning Commons construction.They have made contributions and feel some sense of ownership.
- **Experimentation** – A place to learn, test and share new strategies, test technology or software, develop special projects; the center of professional development.
- **Technology** – Recognition that the Learning Commons is the source of their connection to the digital world that extends into their classroom.
- **Activities and Exhibitions** – They remember and can describe a variety of activities they have seen happening and know that their student's work and productions are a part of the digital museum of the school.
- **Most importantly, they do not feel they are alone in the challenge of elevating every learner toward excellence. They are part of a**

teaching a learning team that merges classroom teachers and specialists in a mutual quest.

In other words, teachers recognize the advantages of building and maintaining a client-side Learning Commons and feel at ease in the give and take of the idea of the Experimental Learning Center.

The Leadership Teams

A visitor might well ask: How has this all come about? What is the organizational structure that keeps it all running? In a prominent location, one might observe an organization chart similar to the one below that details the collaborative nature of a school community team:

The Learning Commons Partnership Teams

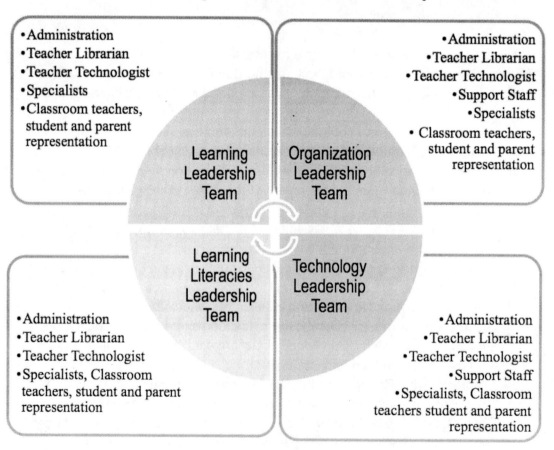

- Administration
- Teacher Librarian
- Teacher Technologist
- Specialists
- Classroom teachers, student and parent representation

Learning Leadership Team

Organization Leadership Team

- Administration
- Teacher Librarian
- Teacher Technologist
- Support Staff
- Specialists
- Classroom teachers, student and parent representation

- Administration
- Teacher Librarian
- Teacher Technologist
- Specialists, Classroom teachers, student and parent representation

Learning Literacies Leadership Team

Technology Leadership Team

- Administration
- Teacher Librarian
- Teacher Technologist
- Support Staff
- Specialists, Classroom teachers student and parent representation

This diagram is one example of the possible orchestration of a school leadership organization. Each school will need to design their own partnership structures based on school improvement goals and specific school needs. The triad of administration, teacher librarian and teacher technologist need to be the constant element for each team. Other specialists, support staff, classroom teachers, students, and parents enrich the dynamics of each team with their particular expertise and interests. The sense that the school is a learning organization becomes quite clear here at the center, the hub, the place of excellence.

As we continue our tour we will examine program elements in the Learning Commons. In the following chapters, we explore the four major program elements of the Learning Commons as pictured below. Each of these elements will be present in both the physical and virtual parts of the Commons.

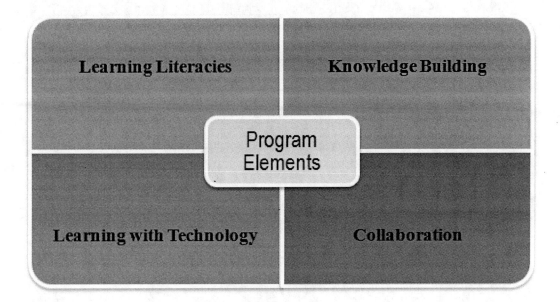

Scenarios of the Learning Commons in Action

- **Blow Your Horn** Valerie Diggs is an early adopter of the Learning Commons approach. She is a real advocate, hosting sessions in her transformed spaces at Chelmsford High School, and writing articles and speaking at workshops and conferences around the country. In a recent article for the journal, *Teacher Librarian,* she offers this advice to teacher librarians embracing the Learning Commons: "Keep learning, keep an open mind, and work hard to open the minds of your fellow colleagues and the students in your school. Start small, one baby step at a time. Soon you will be moving your program ahead by leaps and bounds. And, don't be afraid to blow your own horn. Know who to contact at the offices of one of the major

newspapers in your area, and befriend local reports. A picture and a few words will work wonders." Here is a link to one of her many presentations. It is a little long but she has big story to share.
http://www.slideshare.net/valeriediggs/from-library-to-learning-commonsnyslideshare

- **It's Actually Happening** In her 2010-2011 annual report Joyce Valenza, teacher librarian at Springfield Township High School, captures a moment in time in her center. 'Visitors to our library continue to note its energy, its spirit, and its coziness. During the video our students produced for the State Legislative Breakfast promoting school libraries, one student noted, "It's the closest thing we have to Starbucks". During a single block you will see students working in groups or independently as they create instructional videos, record podcasts, search scholarly journal databases, tell digital stories, present with our SmartBoard, write posts in curricular blogs, and collaborate using such on-line applications as wikis and Nings and Google documents. You will also see our students writing traditional papers and reading books and magazines."
This report is featured in both print and video format from the virtual library site http://springfieldlibrary.wikispaces.com Joyce Valenza celebrates the fact that her Learning Commons continues to morph and grow.She perceives it as the 'Libratory' where learners enter library spaces through both the physical and virtual doors to learn in dynamic hybrid experiences.

- **District Support** The Calgary Board of Education in Alberta, Canada has developed a special section of their central site for Innovative Learning to help schools move forward with the Learning Commons concept. http://www.innovativelearning.ca/sec-rlc/slib-index.asp.Two schools have posted videos to document their beginning journeys:
  - Belfast School
    <http://media.stream.cbe.ab.ca/media/LearningCommons/BelfastLC.wmv>
  - Monterey Park School
    <http://media.stream.cbe.ab.ca/media/LearningCommons/ElemLC.wmv>

- **Proud Principal** Rich Lane, Principal of Crescent Heights High School in Medicine Hat, Alberta, is very proud of the impact his teacher librarians make on teaching and learning at his school. He realizes that his teacher librarians are in a unique position to support and lead innovations in all disciplines. In a video link below he exudes his enthusiasm with this statement, "School is about the excitement of learning that can happen when we are all learning together."

- CHHS Learning Commons Part 1
    <http://www.youtube.com/watch?v=lo0gaTzU0qw> ,
- CHHS Learning Commons Part 2
    http://www.youtube.com/watch?v=nVipfjDk6A8&feature=related

- **Reggio Inspired Learning Commons** Sandra Becker, the teacher librarian, and other staff members at Elizabeth Rummel Elementary in Canmore, Alberta are exploring how the Reggio Philosophy links to their vision of a Learning Commons .They have discovered that just like Reggio, thoughtful use of space (environment as the Third Teacher), focus on inquiry and research, and the idea of documentation as a way to further thinking about teaching and learning are also grounding elements for building a Learning Commons. They have built a Google site as a virtual learning community to explore together and plan their transitions. Enjoy their first steps in this delightful video http://www.youtube.com/watch?v=EpwhQYafNp4
If you are interested in finding out more about designing and building an environment as the Third Teacher, consult this helpful book ,*The Third Teacher: 79 Ways You Can Use Design to Transform Teaching & Learning,* and the collaborative website http://www.thethirdteacher.com/

- **A Learning Landscape** While not a true scenario of the construction of a Learning Commons, we are fascinated by attempts across the continent to design and redesign learning and learning spaces in which learners win. Enjoy the creative application of design at this site in North Carolina: http://www.ted.com/talks/emily_pilloton_teaching_design_for_change.html

Resource TIP We are asked regularly for places and examples of real Learning Commons in both the U.S. and Canada. Since the original publication of this book in 2008, we have been following to some extent the development of the Learning Commons ideas wherever we could. Since David Loertscher is the co-editor of the journal *Teacher Librarian*, a number of articles have appeared since 2008 that spotlight certain characteristics of the Commons. We recommend subscribing to that magazine since we will continue to bring creative and outstanding developments to readers. In 2010, the editors collected the various articles that centered on the Learning Commons up to that point in a single publication, *Learning Commons Treasury*. This collection is available from http://lmcsource.com . We have sprinkled citations to specific articles in the magazine and in the collection in the various chapters of this book where possible.

Over to You Discuss with your group and with the authors:

- Are there any features of your own school library or computer lab that pushes it over toward a client-side environment?

- Make a list of features in this tour of the Learning Commons that intrigue you and find places in the text where those ideas are covered. How could these characteristics be implemented in your school?

References

- "From the Brain Trust, Teacher Librarians are Education: Thoughts from Valerie Diggs". *Teacher Librarian* 38, no.5 (June 2011): 56.

- Ontario Library Association. 2010. *Together for Learning: School Libraries and the Emergence of the Learning Commons.* http://www.accessola.com/data/6/rec_docs/677_OLATogetherforLearning.pdf

- Valenza, Joyce. 2011. *Annual Report, June 2011.* Springfield Township High School Virtual Library. http://springfieldlibrary.wikispaces.com

Resources

- Loertscher, David V. and Elizabeth "Betty" Marcoux, eds. 2010. *Learning Commons Treasury.* Bowie, MD: Teacher Librarian Press.

- O'Donnell Wicklund, Pigozzi, and Peterson Architects Inc, VS Furniture, and Bruce Mau Design. 2010. *The Third Teacher: 79 Ways You Can Use Design to Transform Teaching & Learning.* New York: Abrams Books.

Chapter 3

Knowledge Building
and the Learning Commons

How do we prepare students to be active participants in their future?
Above & Beyond tells the story of how the 4Cs -- communication, collaboration, critical thinking and creativity - complement and strengthen traditional school instruction.
Consider the skills featured in this film and Knowledge Building in the Learning Commons as this chapter unfolds:
http://www.youtube.com/watch?v=7KMM387HNQk

———————————— ❋ ————————————

Historically, there has often been a division between those who feel that young people should have a broad introduction to content in various subject areas versus those who believe that deep understanding and knowing how to learn are paramount. In the past decade, widespread testing that has focused on factual knowledge has driven many teachers to emphasize content coverage over inquiry. The concept of a Learning Commons argues for the development of personal expertise and collaborative construction of deep understanding.

Teachers and students experience a pedagogical merger of classrooms and library/lab facilities. As an extension of all classrooms, the Learning Commons can round out the entire spectrum of learning. The use of guided inquiry and other problem-based learning experiences in the Learning Commons not only engages students but also effectively releases students to take command of their own learning, doing, knowledge building and sharing. This approach prevails for formal education, online education, or informal learning experiences.

In both the Open Commons and the Experimental Learning Center, a continuous stream of learning units are brought by classroom teachers to take advantage of various learning specialists and the rich resources and technologies which are available. Whether experimental in nature or "mature" learning units, the focus is on inquiry-based learning journeys. These journeys can be personal in nature, small-group projects, or whole-class learning experiences guided by the classroom teacher and one or more learning specialists. In the Experimental Learning Center, new ideas, strategies, experiments, and initiatives are being tested and modeled for the school. The major question is whether learners thrive better than with previous strategies. In the Open Commons, previously tested strategies are practiced on a regular basis.

For any of the learning specialists and, in particular, the teacher librarian, the curriculum of the specialist is being integrated with the learning standards required by the classroom teacher. This "just in time" and "need to know" instruction helps learners build their knowledge base and at the same time helps them learn more efficiently. Examples of such integration might include students learning how to judge the differences between fact and opinion as a political issue is being explored; students learning how to think critically about conflicting media messages encountered on the topic; students learning how to paraphrase by selecting major ideas in a variety of texts; and students learning how to use a wiki to collaboratively build a case for a position the group is creating. In another example, the reading specialist might be assisting learners handle more and more complex texts so that the subject at hand is more easily understood. As these learning journeys occur, the adults are watching, coaching, and assessing progress to insure that every learner either meets or exceeds the learning expectations. In other words, the Learning Commons supports a school-wide culture of inquiry fostering 'habits of mind' and 'learning dispositions' conducive to success.

> **Challenge** Many classroom teachers have a different mindset.
> One of the problems teacher librarians or any other specialist face in trying to align with classroom program is that it is often based on a behaviorist approach where the adult coaches prescribe:
> - What students must learn, both broadly and in depth
> - What skills students must build and be able to demonstrate
> - Products that will demonstrate the students' knowledge and skills
> - The acceptable level of performance on any assessment

Critics point out that such education constitutes a "cookie cutter" approach where gifted students are unchallenged, and average students are bored because the emphasis is on bringing the challenged up to an acceptable bar. In this scenario, the teacher librarian works in the supportive role of helping students reach benchmarks or minimums through information tasks that are often low level 'find and deliver' types of assignments.

The Learning Commons recognizes the major shift in the worlds of information and technology. Today's learners are growing up in quite a different world than their adult coaches did, and face a very uncertain ever changing and challenging future. Here, the Learning Commons is "natural" as it focuses on constructivist ideas, learning literacies, and technologies, as learners gradually take more and more control over their learning.

The emphasis is on turning superficial understanding that leads to uninformed decision making into thoughtful and deep understanding designed to develop an informed

Discussion Point Many writers have explored the new digital generation and how today's learners exhibit quite different behaviors than in previous generations. Nicholas Carr points to these learning differences in an interesting video history of technologies and learning. http://www.nicholasgcarr.com/ As Carr points out, each major change in technology has had a deep impact on the way we learn. What are the implications for learning with new technologies in your school?

citizenry. The bottom line is that teacher librarians need to help teachers transform low level projects. As Alison Zmuda has stated at the Treasure Mountain research retreat in 2007, they cannot continue to be an "accomplice to mediocrity".

Evolution of Learning

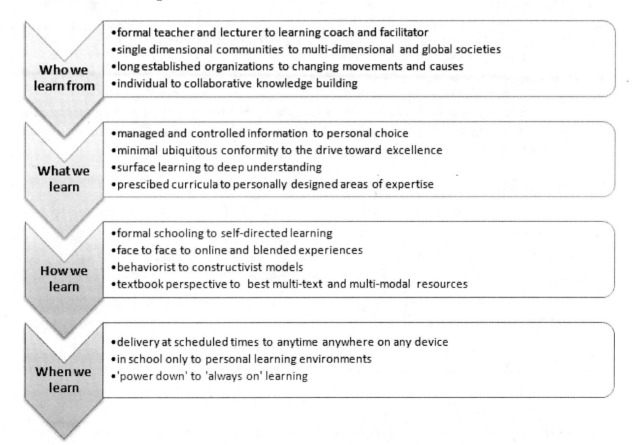

As educators turn away from the prescriptive view of teaching and learning toward the more open view, the Learning Commons can contribute and thrive. The prescriptive stance seems to exist in a narrow information environment while the constructivist stance flourishes in an expanded information and technological environment.

> *Teachers who are shifting their practices to meet the needs of our times talk about how they're remixing the coverage of content with the uncovering of ideas and concepts, how they're balancing their time between being the "sage on the stage" who presents, explains, answers questions and being the "guide on the side," who supports students' research, discovery, and sharing of their own findings in learning projects. As one teacher has put it," I had to unlearn the idea that teaching was about my content; I had to learn it was about **their** thinking and **their** skills."*
> Trilling and Fadel (2009, 39)

Learners of today need to build enough personal expertise to enable them to succeed in a world where personal efforts are combined to build collaborative intelligence. For example, a great film such as the movie, UP, requires the combined expertise of engineers, animators, script writers, directors, and many others who develop what a single individual could not have produced. Forecasters of the future herald personal expertise building as a life-long endeavor in view of the rapid change across many employment sectors.

> **Digging Deeper** How can the Learning Commons help learners build individual expertise?
>
> An interesting example is provided by Salman Khan, a former Wall Street hedge fund analyst who has used his personal mathematical prowess and teaching method to create brief mathematical video demonstrations. His TED talk is at: http://www.youtube.com/watch?v=nTFEUsudhfs

In a radical career switch, Salman Khan has developed the Khan Academy, www.khanacademy.org, a full organization devoted to teaching basic mathematical ideas and essential skills using short online video modules complete with repeatable tests. The academy has expanded to include video modules in history, finance, physics, chemistry, biology, astronomy, economics and computer science. These free YouTube videos have been an online sensation and have inspired a practice known as Flip Teaching where content and skill development happens as homework, and where teachers are freed up during class time to engage the learners in more constructivist projects. For other classroom teachers' experiences using the Flip Classroom, see: http://teachingwithted.pbworks.com/w/page/37315118/Flipping-the-Classroom and locate the Flipped Classroom on the following blog: https://usergeneratededucation.wordpress.com/

Challenge: Invite students to surprise you!
Here is the story of a teacher who supported students in their desire to teach others as Salman Khan did. http://mindshift.kqed.org/2011/08/move-over-sal-khan-sixth-graders-create-their-own-math-videos/
His advice for other teachers, "Don't put technology behind glass. Let them touch the computer, ...That's how the world changed for me, for all of us. If you give kids a little bit of trust and let them try out some stuff, they're going to come up with fascinating things that will surprise you."
Bernard (2011)

Technology Transformed Learning Environments

In fact, in the tech-infused learning environment, the teacher should regularly be saying, "Surprise me!"
*The bottom line is that we will see learners becoming responsible to their peers, audiences, and communities for their learning. ..and that responsibility will not be based on a measure of their learning (**how much** or **how well**), but on **what they have learned** and **what they can do** with what they've learned.*
David Warlick (2010)

In the world of the Learning Commons, both adults and learners stimulate each other in the ownership of their personal learning and in the creation of expertise, creativity, in problem solving, and in the development of collaborative intelligence. Thus, if you want to tour the school whether as a physical place or a virtual place, begin at the Learning Commons to get a glimpse of what excellence looks like in teaching and learning.

Discussion Point: Why the focus on Inquiry and Problem-Based Learning?

Lest the reader debunk inquiry or project-based learning as having been tried before, consider John Larner's list of five major misconceptions about project based learning in his article for *Edutopia* at:
http://www.edutopia.org/blog/debunking-five-pbl-myths-john-larmer

At Lehman's Science Leadership Academy, a public high school in Philadelphia where Larner is the principal, students develop five core values that turn them from passive students into enthusiastic and dedicated students. These values are:

- Inquiry
- Research
- Collaboration
- Presentation
- Reflection

As one interviews the students at this high school, the sense is clear that individual students have taken command of their own learning. They keep reminding us that they are a different breed of learner:
http://www.teachertube.com/viewVideo.php?video_id=448&title=Pay_Attention

Focusing on the Learner

Inquiry in the Learning Commons is a dynamic learner centered process. Teacher librarians, other faculty, and support staff provide 'just in time' and 'just for me' support and learning advice. Evidence of success includes:

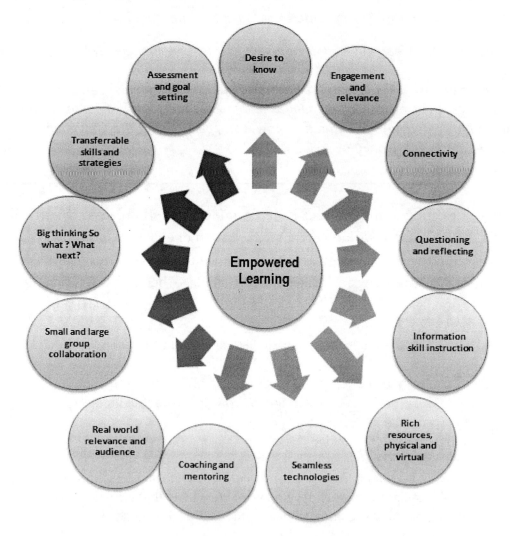

As suggested by major foundational documents, learning becomes a quest, a journey. We can measure success in this journey by considering the following indicators:

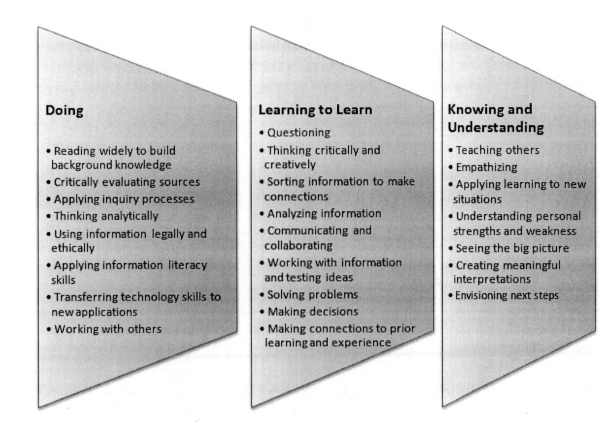

Fostering Self-Directed Learners

For every learner in this new information and technological environment, the essential components of expertise are organization, efficiency, and control. So, whether the learner is a child, a teen, or an adult, the ability to build one's knowledge, track it, and share it , can be beyond even the most organized mind. All learners need strategies and technology to record what they know, to see how they are progressing, and to discover how to build both a private organizational routine and a public face for what they know and are able to do. As the Internet has grown, so have the tools to handle the onslaught of information. More on this will be discussed in the technology chapter and the personal learning environments chapter of this book, but the essential idea belongs here.

- **Personal Organization Spaces** The tools now exist to help every learner come into command of their own information space. Learners can use such tools as an iGoogle page, a Start Page (in Google Apps for Education), a LiveBinder, a private web site, wiki, or blog to be their personal and private or semi-private place where they keep themselves organized. Here, they can have projects they are working on, school assignments, calendars, voices they wish to pay attention to on a regular basis, family stuff, and fun - whatever they need to help them cope with family, school/work, and personal interests. Such an information space is their own filter of the information world. They let in what they want, communicate with whomever they please, explore as they wish, and shut out unwanted pressures vying for their attention. For an example, see *Welcome to my Personal Learning Environment* http://www.youtube.com/watch?v=YEls3tq5wIY

- **Personal Technology Access.** All learners must build access to the information and technology they need to access and flourish in the current world. They figure out what devices they will own, how they can be connected to networks in a reliable fashion, and how they are going to exhibit digital citizenship in the virtual world, just as they are learning to succeed in the physical world. As well, they need to protect themselves and their work from technological malfunction or malicious snooping. They need to build a cadre of tools that help them be efficient and boost their ability to learn quickly and deeply. Of course, they will need reliable mentoring from peers and coaches in order to keep up. In today's world, this is the construction of a personal learning network.

- **Building a Public Face and Image.** Learners are conscious of the public nature of the web and how to control what others know about their personal expertise and who they really are. The tools they need to enable them to build a personal e-portfolio of what they know and can do are readily available and free. Some refer to this personal e-portfolio as digital curation, the preservation of learners and their accomplishments; their projects; their interests; their abilities; and, hopefully, the real people. This is necessary for both their personal interests and their academic prowess. For instance, a learner's collaborative projects at school may appear on the school's Virtual Learning Commons, but they also appear on the learner's personal website or e-portfolio.

In other words, Learners learn how to be in control, understanding the major differences between private, partial, and public sharing in a digital world. They are their own librarians. They are their own publishers. They are their own communicators. They pay attention to what really matters to them. They know where they are going and how to get there. But they also understand their role in community and culture.

See an example of learner led education: *The Independent Project* http://www.youtube.com/watch?v=MTmH1wS2NJY&feature=player_embedded#at=2

See also: *What did you do in school today?* View the student interview video - *A Student's Role in Teacher engagement*
http://www.cea-ace.ca/programs-initiatives/wdydist

Resource TIP: In Command! *Kids and Teens Build and Manage Their Own Information Spaces, And... Learn to Manage Themselves in Those Spaces.*

Empowering the Teaching Team

As the classroom teacher and the learning specialists build and deliver these collaborative learning experiences, they are constantly assessing their own progress to ensure they are:

- Guiding and supporting **inquiry learning**
- Stimulating **critical** and **creative thinking**
- Building cross **curricular literacy** skills and **new literacies**
- **Engaging** and **effective**
- Empowering students to build **deeper understanding**
- Providing **knowledge building** learning experiences
- Employing a framework for designing **successful assignments**
- Effectively utilizing information and technology **rich learning environments**
- Providing **differentiated instruction** to ensure learning success for all
- Utilizing current technologies to **enhance the learning process**
- Stimulating excellent performance on both **formative and summative assessments** of either content knowledge or learning skills

Both the specialists and the classroom teacher follow the advice of W. James Popham as they watch a learning experience unfold. He suggests four levels of formative assessment that monitor the learning experience as it happens.

1. Changing the structure of the learning experience if the learners are not building the sub-skills needed to accomplish the larger goal
2. Learners changing their learning to learn strategies as they progress through a learning experience.
3. The whole classroom/Learning Commons atmosphere changes to accomplish a particular learning experience and experiences over time.
4. Changes occur in the entire school climate as more effective strategies are developed along the way.
   W. James Popham (2008, 53)

Creating Collaborative Environments and Knowledge Building Centers

One of the best ways to create engaging project or problem based learning experiences is to build them within a collaborative digital environment. This has become very easy to do using a variety of Web 2.0 tools that are free and available 24/7 on almost any digital device. When there is a collaborative digital environment, everyone, including learners and adults can be working together. So, instead of the teacher using the Internet to provide a one-way assignment stream with perhaps lecture and submission of work with assessment feedback, the digital learning experience provides a place where everyone is talking, working, helping, constructing, submitting, critiquing, and producing resulting in assessment. This is true whether the class is a face to face one or totally online or mixed.

We recommend the use of Google Sites as a website where the collaborative learning experience happens. Other technologies such as Moodle, blogs, or wikis can also be used. Below is a picture of the template for constructing what we term knowledge building centers. The template can be downloaded at:

<u>Virtual Knowledge Building Center Template</u>

In the center of the template, the adults put the project question and then around that problem description are "rooms" where the learners and adults work together from the beginning of the project until its conclusion.

Examples of constructed learning experiences using the knowledge building center format have been constructed by graduate students at San Jose State University as they have transformed older style learning experiences into inquiry projects. Many of these transformations are available at the following website (note: the higher the transformation number, the more developed the learning experience is. A Module 3 learning experience is the most developed of all). Start your examination at the lesson plans tab. https://spreadsheets.google.com/ccc?key=oAkkdWYq2foWvdENEZmpJao NyTHFoMzJndktIejV3dkE&hl=en#gid=o

An example of an adaptation of the template shows a knowledge building center where adults and students are recreating the school yard.

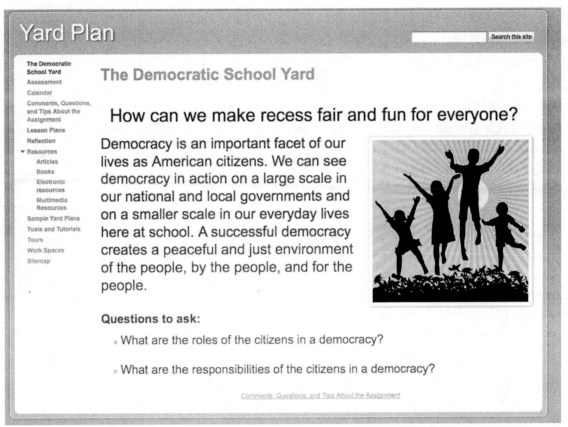

As well as Google Sites and Moodle, Richard Byrne, who writes the Free Technology for Teachers blog, recommends the following tools:
- Sakai
- Canvas
- OLAT
- A Tutor
- Google's Cloud Course

The teacher librarian or the teacher technologist can easily design the virtual environment in such a way that collaboration is a "natural" rather than a forced experience. Who can help with the re-conceptualization of the school yard? Of course, the classroom teachers and the students, but also other adults could help. The teacher librarian? An outside expert? An administrator? Parents? A community planner? The special ed class at the school? Obviously, the environment itself encourages participation rather than just individuals filling out an assignment. And, the likelihood that this plan will actually be carried out makes the learning experience real and engaging.

Another collaborative experience can be constructed using any type of text, video, poem or other material. Consider the Book2Cloud experiment using a Google Site where students can creatively study the Gettysburg Address line by line or phrase by phrase to construct their own sense of deep meaning:
https://sites.google.com/site/gettysburgaddressb2c/

In the next two sections, we will discuss the necessity of using sound instructional designs and a Big Think metacognitive activity at the end of the learning experience, but before we do that, consider the power of helping children and teens learn what collaborative intelligence and team functioning can do to elevate what we all know and can do.

> **Digging Deeper** Consider the following articles:
> http://www.ere.net/2011/01/17/cross-functional-collaboration-discovering-its-value-and-the-genius-of-google/
> and also Christopher Barlow's white paper:
> http://issuu.com/gfbertini/docs/creativity_and_complexity_in_cross_functional_te am?mode=a_p&wmode=0

 globalearner Alan November
#edtech #edchat Do we really need to memorize the fifty state capitals? What is the new creative, motivating, rigorous assignment?
4 hours ago

Incorporate a Sound Instructional Design into a Knowledge Building Center

Once classroom teachers realize that two heads are better than one, they plan, schedule and assess learning experiences which utilize the rich resources and adult specialists that the Learning Commons provides. The Learning Commons promotes an environment where every child or teen can flourish as a creator, investigator, critical thinker, or communicator. Building on the principles of backwards planning promoted by Wiggins and McTigue in *Understanding by Design*, teachers and learners can apply the

Loertscher/Koechlin/Zwaan Think Models to push thinking far beyond the cut/paste/present tradition. These models find applications in both the Open Commons and the Experimental Learning Center depending on whether the learning units are being tried and tested or whether they have been adopted widely. The 18 Think Models that stimulate high-level thinking are:

- **Background to Question Model**—where learners build enough background knowledge on a topic to formulate intelligent and engaging questions for themselves
- **Sensemaking Model**—where the learner takes a group of facts, ideas, or opinions and makes sense through visualization, classification, or synthesis
- **Read, View, and Listen Model**—where learners read, view, and listen widely on a topic and combine what they learn with what others know
- **Advice to Action Model**—where learners consult a wide variety of advice and discern what are the wisest courses of action
- **Compare and Contrast Model**—where people, places, ideas, time periods, issues or solutions to problems are analyzed and compared to gain understanding of varying perspectives
- **Concept Jigsaw Puzzle Model**—where groups build expertise on subtopics and then combine their expertise to build a big picture across what everyone has discovered
- **Problems/Possibilities Jigsaw Puzzle Model**—where learners build expertise in various parts of a problem and then combine their expertise to solve the larger problem.
- **Decision Matrix Model**—where learners assemble facts, ideas, or opinions in a spreadsheet-type of matrix that enables them to do a comparative analysis in order to make an informed rather than a subjective decision
- **Patterns & Trends Matrix Model**—where learners assemble facts, ideas, or opinions in a spreadsheet type of matrix that enables them to look for patterns or trends across the data collected
- **The Timeline Model**—where learners arrange ideas, events, or data in chronological order to enable comparisons, sequences, contrasts, or developments in order to see a larger picture of what is or what was happening.
- **History & Mystery Model**—where learners try to determine what happened, really happened, or find explanations to mysterious happenings
- **Take a Position Model**—where learners take positions based upon careful study rather than upon whim

- **Re-Create Model**—where learners create authentic reproductions whether literary, real, artistically, or creatively as possible
- **Reinvent Model**—where learners try to invent new ways of doing things, processes, environmental systems as close to the real world as possible
- **Learn By Doing**—where learners create apprenticeships, experiments, mockups, or performing tasks in the real or simulated world
- **Teacher-Directed Quest Model**—where learners do research projects under the teacher and learning specialist's direction such as:
    - Online Quest Projects
    - The Report
    - The Research Paper
    - The WebQuest as a Research Model
- **Learner-Directed Quest Model**—where learners take the initiative with adult shadowing of research projects such as:
    - Hero's Journey
    - Become an Expert
    - I Search
- **Mix It Up! Model**—where learners mix and match any of the models above

Resource TIP Loertscher, David V., Carol Koechlin, and Sandi Zwaan. *Beyond Bird Units*. Learning Commons Press, 2010. http://lmcsource.com

When It's Over, It's Just the Beginning of Learning: The Big Think – Building Collective Intelligence

To reach the full potential of their inquiries learners need to explore the bigger impact of their work. Often the concepts and ideas learned are essentially those targeted in learning standards. As individual or group inquiries are completed and presentations given, learners realize that they have considerable expertise in the curriculum topic they have just explored. They have heard, seen, and experienced the findings of others and are ready to examine the collective knowledge of the class. These products or presentations are not the end of the inquiry project but the beginning of a Big Think. Through collaborative knowledge building, learners take this opportunity to transform their learning into something new.

The Big Think is divided into two parts. The first helps learners reflect on the content knowledge they have built. To do this, they might:

- Conduct an active discussion about what they now know as a group vs. what they researched as individuals
- Attack a more difficult problem or challenge using the expertise of individuals to create an inventive solution
- Challenge the group with a new question requiring combined expertise
- Create a new question that leads them into the next learning experience
- Write about larger ideas and concepts learned by the group
- Collaboratively build charts, diagrams, maps, mind maps, plans, or action items based upon both individual and collaborative expertise
- Interact with an expert in order to compare what they have learned with what the expert knows about a topic and ways they might become experts themselves
- Take action on a problem or issue that surfaces during the learning experience
- Participate in related real world events that exhibit what they know and can do

Thus, as they reflect on their knowledge, they can clearly state or demonstrate:

What I Know ↓ **What We Know** ↓ **What I Understand Better**	**What I can Do** ↓ **What We Can Do** ↓ **What I Can Do Better**

Digging Deeper What should learners try to understand as they reflect back on a learning experience?

Have the students experienced collaborative intelligence (excellence) in the following two videos?
http://www.youtube.com/watch?v=D7o7BrlbaDs&feature=player_embedded
and
http://www.youtube.com/watch?v=6WhWDCw3Mng&feature=player_embedded

Can they learn to tell stories unique to their own experience? See the video at:
http://mediastorm.com/publication/african-air

and the Periodic Table of Storytelling at:
http://computersherpa.deviantart.com/art/Periodic-Table-of-Storytelling-203548951

Can they build visualizations of their work? Check out Kathy Schrock's excellent bibliography about infographics at:
https://sites.google.com/a/kathyschrock.net/infographics/links

and an excellent example titled the Periodic Table of Visualization Methods at:
http://www.visual-literacy.org/periodic_table/periodic_table.html

The second part of the Big Think is to design an activity that will press students to think about the learning process they have just encountered. This activity could include reflection, questioning, and assessing techniques. A Big Think about the learning process should result in transference of skills and knowledge to other or new situations, self and peer evaluation, and goal setting. Together, learners might:

- Develop a visual map of their learning journey and/or the information networks they used during the process.
- Chart individual emotions during the learning process on line graphs and layer the graphs to analyze for group or class patterns. Suggest learning tips for dealing with emotions, work habits, dispositions, and organization skills.
- Compare self-assessments and look for similarities or major differences. Use this data to set individual and class goals.
- Discuss and chart how their skill development applies to future work at school and in their personal lives.
- Explore careers that require inquiry process skills and begin a career database for future reference.

- Create a how-to presentation for another group of learners, e.g., best search strategies, notemaking techniques, presentation tips, etc.
- Develop questions to assess collaborative learning experiences and then develop criteria for better team work.
- Analyze the effectiveness of available time, resources, and equipment, and then prepare a needs assessment report for the Learning Commons
- Reflect as a group: Are we getting better as learners? How can we learn more in less time? What technologies will help us learn better?

Thus, as they reflect on their learning journey, they can clearly state or demonstrate:

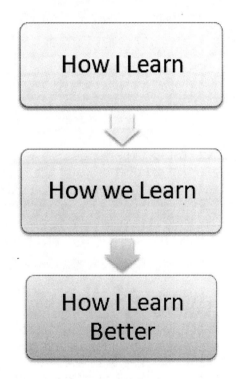

Challenge

Would it really be possible to bend our social media skills over into our academic skills as illustrated in the following infographic? (Hint: click on the graphic to enlarge it): http://w3protokol.com/blog/2011/03/conversations-in-social-media/

The third part of the Big Think is designed as a review by the teaching partners of data gathered from the learner, learning unit activities, and learning organization practices. Combined, this evidence will provide teaching partners with powerful data for refining or redesigning future learning experiences. See the Chapter 9 - School Improvement for further details.

The bottom line, known as the Big Think, is that the traditional end to a learning activity—passing in a paper, a project, or making a presentation—is now a springboard to keep the thinking and learning flowing.

> **Resource TIP** In the book, _The Big Think: 9 Metacognitive Stratagies That Make the End Just the Beginning of Learning_ by David V. Loertscher, Carol Koechlin, and Sandi Zwaan, nine strategies have been developed for collaborative reflection by classroom teachers, students, teacher librarians, teacher technologists, other adult specialists, experts, and/or parents.

 willrich45 Will Richardson
I'd love to see a site like this for schools and kids...real problems that need real solutions. http://bit.ly/dt6SSU #edchat #edreform
20 Jun

Open IDEO http://www.openideo.com/

Activity
Characteristics of Super Learning Experiences
Take action: Compare a learning experience you have recently participated in to the characteristics listed below. What strategies did you experience that would exceed any of these characteristics? In what areas could the learning experience have improved? What areas seem difficult or unfamiliar? What experimentation could happen to test the various characteristics for an improved result in your school?

Characteristics of Super Learning Experiences
- The learning experience happens in a physical/virtual environment conducive to active investigation under the direction of adult coaches.
- Standards and learning outcomes are selected from state/provincial/national documents that provide minimums the learners are to surpass
- The problem, project, or quest engages the learners; they are engaged because the task is relevant and meaningful.
- Learners encounter a wide range of information from which they must develop deep understanding
- Learners use quality information and media in their learning journey
- Each learner develops personal expertise in the topic at hand and adds that expertise to the pool to create collaborative intelligence
- Adult coaches facilitate learning collaboratively (classroom teacher, teacher librarian, teacher technologist, reading specialists, counsellors, outside experts, other specialists, parents, etc.)
- The technology used supports the active investigation of the problem/project and actually contributes to the learning and to learning how to learn.

- Sound instructional designs are used to spur active inquiry, higher-level thinking, habits of mind, and creativity
- Products include both individual and collaborative creations in written and multimedia formats
- 21st century skills are taught "just-in-time" to spur content knowledge
- Sharing both individual and group work takes many forms and a variety of events
- Differentiation allows for multiple routes toward excellence
- Almost without exception, every learner meets or exceeds expectations for the learning experience
- A variety of formative and assessment measures chart progress of individuals and groups of learners.
- After the unit is complete, the adult coaches and learners participate in a metacognitive Big Think and decide how they can do better during the next learning experience together.

The Learning Leadership Team

The school administrator, representatives of grade level or department faculty, student representatives, and learning specialists, including the teacher librarian, constitute the Learning Leadership Team. This professional learning community plans the professional development for the school, centers it in the Experimental Learning Center, encourages and promotes experimentation in the Center, and draws attention to exemplary teaching and learning in the Learning Commons and throughout the school. They conduct action research on experimental learning approaches, school or district initiatives, and guide assessment practices and progress toward achievement.

Kuhlthau, Maniotes and Caspari in their book, *Guided Inquiry: Learning in the 21st Century*, describe the guided inquiry team as the group who:
- Understands the constructivist approach.
- Embraces the team approach to teaching.
- Includes administrators.
- Considers inquiry central to curricular learning.
- Commits to the development of information literacy.
- Allocates time for team planning.
- Defines clear roles for each team member.
- Designs assignments that enable and enhance inquiry learning.
- Allocates time for extended learning.
- Commits to guiding students through inquiry.
- Adopts a flexible approach.
- Endorses innovation and creativity.

Kuhlthau, Maniotes and Caspari (2007, 60)

The collegial relationships among team members that extend into the whole school faculty will be an important factor if experimentation and action research are to become part of the whole school culture.

Systems and Networks that Support Learning and Experimentation

The Learning Leadership Team cannot operate in a vacuum. They require the resources to pursue initiatives, professional development, action research, and ongoing relationships with outside experts. Given these conditions the team affects the growth of the whole school as a learning environment that has its vision centered on long-term improvement rather than on short term dictates. The teacher technologist, as part of the Learning Leadership Team, provides the latest systems, hardware, software, and support to facilitate the growth of knowledge building.

BRIGHT Ideas to Build On

- There are hundreds of tested ideas that engage learners in higher order thinking. Try the list generated by the Generation YES blog authors at: http://constructingmodernknowledge.com/cmk08/?p=1099

- Adopt Blooms Taxonomy at HOTTS Higher Order Thinking Technology Skills
http://www.freetech4teachers.com/2011/04/hotts-higher-order-thinkingtechnology.html

- What is the relationship between student engagement and achievement levels ? This Canadian research study, *What did you do in school today?*, explores the connection. http://www.cea-ace.ca/sites/default/files/cea-2009-wdydist.pdf

- This study was followed up with a teacher effectiveness framework ,developed by Sharon Friesen, that provides five principles for teachers to apply plus a useful rubric to help teachers improve their design of learning experiences.
    - Principle 1 – Teachers are Designers of Learning
    - Principle 2 – Work Students are Asked to Undertake is Worth Their Time and Attention
    - Principle 3 – Assessment Practices Improve Students Learning and Guide Teaching
    - Principle 4 – Teachers Foster A Variety of Interdependent Relationships

- **Principle 5 – Teachers Improve Their Practice in The Company of Their Peers**
http://www.cea-ace.ca/publication/what-did-you-do-school-today-teaching-effectiveness-framework-and-rubric
Sharon Friesen (2009)

- As the learners approach a new topic, would they be able to generate better and better questions that could be prompted by working in the following matrix?
https://spreadsheets.google.com/spreadsheet/ccc?key=0Ap3yb3UOI0Ycd E2M1dtNGdwcUxWaG1IdjgzTWN4NUE#gid=0

- Or, if they were to encounter a huge number of resources on a current topic, would they know how to sort through the jungle?
http://zomobo.com/

- Sharon Nelson shares her recommendations for assisting students in the building of e-portfolios at:
http://thejournal.com/articles/2011/06/29/3-keys-for-a-successful-eportfolio-implementation.aspx

- Explore Paul Saffo's notion of a third kind of knowledge (what really matters) at: http://stupidgoogle.wordpress.com/2010/09/14/the-third-kind-of-knowledge/

- Discover Eli Pariser's warning about Web Personalization:
http://www.thefilterbubble.com/ted-talk

- Study the Partnership for 21st Century Learning's Common Core Toolkit at:
http://www.p21.org/index.php?option=com_content&task=view&id=1005& Itemid=236

- A Brief History of Knowledge Building uncovers knowledge building principles http://www.cjlt.ca/index.php/cjlt/article/viewArticle/574

- Success in deep learning is being reported when learners study a topic throughout their schooling at: http://www.ierg.net/LiD/

- Check out the myths about Project Based Learning at:
http://www.fluency21.com/blogpost.cfm?blogID=2092&utm_source=Com mitted+Sardine+Blog+Update&utm_campaign=da3eba5afc-RSS_EMAIL_CAMPAIGN&utm_medium=email

- Gary Sager's rules learned from Seamour Papert's final work: http://blog.genyes.org/index.php/2011/06/08/8-big-ideas-of-the-constructionist-learning-lab/

- Explore how to build a Human Library http://humanlibrary.org/

Scenarios of Knowledge Building In Action

- **A Major Decision**. Every year, the sixth graders chose a location for a class excursion, but the teacher noticed that the decision was usually based on popularity and whim rather than sound decision-making practice. Enlisting the support of the teacher librarian and the district technology coordinator, a research project ensued. Using a Google spreadsheet so that everyone could be working simultaneously, the students collected facts about specific locations on class-designed acceptability criteria: travel time, cost, fun factor, accessibility for all students etc. The teacher librarian taught not just how to find the answer to put into the spreadsheet but why accurate information was so very important. All three teachers became coaches. When the spreadsheet columns and rows were filled with data, the coaches asked the students what they should do now. The idea of reducing the size of the matrix developed, since any remote location, for example, would eliminate that excursion from consideration. Locations were eliminated until the last remaining were those that met all criteria. Accurate information and the process of decision-making were talked about over and over. Students ended up being confident that they had chosen the right excursion and they understood the basis on which good decisions are made.

- **A Big, Big Think.** When the state governor made a proposal to the regional state governors that they move on multiple fronts to work on the energy crisis, one school's science teacher thought that teenagers just might make a contribution. Mentioning the governor's idea, the science teacher suggested that the entire high school, and perhaps surrounding high schools could take on the governor's challenge. The school principal presented the idea at the first meeting of the professional learning community and there was a round of applause, and a "let's do this" from the entire faculty. Specialists, classroom teachers, community, experts, and excited students began the plans. The professional learning community demanded that the project be based on two major principles: careful research to produce deep understanding of the energy crisis, and a year-long reflection on the skills needed by the students that would enable them to make a sound contribution to a major problem. Thus began their journey. Every week rotating class reflections were scheduled: What do we know now? What skills do we need to advance further? What do you, as a reader, think could have happened? And just why is metacognitive activity done on a regular basis?

- **Action!** In a meeting of the professional learning community, the math teacher was warning that more attention be devoted to math in the school. The P.E. teacher noted that 9 year olds needed more time in physical activities because of a major national study showing a drop in activity at that age, and, the teacher librarian demanded more time for the kids to connect to literature in order to raise reading scores. The technology director suggested to the group that all three competing agendas be combined into a single initiative. There was silence. Then, ideas! They named the project "Run a Chapter". A class committed to run daily while listening to a whole chapter of a book on MP3 players, taking and recording data of heartbeats before and after the run, then calculating individual performance, group performance and school performance as part of an effort to build understanding of applied math. Reflection sessions held once a week did data analysis, had discussions about math operations, principles of health, and of the stories to which they were listening. Students invited the mayor to the school for a tour of the entire project, and he presented the students with a special fitness award at a final assembly of the year. He also passed out coupons to the city recreation center for summer fun, and the public library linked their summer reading program into the recreation center program.

- **Way Beyond all About**. The primary division in a remote rural school met with the teacher librarian to plan a unit on Cultures of the World. New books were ordered and appropriate video and web materials sourced. During a final planning meeting one of the teachers happened to mention a web site she had just discovered where a primary teacher, Kathy Cassidy, was using a wiki and connecting with other classes around the world to reinforce math concepts. She shared the link http://primaryweb2.wikispaces.com/ and it sparked all kinds of ideas for learning with other cultures, not just about them.

Over to You. Discuss with your group or the authors:

- What experiences have you had with learning units co-taught by classroom teachers and specialists? What were the successes? The challenges?

- Have you had experiences with the Big Think at the end of a learning unit that help learners explore both the collaborative intelligence of what they know, but also the metacognitive journey in getting there?

- If you are having trouble engaging students, consider Brian Harris' seven ways to go from on-task learners to engaged learners at: http://ascd.typepad.com/blog/2011/06/on-task-doesnt-mean-engaged.html

References

- Bernard, Sara. 2011. "Move Over, Sal Khan: Sixth-Graders Create Their Own Math Videos!" *Mind/Shift How We Learn*. August 11, 2011. http://mindshift.kqed.org/2011/08/move-over-sal-khan-sixth-graders-create-their-own-math-videos/

- Friesen, Sharon. 2009. *What did you do in school today? Teaching Effectiveness: A Framework and Rubric.* Canadian Education Association. http://www.cea-ace.ca/publication/what-did-you-do-school-today-teaching-effectiveness-framework-and-rubric

- Kuhlthau, Carol C., Leslie K. Maniotes, and Ann K. Caspari. 2007. *Guided Inquiry:Learning in the 21st Century.* Westport, CT: Libraries Unlimited.

- Larner, John. 2011. "Debunking Five Myths About Project-Based Learning" . *Edutopia.* 7/1/2011. http://www.edutopia.org/blog/debunking-five-pbl-myths-john-larmer

- Popham, W. James. 2008. *Transformative Assessment.* Alexandria, VA: Association for Curriculum Supervision and Development.

- Trilling, Bernie and Charles Fadel. 2009. *21st Century Skills: Learning for Life in our Times.* San Francisco, CA: Jossey-Bass

- Warlick, David. 2010. "Technology-Transformed Learning Environments". *2 cents worth.* March 12, 2010. http://davidwarlick.com/2cents/?p=2294

Resources

Foundational Ideas

- Popham, W. James. 2008. *Transformative Assessment*. Alexandria, VA: Association for Supervision and Curriculum Development.

- Sawyer, R. Keith, ed. 2005. *The Cambridge Handbook of the Learning Sciences*. New York: Cambridge University Press.

Foundational Documents

- American Association of School Librarians (AASL). "Standards for the 21st-Century Learner". http://www.ala.org/ala/aasl/aaslproftools/learningstandards/standards.cfm

- Anderson, Lorin W., David R. Krathwohl, and Benjamin Samuel Bloom. 2000. *A Taxonomy for Learning, Teaching, and Assessing: A Revision of Bloom's Taxonomy of Educational Objectives*. Upper Saddle River,NJ: Longman. A revision of the popular taxonomy.

- International Information and Communication Technologies (ICT) Literacy Panel. 2007. "Digital Transformation: A Framework for ICT Literacy." Princeton, NJ: Educational Testing Services. http://www.ets.org/Media/Tests/Information_and_Communication_Technology_Literacy/ictreport.pdf

- Marzano, Robert J. and John S. Kendall. 2008. *Designing & Assessing Educational Objectives: Applying the New Taxonomy*. Thousand Oaks, CA: Corwin Press. An elaboration and restructuring of Blooms Taxonomy from a different perspective.

- The Partnership for 21st Century Learning. *The Intellectual and Policy Foundations of the 21st Century Skills Framework*. http://www.p21.org/route21/images/stories/epapers/skills_foundations_final.pdf

- Wilson, Timothy D. 2002. *Strangers to Ourselves: Uncovering Adaptive Unconscious*. Cambridge, MA: Harvard University Press. A major psychological tour of how we behave and make decisions.

Professional Organizations

- Association for Supervision and Curriculum Development (ASCD) http://ascd.org

- American Association of School Librarians
  http://www.ala.org/ala/aasl/aaslindex.cfm

- International Society for Technology in Education (ISTE) http;//isteorg

- Canadian Association for School Libraries (CASL)
  http://www.cla.ca/AM/Template.cfm?Section=CASL2

- Galileo Professional Network http://www.galileo.org/inquiry-what.html

- International Association of Learning Sciences http://www.isls.org/index.html

Professional Resources

- Blos, Susi, and Jane Krauss. 2007. *Reinventing Project-Based Learning: Your Field Guide to Real-World Projects in the Digital Age.* Washington, DC: International Society for Technology in Education

- Callison, Daniel and Leslie Preddy. 2006. *The Blue Book on Information, Age Inquiry, Instruction and Literacy.* Westport, CT: Libraries Unlimited.

- Danielson, Charlotte. 2007. *Enhancing Professional Practice: a Framework for Teachers*, 2nd edition. Alexandria, VA: Association for Supervision and Curriculum Development.

- DuFour, Rebecca, Richard DuFour, and Robert Eaker. 2006. *Professional Learning Communities at Work Plan Book.* Bloomington, IN: Solution Tree Press.

- DuFour, Richard, Rebecca DuFour, and Robert Eaker. 2006. *Learning by Doing: A Handbook for Professional Learning Communities at Work.* Bloomington, IN: Solution Tree Press.

- DuFour, Richard, Rebecca DuFour, and Robert Eaker. 2008. *Revisiting Professional Learning Communities at Work: New Insights for Improving Schools.* Bloomington, IN: Solution Tree Press.

- *A Framework for K-12 Science Education: Practices, Crosscutting Concepts, and Core Ideas.* 2011. Washington, DC: The National Academies Press. PDF version available online at http://www.nap.edu/catalog.php?record_id=13165

- Habits of Mind http://www.habits-of-mind.net/

- Jensen, Eric. 2008. *Brain-Based Learning: The New Paradigm of Teaching.* 2nd edition. Thousand Oaks, CA: Corwin Press.

- Koechlin, Carol and Sandi Zwaan. 2003. *Build Your Own Information Literate School.* Salt Lake City, UT: Hi Willow Research and Publishing.

- Koechlin, Carol and Sandi Zwaan. 2001. *Info Tasks for Successful Learning.* Markham, ON: Pembroke Publishers.

- Koechlin, Carol and Sandi Zwaan. 2006. *Q Tasks: How to Empower Students to Ask Questions and Care About Answers.* Markham, ON: Pembroke Publishers.

- Kuhlthau, Carol C., Leslie K. Maniotes, and Ann K. Caspari. 2007. *Guided Inquiry: Learning in the 21st Century.* Westport, CT: Libraries Unlimited.

- Loertscher, David V., Carol Koechlin, and Sandi Zwaan. 2005. *Ban Those Bird Units: Thinking and Understanding in Information-rich and Technology-rich Environments.* Salt Lake City, UT: Hi Willow Research and Publishing.

- Loertscher, David V., Carol Koechlin, and Sandi Zwaan. 2007. *Beyond Bird Units. Thinking and Understanding in Information and Technology Rich Environments.* Salt Lake City, UT: Hi Willow Research & Publishing.

- Loertscher, David V., Carol Koechlin, and Sandi Zwaan. 2011. *Beyond Bird Units: 18 Models for Teaching and Learning in Information-rich and Technology-rich Environments.* Refresh edition. Salt Lake City, UT: Hi Willow Research and Publishing.

- Loertscher, David V., Carol Koechlin, and Sandi Zwaan. 2009. *The Big Think: 9 Metacognative Strategies That Make the End Just the Beginning of Learning.* Salt Lake City, UT: Hi Willow Research and Publishing.

- Marzano, Robert J. 2007. *The Art and Science of Teaching: A Comprehensive Framework for Effective Teaching.* Alexandria, VA: Association for Supervision and Curriculum Development.

- Marzano, Robert J. and Debra Pickering. 2010. *The Highly Engaged Classroom.* Bloomington, IN: Solution Tree Press.

- McKenzie, Jamie. 2009. *Beyond Cut-and-Paste: Engaging Students in Making Good New Ideas.* Bellingham, WA: FNO Press.

- Montiel-Overall, Patricia and Donald C. Adcock. 2007. *Collaboration.* Chicago, IL: American Library Association.

- Small, Gary and Gigi Vorgan. 2008. *iBrain: Surviving the Technological Alteration of the Modern Mind.* New York: Collins Living (Harper Collins Publishers).

- Tomlinson, Carol Ann, Kay Brimijoin, and Lane Narvaez. 2008. *The Differentiated School: Making Revolutionary Changes in Teaching and Learning.* Alexandria, VA: Association for Supervision and Curriculum Development.

- Thompson, Clive. 2011. "How Khan Academy Is Changing the Rules of Education". *Wired.* August 2011. http://www.wired.com/magazine/2011/07/ff_khan/

- Trilling, Bernie and Charles Fadel. 2009. *21st Century Skills: Learning for Life in Our Times.* San Francisco CA: Jossey-Bass.

- Wiggins, Grant and Jay McTighe. 2005. *Understanding by Design.* Expanded 2nd edition. Upper Saddle River, NJ: Prentice Hall.

- Williams, Anthony D. and Don Tapscott. 2010. *Wikinomics: How Mass Collaboration Changes Everything.* New York: Penguin Group.

- Williams, Robin T. and David V. Loertscher. 2008. *In Command! Kids and Teens Build and Manage Their Own Information Spaces, And... Learn to Manage Themselves in Those Spaces.* Salt Lake City, UT: Learning Commons Press.

- Zmuda, Allison and Violet H. Harada. 2008. *Librarians as Learning Specialists: Meeting the Learning Imperative for the 21st Century.* Westport, CT: Libraries Unlimited.

Chapter 4

Learning Literacies
and the Learning Commons

What counts as literacy?
Transliteracy is a term gaining more and more attention with teacher librarians and reading specialists. View this brief slide show to find out why.
http://www.youtube.com/watch?v=sk4Cw8vrDuM&feature=player_embedded. Visit Libraries and Transliteracy blog to find out more.
http://librariesandtransliteracy.wordpress.com/what-is-transliteracy/

———————— ❇ ————————

Defining literacy is a process of continuous negotiation that is fueled by social, economic, and technological changes. To be literate is to have the skills and knowledge to make meaningful connections between what one knows and what one is trying to understand, apply, or communicate. Reading, writing, speaking, listening, and communicating are foundational but the term literacy, however, has matured. An elastic definition of literacy now encompasses textual, digital, visual, media, informational, cultural, and global literacy under this broad learning umbrella. It could be argued that the umbrella term literacy now means learning literacy with all of the above nestled together. New literacies will continue to evolve as technologies appear and disappear and as global and societal pressures shift the focus on specific information and learner needs. It isn't the label that is the critical issue, but the understanding of the need to bring Learning Commons into the 21st Century as evolving centers for literacy excellence.

Just as predicted in the original version of this text, "New Literacies" are evolving to better address the skills needed to work and play with new modes and modalities of information creation, storage, and sharing. Experimentation with technologies, discovery and inquiry based learning, and collaborative environments make the Learning Commons a natural incubator for fostering new literacies. Teacher librarians and other teaching specialists need to keep pace with multi literacy research and best practice.

Digging Deeper Toward A Definition of 21st-Century Literacies

Literacy has always been a collection of cultural and communicative practices shared among members of particular groups. As society and technology change, so does literacy. Because technology has increased the intensity and complexity of literate environments, the twenty-first century demands that a literate person possess a wide range of abilities and competencies, many literacies. These literacies—from reading online newspapers to participating in virtual classrooms—are multiple, dynamic, and malleable. As in the past, they are inextricably linked with particular histories, life possibilities and social trajectories of individuals and groups. Twenty-first century readers and writers need to
- *Develop proficiency with the tools of technology*
- *Build relationships with others to pose and solve problems collaboratively and cross-culturally*
- *Design and share information for global communities to meet a variety of purposes*
- *Manage, analyze and synthesize multiple streams of simultaneous information*
- *Create, critique, analyze, and evaluate multi-media texts*
- *Attend to the ethical responsibilities required by these complex environments*

     NCTE Executive Committee (2008)

The following chart identifies the many learning literacies fostered in the Learning Commons and provides brief examples of implementation.

Information Literacy	• is the ability to discern what you need, find the best information and through analysis and synthesis transform the information to personal knowledge. • in the Learning Commons personal expertise is then shared with others to build collective knowledge and encourage innovation and creativity.
Media Literacy	• is the ability to access, analyze, interpret, create and communicate media messages in a variety of forms. • in the Learning Commons opportunities to build media literacy competencies are woven into authentic tasks and demonstrations of learning.
Visual Literacy	• is the ability to derive meaning from visual information or to "read images" and conversely the ability to create visual formats to demonstrate or communicate information and ideas. • in the Learning Commons there are both physical and virtual opportunities to hone this literacy.
Digital Literacy	• is the ability to use current technologies to the best effect to support needs. • in the Learning Commons this also encompasses the ability to teach others.
Critical Literacy	• is the ability to think deeply and analytically about information and ideas. • in the Learning Commons a focus on questioning skills enables effective critical literacy development.
Cultural Literacy	• is the ability to build knowledge of self and others. • in the Learning Commons all relevant perspectives are explored and learning is designed to build diversified understandings and empathy with others.
Multi-modal Literacy	• is the ability to express and communicate knowledge in many formats both physical and digital. • in the Learning Commons learning spaces and technologies are in place to encourage experimentation with multi-modal expression.
Transliteracy	• is the ability to read, write and interact across a range of platforms, tools and media from signing and orality through handwriting, print, TV, radio and film, to digital social networks. • a major goal in the Learning Commons • (http://librariesandtransliteracy.wordpress.com/what-is-transliteracy/)
Evolving Literacies	• Environmental, Civic, Financial, Health and Global. • in the Learning Commons the program and excellent resources and technologies provide a rich playground for developing evolving literacies.

Learning to Learn

It isn't the literacy label that is the critical issue, but the need to establish the Learning Commons as an **evolving center for literacy excellence**. This is accomplished as illustrated in the figure below by applying learning literacies to projects and tasks that are relevant and real world for learners. Competency with multiple literacies puts more tools in the learning to learn toolbox.

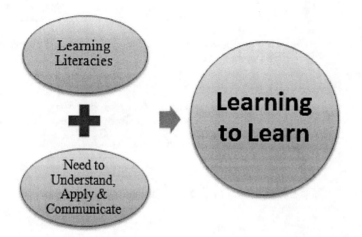

Discussion Point Learning to learn means that one is getting better and better as a learner. **21st Century Fluency** is the unconscious and seamless demonstration of learning literacy skills proficiencies, specifically information, media, creativity, collaboration and solution fluencies. Visit the project site for more information. http://21stcenturyfluency.com/index.cfm

What is it that we want students as the rising generation to know and be able to do? Educators have developed multiple content standards for every discipline and every grade level. Naturally, teachers and students are overwhelmed by the required content. Robert Marzano has spoken of an analysis done by McCREL noting that if just the state content standards were actually taught, elementary and high school would take 22 years to complete. Clustering expectations and examining existing curriculum for what Wiggins and McTighe term 'enduring understandings' is definitely needed. But the question remains, should it be content alone that drives our curriculum? Some organizations, as indicated in the chart below, have developed standards and processes to empower 21st century workers and learners, not with the content to be mastered, but with the skills required to learn how to learn.

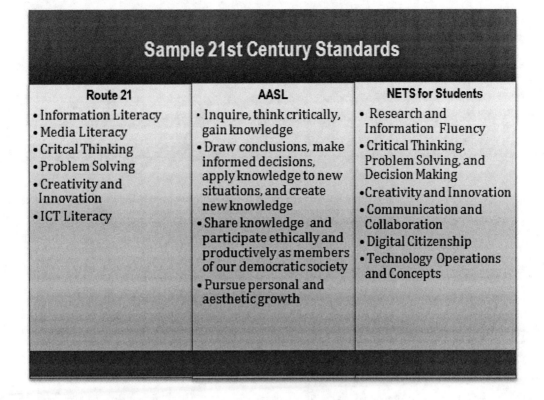

Sample 21st Century Standards

Route 21	AASL	NETS for Students
• Information Literacy • Media Literacy • Critcal Thinking • Problem Solving • Creativity and Innovation • ICT Literacy	• Inquire, think critically, gain knowledge • Draw conclusions, make informed decisions, apply knowledge to new situations, and create new knowledge • Share knowledge and participate ethically and productively as members of our democratic society • Pursue personal and aesthetic growth	• Research and Information Fluency • Critical Thinking, Problem Solving, and Decision Making • Creativity and Innovation • Communication and Collaboration • Digital Citizenship • Technology Operations and Concepts

These organizations are leading the way for educators to refocus student preparation for a changing world; a world where information is no longer the driving force. We have left the Information Age, where data and computer savvy ruled, and are now already immersed in a world of knowledge building and big Ideas. Preparing students with learning literacies is now paramount. By knowing how to learn students will be able to take informational content in any form and work it until they have deep understanding. They will know how to evaluate information and analyze it for relationships, discrepancies, perspectives, and bias. They will know how to use information and ideas critically and creatively to build personal knowledge, solve problems, and make decisions. The truly literate of the 21st century will have the know how to keep on learning, creating, and sharing in spite of, or perhaps because of, the increasing complexity and challenges of information, technologies, and global issues.

Resource TIP

- *AASL Standards*
  www.ala.org/ala/mgrps/divs/aasl/guidelinesandstandards/learningstandards/standards.cfm

- *Mile Guide for 21st Century Skills*
  www.p21.org/downloads/P21_MILE_Guide.pdf

- *NETS for Students* www.iste.org/standards/nets-for-students.asp

- National Council of Teachers of English (NCTE)
  http://www.ncte.org/governance/literacies

- *Together For Learning: School Libraries and the Emergence of the Learning Commons*
  www.accessola.com/data/6/rec_docs/677_OLATogetherforLearning.pdf

- *The Common Core Standards (U.S.)* http://www.corestandards.org/

The best thing we can be teaching our children today is how to teach themselves.
David Warlick

Empowering the Learner

In the Learning Commons, traditional literacies are naturally nurtured through all learning experiences. Teacher librarians continue to apply their special talents to foster the 'reading habit' with all learners. Supporting independent reading is as critical as ever, if not more so, in an era of so much choice.

Reading is still the king of all literacies because it enables progress in all the others. As Stephen Krashen pointed out a number of years ago in his research-based book, *The Power of Reading,* avid readers automatically develop skills in comprehension, vocabulary, spelling, grammar, and writing. In his latest work, *Free Voluntary Reading,* Krashen continues to make the case that pleasurable reading is still the best predictor of successful readers. We might add that children and teens need to read not just narrative works but also need to delve widely into expository texts. Today's readers are not so inclined to pursue lengthy manuscripts as the previous generation. However, even in their consumption of shorter passages from all types of sources on the Internet, they can pursue their interests with many more texts than any library could have supplied just a decade or two ago. Much of the Internet requires skillful reading and very little of it is what some would term leveled reading. However, the rise of e-books connected to a number of personal digital devices gives a whole new opportunity to explore beyond the few books a classroom or a library might contain in printed form.

Activity

Consider the reading literacy goals and objectives for your school and develop a set of complementary Learning Commons goals. The ideas in this visual will help you get started.

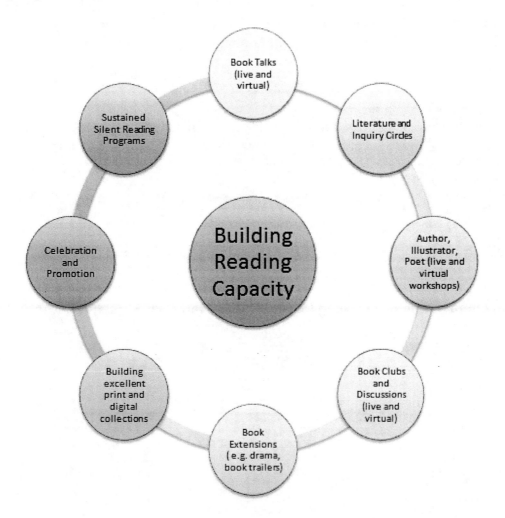

In the Learning Commons, student learning experiences are designed to develop skills and strategies for dealing with a wide range of media, ever changing technologies, and vast amounts of information. Through relevant real world challenges students will develop learning literacies to mirror the changes brought about by the evolution of information and communication technologies. In other words, they will master the learning necessary to learn literacies that will help them master the content knowledge they are asked to learn. In simple terms, learners know a lot and they know how to learn anything they need to learn. Because the resources are plentiful and the technology accessible, as shown in the charts below, learners are developing skills for the purpose of using those skills to learn and, in turn, developing deep understanding. Learners may have mastered the skills of social networking for communicating with friends, but it is only when they blend them in the direction of their academic skills that they begin to develop the globally competitive skills they will need.

Example: Suppose the leadership team notices that listening skills are declining in the face of increased use of social media. They decide to work across the school on listening attention spans. One resource they consult is: <u>Seven ways to improve listening.</u>

> "If schools are to teach students 21st Century skills, educators must collaboratively engage in the process to clarify what those skills are, the indicators they will monitor to ensure each student had acquired those skills, and the best strategies they can employ in helping students develop the skills."
>
> Richard and Rebecca DuFour (2010, 81)

The following chart identifies some of the indicators of the development of learning literacies.

Learning Literacies in the Learning Commons - Indicators of Student Success

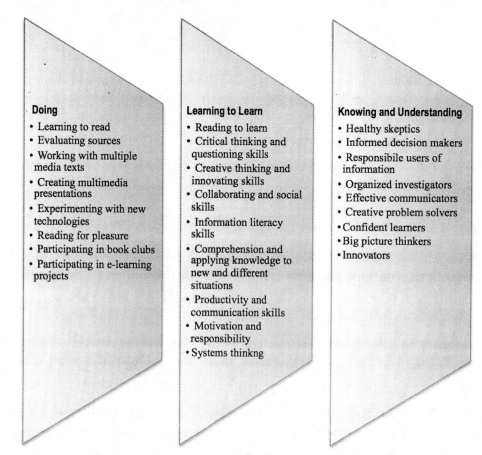

Doing
- Learning to read
- Evaluating sources
- Working with multiple media texts
- Creating multimedia presentations
- Experimenting with new technologies
- Reading for pleasure
- Participating in book clubs
- Participating in e-learning projects

Learning to Learn
- Reading to learn
- Critical thinking and questioning skills
- Creative thinking and innovating skills
- Collaborating and social skills
- Information literacy skills
- Comprehension and applying knowledge to new and different situations
- Productivity and communication skills
- Motivation and responsibility
- Systems thinkng

Knowing and Understanding
- Healthy skeptics
- Informed decision makers
- Responsibile users of information
- Organized investigators
- Effective communicators
- Creative problem solvers
- Confident learners
- Big picture thinkers
- Innovators

In the U.S. the Governors of most states have sponsored the Common Core Standards that center literacy in reading, writing, speaking and listening around doing short research projects linked to various disciplines. Such regular learning activities would put the use of the Learning Commons front and center in both school improvement initiatives and into the lives of each student across the grade levels. National tests designed to test this idea are to appear in 2014.

The Learning Skills Journey

We should explain to learners that a combination of learning to learn and subject content results in a journey that combines the skills and knowledge needed to propel them to success. Thus they are able to pass almost any kind of assessment thrown at them. They can pass a knowledge test of the topic at hand. They can also demonstrate their use of tools to help them be critical or creative thinkers, and they can turn their knowledge into "doing" by exhibiting an action, a project, an action plan, or any other real-world event. As learners, they become more and more in command of their own learning. They become independent learners, learners who appreciate and expect coaches, but have the ability to make progress themselves. As shown in the following pathway, they can actually document their journey toward mastery and excellence and reflect regularly about whether they could be more efficient learners.

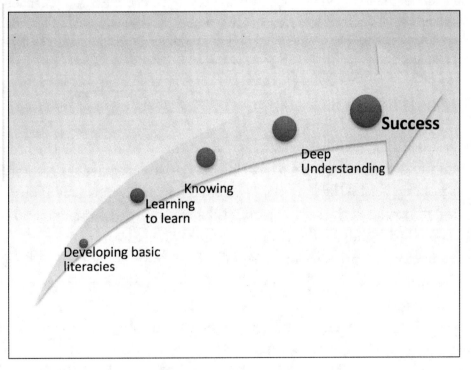

Learning Literacies Take Me on a Journey

For example, the Kentucky State Library has developed an interactive map of the research process at: http://www.kyvl.org/kids/homebase.html as shown below:

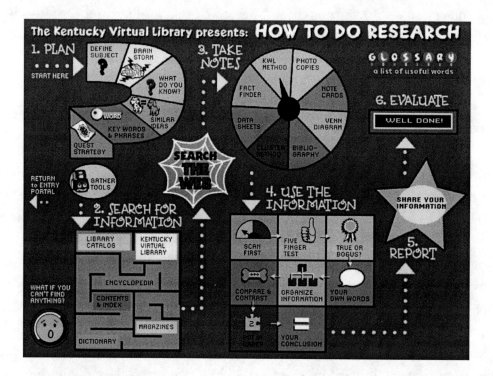

Challenge Using your local inquiry model, create an interactive research expedition for the teachers and learners in your jurisdiction. Embed reflection throughout and high level analysis and synthesis strategies to ensure knowledge building. A simple tool to create such an interact diagram is to use the software program Glogster.

Empowering the Teacher

During the last decade, much has been made about the need to raise basic literacy to prescribed minimal levels. The results have been less than spectacular. As Stephen Krashen has pointed out in *The Power of Reading*, today's youth read at about the same level as their parents did at the same age, but the problem is that the demand for literacy has risen. Coupled with the need to embrace more than just reading literacy, classroom teachers have felt intense pressure in spite of the rising number of English language learners and continuing poverty pressures.

Teachers at all levels have been urged to make the various literacies a part of their daily teaching routine, something that some secondary subject specialists have challenged. However, if progress is to be made helping learners exceed reading expectations along with helping them develop other literacies, then classroom teachers cannot be expected to succeed alone just because they are being told to do so.

Empowering classroom teachers means that the entire school develops a plan and an atmosphere conducive to literacy excellence and that all the specialists work collaboratively to help achieve the goal. Teacher librarians supply every reader with a wide selection of materials that learners want to read and strive to develop a love of reading. Reading coaches work alongside classroom teachers, both elementary and secondary, to model and demonstrate the best strategies. Teacher technologists make wide reading far beyond the printed text appealing and available to learners. In other words, the school develops a reading culture in addition to emphasizing that it is just not enough to read at a minimal level. In addition, there are numerous other learning literacies that are stressed.

The Open Commons is the space for all the literacies to be implemented. The Experimental Learning Center is the space where the entire faculty comes together to make literacies happen. The diagram below suggests some of the possibilities to empower all teachers through a whole-school sustained effort.

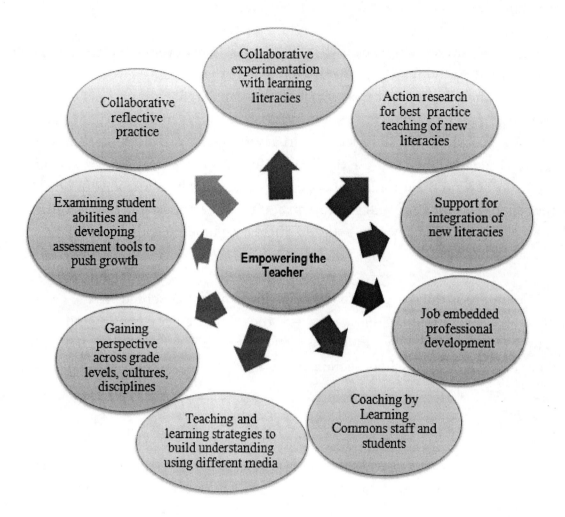

The Learning Commons as Literacy Central

The approach to literacy in the Learning Commons differs from the skill development and testing of the classroom. The Commons is at the center of literacy for a school because programs are more holistic and focus on interest, excitement, engagement, and relevance as the central raison d'être. Everyone desires literacy in all its many forms because they want to be involved, they want to learn. How does that happen? What transformation toward a client-side organization causes the switch from drill to thrill? A starter list might include:

- The Commons reading collection circulates to every classroom and to every learner in unlimited amounts. Thus, teachers are able to change their rotating classroom collections as often as need and interest dictate. For learners, the

Commons has what they want to read and they too are free to exchange as often as they wish.

- The Commons is the center of reading and other literacy initiatives for the entire school. Amount read, viewed, and listened to begin with interest and curricular needs as the key factors. Everyone becomes a critic of literature, film, Internet content, mass media, and the events surrounding new releases.

- Learners research and develop exhibitions in a wide variety of media, and, in the process, develop information literacy, critical thinking, and creativity, as they build expertise. Learners take pride in their creations because they are archived in the Commons and available to the world.

- Learners build skill in creating and using the wide variety of technologies that enhance the learning experience, helping them communicate their knowledge across the room, across the school, or across the world.

- Learners build skill not just in working with printed text, but also in audio, video, and mixed media. They build these skills during collaborative creations, projects, and events both locally, nationally, and globally.

- Learners know that no matter the culture, the skill level, the interest level, the language ability, the disability or the super ability, the Learning Commons is the cool place where what they need and want is available in abundance. They feel ownership because they help build the collection. For teachers, this abundance, along with 'just in time' skill instruction, makes the Learning Commons THE ONLY place that makes the literacies possible when differentiated instruction is emphasized.

Given the underlying policies that support literacies in the Learning Commons, visitors who spend time there might list the following as evidence that literacy skills are being transformed into knowledge building:

- A team of students deconstructing advertising samples to identify techniques that were used to deliver a message.

- A class learning how to experiment with graphs to effectively represent the data they have gathered on recycling in their community.

- A group of English learners viewing a movie version of a piece of literature or a book trailer of the piece in order to get the basics of the story in their heads before attacking the full text in English.

- A class searching the web, to find authoritative sources on an issue they are studying, and building their own "trusted" list to use in their next research session.

- The technology teacher coaching a group of students on use of a new camera as they make a video tutorial for other students.

- The fantasy book club having a brown bag lunch in simultaneous discussion with the same club in a different school across the city.

- A class talking with an invited expert comparing what they know with what the expert does in real life.

- A group of students leaving for the local bookstore where they are choosing graphic novels based on selection criteria they have developed.

- E-readers are signed out by a special education teacher for his students to use for pleasure reading.

joycevalenza Joyce Valenza

Some of the real learning is in having the kids plan & moderate the questions & discussion & manage the debriefing #yalitchat #tlchat

2 hours ago

The Learning Literacies Leadership Team

The school's Learning Literacies Leadership Team has student representatives and solicits a variety of advice from all the learners in the school as everyone contributes to the construction of the policies and practices of the Learning Commons. Administrators, classroom teachers, and specialists, including the teacher librarian and reading specialists, constitute this leadership team. A sense of inclusion keeps both teachers and students confident that they are contributing, sharing, and working collaboratively. It is a professional learning community that involves its clientele. Together the team will:

- Collaboratively build a print-rich environment for students
- Promote and celebrate the reading habit
- Timetable sufficient time for free voluntary reading
- Design learning experiences to focus on reading for meaning
- Empower students to develop their own learning lifestyle
- Utilize technologies to *build* literacy competencies
- Integrate cross curricular learning literacies
- Apply information literacies to knowledge building
- Collaborate to explore and experiment with new literacies
- Facilitate job embedded professional development
- Design assessment tools to foster growth of multiple literacy skills
- Observe, track, and analyze growth of learning literacies across grade levels and disciplines
- Support action research projects (individual and collaborative)
- Review, reflect, and redesign literacy initiatives
- Make literacy fun and irresistible.

Systems and Networks that Support Learning and Experimentation

The system that will sustain a literate and learning community begins with a vision by the entire school leadership team. Rather than a one-size-fits-all model or a top-down initiative, a purposeful collaborative is needed to make a sustainable change. The walls between the old library, the computer labs, and the classroom must crumble as client-side policies replace command and control. Everyone understands the needs of the learners because the learners have a voice. The classroom teachers embrace the specialists of the school in these massive initiatives in various literacies. The system accepts the notion that literacy is not dictated but is an integral part of fascinating learning activities that motivate learners to build the skills they need to participate. Excellence rather than minimums is the focus.

The Experimental Learning Center is the place for the documenting of school-wide initiatives. Data walls demonstrate the progress of the experimentation and of the initiatives currently under way. The ELC becomes one more place around which to unite the entire faculty in school improvement.

> *Our students must learn:*
> - *How to make meaning with overwhelming amounts of information*
> - *How to work with people around the world (empathy)*
> - *How to be self directed, interdependent and a superb lifelong learner*
>   Alan November (2010, 279)

BRIGHT Ideas to Build On

- New Media Literacies Project PLAY (Participatory Learning and You)
  http://playnml.wikispaces.com/
  More by Henry Jenkins
  Shall we Play Part 1 http://henryjenkins.org/2011/05/shall_we_play.html
  Shall we Play Part 2
  http://henryjenkins.org/2011/05/shall_we_play_part_two.html

- Media Literacy lessons and resources for teachers, parents and students
  http://www.media-awareness.ca/english/index.cfm

- Teaching students to ask their own questions
  http://www.hepg.org/hel/article/507#home

- New Internet Literacies by Will Richardson
  http://weblogged.wikispaces.com/New+Internet+Literacies

- Applied ISTE standards for framing teacher PD Webinary April 25, 2011 from
  Osseo MN, Tim Wilson and Dawn Nelson at:
  https://nexus.sjsu.edu/play_recording.html?recordingId=1267553046153_130377
  4448320

- E projects to build global literacy
  Free the Children http://www.freethechildren.com/
  Global School Net http://globalschoolnet.org/
  Be the Change http://www.accessola.com/osla/bethechange/home.html

- Activities to build Financial Literacy
  - Get Smart About Money http://www.getsmarteraboutmoney.ca/education-
    programs/for-students/Pages/default.aspx
  - PBS Financial Literacy for Children
    http://www.pbs.org/nbr/site/onair/transcripts/financial_literacy_for_children
    _110207/
  - Kids Lit and Financial Literacy http://econkids.rutgers.edu/

- Central Learning Commons to ensure all learners have access to Information
  Literacy skills and help http://library.wrdsb.ca/

- Transliteracy presentation by Buffy Hamilton
  http://www.slideshare.net/buffyjhamilton/participatory-librarianship-creating-
  possibilities-through-transliteracy-learning-and-linchpins-6008238

- Building visual literacy skills with feeds on your virtual LC site:
  - Infographic-a-Day http://davidwarlick.com/graphicaday/
  - Video-a-Day http://davidwarlick.com/vidaday/

- Kathy Schrock's Everything about Infographics
  https://sites.google.com/a/kathyschrock.net/infographics/links

Scenarios to SPARK Your Thinking About Learning Literacies

- **Book Bags** In a poor urban neighborhood, languages were diverse and reading scores in the basement. The school literacy team met to consider what they could do to address this major problem. The teacher librarian, who was in graduate school to get her masters degree, had heard in class of the success of the book bag program. She convinced her peers to try it. The district library department was anxious to help so they purchased enough red canvas bags for all kindergarten and first grade students in the school and were able to find some funds to purchase high interest books for this age group. Each month each class would come to the library and the children would select two books for their book bag, one they could "read" themselves and one that could be read to them. The bags were numbered and every day, the classroom teacher would send a bag home with each child and it would come back the next morning, to be exchanged with a fresh one. At ten books read per week, each child was reading 300-500 books a year. Book loss was minuscule. Reading scores jumped. The book bag program became a mainstay of the entire reading initiative.

- **SSR with a Twist** A high school chemistry teacher complained to the teacher librarian that Silent Sustained Reading time was wasted time in his classroom and he was going to recommend that it be discontinued. The teacher librarian suggested they try a fresh approach. Taking the topic about to be studied by all the beginning chemistry classes, the pair pulled all the related, "fascinating" books from the library collection, borrowed interesting books from the public library, and used the library credit card to purchase duplicate copies of a few titles from the local bookstore as well as science journals. The students helped find interesting topic related online articles. Every day for the first week, the teacher and the teacher librarian introduced a few new items to the class and modeled the SSR time with the students, saving the last five minutes of SSR to share what they were reading. They also invited students to trade ideas and books. SSR became a popular activity again and general background knowledge was increased.

- **Blog to Write.** The literacy coach was arguing for more opportunities for middle schoolers to write, but the students had lost interest in doing quick writes. The teacher technologist and the teacher librarian offered to work with the eighth grade language arts teachers to infuse new life and interest in writing. First they polled the reading interests of the students, and then introduced the idea of forming book clubs with students blogging about what they had read. Every student was invited to join and assist with an interest blog. Motorcycles, makeup tips, true survival, movie-book tie ins, and fantasy were the most popular first blog topics. Students, with the help of the teachers and specialists, collected books and passed them around. They read during SSR time and blogged after every free reading SSR period. Club topics and bloggers changed monthly under the supervision of a student leadership team, with all the adults assuming coaching positions in the initiative. The literacy coach and teacher technologist had teams of students create some short videos giving writing tips for "selling" a book to another person on the blog. A reading community and writing community emerged.

- **Going Green** The principal attended the specialists' professional learning community and asked what they could do to push the school's going green initiative. A brainstorming session with students, faculty, parents, and community experts generated a slogan for the project as well as a long list of initiatives. The students on the committee were intrigued with the idea of getting the message out so they asked the teacher technologist for help. She showed them examples of different kinds of media formats. The teacher librarian connected them with media literacy websites where they discovered how they would need to consider their message and their audience, and match those to the best format. A production team went into full swing and what had begun as a school project to save energy developed into a major student-produced media blitz of the local community.

- **Role Models** Several reports of harassing and bullying of students on social networking sites led to demands from the parent council for action. The Health specialist invited the police department into the school to consult with staff and to provide workshop material for student awareness sessions. A comment made by the police officer clicked with the teacher librarian and technology teacher. The officer had said that on the social networking sites that young people frequent, there is often misbehavior and inappropriate mimicking because they only have each other as role models. Adults do not tread in these spaces. The specialists had failed in their efforts to encourage teachers to use blogging with students in spite of all the evidence they had gathered that showed how engaged students are on the read/write web. They now proceeded to help teachers see the contributions they could make by providing good role models as well as some parameters for social networking. Blogs were set up for those interested, with social networking skills and behaviors embedded. Teachers were amazed by the amount and quality of free writing their students were spinning on the blogs, especially students who normally said very little in class. Specialists were soon bombarded with inquiries about helping teachers set up other uses for class blogs.

Over to You. Discuss with your group:

- How does a school connect reading skills with fun?

- How does every member of the faculty integrate reading, writing, speaking, and listening into almost every learning experience?

- How are learners building their reading skills and other literacies through non-traditional media?

- How can all teachers help develop literacies no matter their subjects taught or grade level?

- The National Council of Teachers of English have recently updated their definition of literacy to include "Twenty-first Century readers and writers should be able to manage, analyze, synthesize multiple streams of simultaneous information." (NCTE 2008). Will Richardson, in a conference talk, added to this definition as follows: "Twenty-first Century readers and writers should be able to [find] manage, analyze, synthesize [produce and share] multiple streams of simultaneous information." To this list, the authors offer an even more complete definition: "Twenty-first Century readers and writers should be able to [build questions], [find], [consume], manage, analyze, synthesize, [produce and share], [and reflect on] multiple streams of simultaneous information." What do you think?

References

- DuFour, Richard and Rebecca Dufour. 2010. "The Role of Professional Learning Communities in Advancing 21st Century Skills". Balanca, James and Ron Brandt. eds. *21st Century Skills: Rethinking How Students Learn*. Bloomington, IN: Solution Tree.

- Krashen, Stephen. 2006. *The Power of Reading*, 2nd ed. Westport, CT: Libraries Unlimited.

- Krashen, Stephen. 2011. *Free Voluntary Reading.* Westport, CT: Libraries Unlimited.

- National Council of Teachers of English. 2008. NCTE Executive Committee Statement. http://www.ncte.org/

- November, Alan. 2010. "Technology Rich, Information Poor". Balanca, James and Ron Brandt. eds. *21st Century Skills: Rethinking How Students Learn*. Bloomington, IN: Solution Tree.

Resources

Foundational Ideas

- Anderson, Lorin W., David R. Krathwohl, and Benjamin Samuel Bloom. 2000. *A Taxonomy for Learning, Teaching, and Assessing: A Revision of Bloom's Taxonomy of Educational Objectives*. White Plains, NY: Pearson Longman. A revision of the popular taxonomy.

- International Reading Association http://www.reading.org/ See their many policy statements on reading and literacy.

- Marzano, Robert J. and John S. Kendall. 2008. *Designing & Assessing Educational Objectives: Applying the New Taxonomy*. Thousand Oaks, CA: Corwin Press. An elaboration and restructuring of Blooms Taxonomy from a different perspective.

- National Council of Teachers of English. http://www.ncte.org/ Various statements on literacies for children and teens.

- National Council of Teachers of English. 2005. *Standards for Middle and High School Literacy Coaches: A Project of the International Reading Association in Collaboration with NCTE, NCTM, NSTA, and NCSS, and with support provided by Carnegie Corporation of New York*. Urbana, IL: National Council of Teachers of English. Just one of the various standards documents published by NCTE. See their website for a complete list at: http://www.ncte.org/

- *National Educational Technology Standards for Students*. 2nd ed. 2007. Washington, DC: International Society for Technology in Education.

- Jenkins, Henry et al. 2007. "Confronting the Challenge of Participatory Culture: Media Education for the 21st Century." MacArthur Foundation White Paper. http://www.projectnml.org/files/working/NMLWhitePaper.pdf

Professional Organizations

- National Council of Teachers of English (NCTE) http://www.ncte.org

- Association for Supervision and Curriculum Development (ASCD) http://ascd.org

- American Association of School Librarians (AASL) http://www.ala.org/ala/aasl/aaslindex.cfm

- International Society for Technology in Education (ISTE) http://www.iste.org/

- International Reading Association (IRA) http://www.reading.org/

Professional Resources

- Booth, David and Jennifer Rowsell. 2007. *The Literacy Principal: Leading, Supporting, and Assessing Reading and Writing Initiatives,* second edition. Markham, ON: Pembroke Publishers.

- Boyes, Karen and Graham Watts, eds. 2010. *Developing Habits of Mind in Elementary Schools*. Alexandria, VA: Association for Supervision and Curriculum Development.

- Braunger, Jane and Jan Patricia Lewis. 2006. *Building a Knowledge Base in Reading,* 2nd ed. Urbana, ILL: National Council of Teachers of English.

- Callison, Daniel and Leslie Preddy. 2006. *The Blue Book on Information Age Inquiry, Instruction and Literacy*. Westport, CT: Libraries Unlimited.

- Costa, Arthur and Bena Kallick, eds. 2009. *Habits of Mind Across the Curriculum: Practical and Creative Strategies for Teachers.* Alexandria, VA: Association for Supervision and Curriculum Development.

- Fogarty, Robin. 2007. *Literacy Matters: Strategies Every Teacher Can Use,* 2nd ed. Thousand Oaks, CA: Corwin Press.

- Harada, Violet H. and Joan M. Yoshima. 2010. *Assessing For Learning: Librarians and Teachers as Partners,* 2nd ed. Westport, CT: Libraries Unlimited.

- Harvey, Stephanie and Anne Goudvis. 2007. *Strategies that Work: Teaching Comprehension for Understanding and Engagement.* 2nd ed. Portland, ME: Stenhouse Publishers.

- Ivey, Gay and Douglas Fisher. 2006. *Creating Literacy-Rich Schools for Adolescents.* Alexandria, VA: Association for Supervision and Curriculum Development.

- Kajder, Sara. 2008. "Reaching the Reluctant Learner," *Educational Leadership,* v. 65, no 6 (March 2008).

- Koechlin Carol and Sandi Zwaan. 2006. *Build You Own Information Literate School.* Salt Lake City, UT: Hi Willow Research and Publishing.

- Koechlin, Carol and Sandi Zwaan. 2008. *Building Info Smarts.* Markham, ON: Pembroke Publishers.

- Krashen, Stephen. 2006. *The Power of Reading,* 2nd ed. Westport, CT: Libraries Unlimited.

- Latrobe, Kathy and Judy Drury. 2009. *Critical Approaches to Young Adult Literature.* New York: Neal-Schuman Publishers Inc.

- Moreillon, Judi. 2007. *Collaborative Strategies for Teaching Reading Comprehension: Maximizing Your Impact.* Chicago, IL: American Library Association.

- Ohler, Jason. 2007. *Digital Storytelling in the Classroom: New Media Pathways to Literacy, Learning, and Creativity.* Thousand Oaks, CA: Corwin Press.

- Roam, Dan. 2008. *The Back of the Napkin: Solving Problems and Selling Ideas with Pictures.* New York: Portfolio (Penguin Group).

- Warlick, David F. 2008. *Redefining Literacy 2.0,* 2nd ed. Santa Barbara CA: Linworth.

- Warlick, David F. 2 cents worth blog at: http://davidwarlick.com/2cents/

Chapter 5

Technology
and the Learning Commons

Does technology impact learning?

The prevailing technologies of a particular place and time have always been intimately linked with education, because a society's tools are both the subject and the means of its learning. Today, the fact that technology pervades almost every sphere of life – from home to work to play – results in profound implications for learning, both in schools and throughout life. Students are able to connect – and create – with their peers, and with the wider world, in ways that were unfathomable just a few years ago. Learning tools – media, telecommunication, and networked technologies coupled with learning science – are rapidly evolving into a powerful support system for acquiring the skills needed for modern life. (Partnership for 21st Century Skills)

How do we keep up with technology trends? A good place to start is the yearly Horizon Report at http://www.nmc.org/pdf/2011-Horizon-Report-K12.pdf . But how do we know technology is an effective tool for learning? A convincing case is found at http://www.ncsu.edu/meridian/winter2011/krugerross/print.html

---

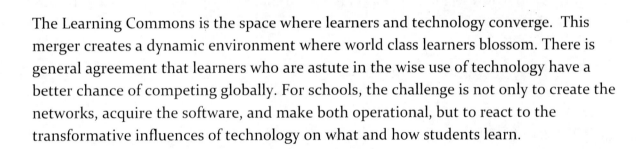

The Learning Commons is the space where learners and technology converge. This merger creates a dynamic environment where world class learners blossom. There is general agreement that learners who are astute in the wise use of technology have a better chance of competing globally. For schools, the challenge is not only to create the networks, acquire the software, and make both operational, but to react to the transformative influences of technology on what and how students learn.

Rapid changes in technologies and communication have opened up new worlds and challenges in education just as they have revolutionized every other organization. We are just beginning to realize the profound impact these changes have on all facets of learning. This is a trend that will only become more pronounced. Technology is already a powerful extension of self and influences what we know and what we do in many ways every day. Leveraging this force to solve problems, shape understanding, and construct and share knowledge to benefit ourselves and others is the future.

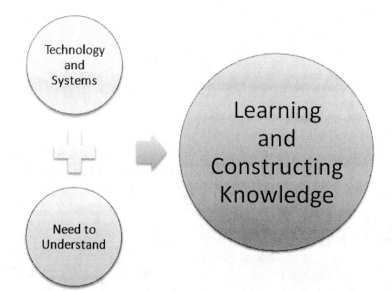

The question arises, how do we take advantage of student comfort with social networking and the interactive technologies that students currently associate with pleasure? How do we apply the personal knowledge, skills, and experiences from the students' worlds to create a school environment that utilizes their abilities; a curriculum where learners find relevance, a place where they can flourish? Early solutions to this challenge were to create computer labs in which technology was taught - a pull out course like an isolated reading skills curriculum.

The Learning Commons concept approaches technology as the natural way of doing business. It supports an environment where everyone, including adults, is learning how to engage in a world of seemingly unending possibilities. To do this, a serious re-conceptualization of the technological environment in a school is required.

Administrative and Instructional Computing: A Re-Conceptualization

It is important to make a distinction between administrative computing in the school and instructional computing. Administrative computing is a tightly controlled space for budgets, schedules, student records, grades, and anything else related to administration. Security for this system is essential.

The instructional computer system that serves the teaching and learning function in the school is quite different from the administrative system. The instructional system is constructed cooperatively. It is a virtual learning community consisting of many different commercial tools, open sources, Web 2.0 applications, and eventually Web 3.0 virtual worlds. This space is built on the Google Model of information systems; the "If *they* build it, they will use it." The virtual learning community may be accessed through district servers, but it is more likely to be a distributed model where various functions are "in the cloud." This means that the actual servers could be anywhere but are accessible through a home page linking the various applications together. The distinction between administrative computing and instructional computing is essential if we expect technology to have an impact on teaching and learning.

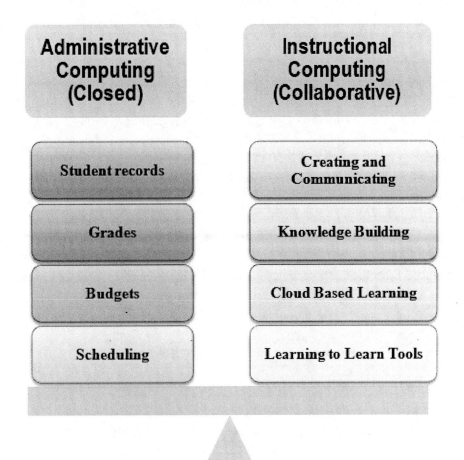

When the two systems are separated, then different policies cover each system. Administrative computing will have rules governing private and secure need-to-know only policies. Instructional computing will have quite a different policy set, pushing open access, collaboration, building, thinking, using, and doing.

Admittedly, over the last decade, there has been a struggle over the openness of instructional computing. This has often depended on the background of the administrator of technology for the school district. Those with a computer science background have tended to lock down instructional computing, while those with educational backgrounds have tended to prefer much more open and collaborative systems. Federal and local laws, plus fear factors, have often ruled out open access.

Resource TIP
Do fear and exaggeration increase risk? This thought provoking slideshow by Larry Magid, co-director of ConnectSafely.org and founder of SafeKids.com, will help your school explore this issue.
http://www.slideshare.net/larrymagid/do-fear-and-exaggeration-increase-risk

Digging Deeper
Finally, in 2011, ISTE, the International Society for Technology in Education, issued specific role definitions that concentrate on transforming learning through technology. See ISTE NETS for coordinators and technology coaches at:
http://www.iste.org/Libraries/NETS_Refresh_Toolkit/NETS_for_Technology_Coaches.sflb.ashx

See also, ISTE NETS for Administrators and Technology Directors at:
http://www.iste.org/Libraries/NETS_Refresh_Toolkit/NETS_for_Educational_Technology_Directors.sflb.ashx

Now watch how professionals use such standards to suggest transformation of learning through technology at:
http://www.youtube.com/watch?v=xiisteObuhk&NR=1

Finally, when there are objections citing CIPA rules, read the following document about web filtering closely:
http://www.lightspeedsystems.com/landing/web-filtering-best-practices.aspx

Challenge Invite students and teachers create their own *I Love School* video like this one from ISTE http://www.youtube.com/watch?v=SqDigEggJkw

As far as instructional computing goes, the trend for Web 2.0 applications is toward more and more secure areas that only a teacher, specialists, invited students, and invited parents can access. Most importantly, these systems are available 24/7/365. District and school teacher technologists regularly facilitate and participate in creating, experimenting with, using, and assessing the impact of the various tools on learning. As members of collaborative teaching and learning teams, teacher technologists focus on access, usability, and learning results. They also research emerging technologies while promoting the creative and clever combinations of current technologies. However, one must plan for instructional computing with the students in mind. In fact, they should be in the loop as systems are proposed, tested, adopted, and discarded in favor of better and better systems. They will be concerned about support of their own personal devices; powering UP in school, rather than powering DOWN. They can and should be involved in all types of policy decisions such as safety, digital citizenship, various platforms and connections, as well as the various software and tools they need to learn and be creative.

Discussion Point How can schools ensure equity of access through the Learning Commons facilities and programs?

Note the hope and dreams of one school system that adopts one-to-one computing:
http://www.youtube.com/watch?v=p-ne03ROH3Q

Consider opening up networks to student and teacher devices and moving to the cloud. Of the systems available at this writing, the one that best exemplifies the concept of instructional computing is Google Apps for Education. This safe and free environment allows the school to concentrate on creating maximum bandwidth rather than having expensive equipment and maintenance staff. A number of videos about the implementation of Google Apps are available at: http://www.google.com/apps/intl/en/edu/k12.html

Resource TIP Consult the book *Google Apps for Education: Building Knowledge in a Safe and Free Environment* by Roger Nevin, Micah Melton, and David V. Loertscher.

As an entire system, administrative and instructional computing inform each other, as administrative computing responds to what is happening in the instructional side and vice versa. For example, low cost web 2.0 tools might replace expensive commercial applications, thus reducing budgets. Likewise, student performance data in the administrative system is used by the learning literacies leadership team to recommend instructional changes as shown in the following illustration.

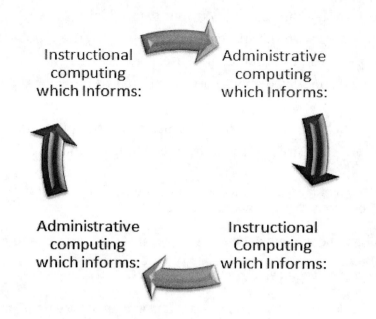

The Learning Commons as Learning Tech Central

The Learning Commons is the center for instructional computing in the school. Everyone feels a sense of ownership while participating in a perpetual beta experiment. For learners, the sentiment is that technology, as an extension of themselves, empowers them to know, do, and understand. To the teachers, technology enables strategies that help them reach every learner and propels the possibilities for achievement far beyond what could be expected in a traditional environment.

The Learning Commons is an open, wireless environment enabling computing devices of various types to be connected instantly. Movable furniture allows for different configurations of teaching or learning groups without regard to connectivity restraints at designated places. As one-on-one computing becomes a reality, a single uniform, device will be replaced by devices of personal preference with robust capabilities.

Technology in the Learning Commons is not only the latest and most extensive, but it has a reputation for reliability. Its many options of formats, media, research, production, and communication possibilities enable individual learning styles and needs. This is the center for support, experimentation, troubleshooting, and sharing of expertise. This is true even when technology is widely available across campus. The Learning Commons is the place everyone knows to go for help, guidance, doing, collaborating, producing, and sharing.

Like at many computer stores, students, adults, staff, and volunteers serve at the Commons expert bar, where technical advice on both hardware and software is available. Students who staff the expert bar might extend their volunteering into industry-standard expertise and licensing, a pathway to a career.

Student content and products are not only created, but also uploaded for assessment and easy display to other students, parents, and perhaps beyond the school networks. Thus, the Learning Commons is not only the production center for demonstrations of current learning (exhibitions, portfolios), but it also serves as museum and archive, as well as an instructional space open to discussion and input from the outside world. It is the extension of every classroom in the school.

The Learning Commons is also the center of online education, where students go to connect to courses beyond school walls; where they receive help and counselling; where they can troubleshoot problems. The Commons provides the connections to college and careers, and to personal learning opportunities. It is the place where collaborative learning experiences across the school, the district, the state, nation, or the world connect. It is both learning central and tech central.

Digging Deeper

The education revolution

1. *is not about new tools. It's a new approach to learning and teaching*
2. *does not separate knowledge, it layers knowledge*
3. *is understanding that learning happens best within a context that is real, has color and flavor, and provokes new questions.*
4. *is alchemy. It is resourcefully, inventively, and responsibly mixing information; boiling it into new knowledge, new action, new relationships, and into richer personal identities, cultural understandings, and greater opportunities.* David Warlick (2011)

To expand on David Warlick's expert views on technology and education see http://davidwarlick.com/2cents/?p=3230 and also Technology-Transformed Learning Environments http://davidwarlick.com/2cents/?p=2294

Empowering the Learner

What is it that technology does for the learner that cannot be done without it? As we test and experiment with technology tools and applications in the Learning Commons, the focus is on strategies that build the capabilities of the learner. What are these strategies and characteristics that boost learning? What is the advantage in learning how to build a personal information space and learning to manage oneself in that space? How can the school culture use technology to raise the challenge but keep the threat level low?

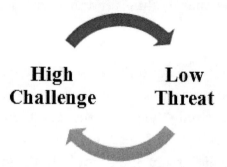

High
Challenge

Low
Threat

Rather than focus on the networks, devices, and applications, attention is squarely on what the technology does to help students know, do, understand, and thus become a better learner, as illustrated below.

Technology in the Learning Commons - Indicators of Learner Success

Consider building assessments, observations, and perform ace demonstrations around the various items listed in the figure below.

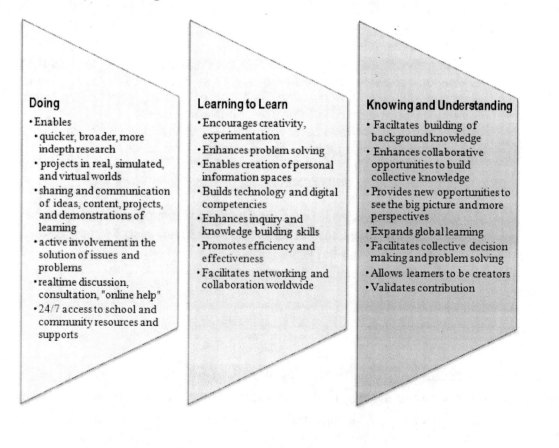

Doing
- Enables
- quicker, broader, more indepth research
- projects in real, simulated, and virtual worlds
- sharing and communication of ideas, content, projects, and demonstrations of learning
- active involvement in the solution of issues and problems
- realtime discussion, consultation, "online help"
- 24/7 access to school and community resources and supports

Learning to Learn
- Encourages creativity, experimentation
- Enhances problem solving
- Enables creation of personal information spaces
- Builds technology and digital competencies
- Enhances inquiry and knowledge building skills
- Promotes efficiency and effectiveness
- Facilitates networking and collaboration worldwide

Knowing and Understanding
- Faciltates building of background knowledge
- Enhances collaborative opportunities to build collective knowledge
- Provides new opportunities to see the big picture and more perspectives
- Expands global learning
- Facilitates collective decision making and problem solving
- Allows learners to be creators
- Validates contribution

84

At the beginning of each school year, learners should build or re-build their own information space using a tool, such as iGoogle, that allows them to take control of the interface between themselves and the world of the Internet. This process continues as learners progress. Loertscher and Williams, in their book *In Command*, demonstrate the various layers of a student's information space. Learners first build a personal information space containing tools and information they need to survive each day—calendars, to do lists, assignments from teachers, RSS feeds, and essential software applications. To this space they add other self-designed pages from group projects, specific classes requiring lots of attention, and even an entry point into the world of the Internet. This constructed space allows them to function in an organized fashion without the overwhelming overload of the entire Internet. Learners are in command, in control, and prepared to succeed at school, at home, or in extra-curricular activities. In cooperation with teachers, teacher librarians, tech specialists, and parents, learners set up the filtering system for their site based on their own responsibility index. Thus, their filter is like a dimmer switch or a rheostat, moving more open or more closed as needed.

Learners use their information space as the foundation to construct their own personal learning system where they are interacting with people, information, and ideas. Interestingly the learner begins to develop various learning spaces for the different projects and activities of life . Thus, they might have their personal network system for their daily routines, another for their reading hobby network, a third for a local history project team, and yet another for gaming. Each of these has a support system of, not one but many, learning commons, organizations, experts and tools. This facilitates user control over what is usually the overwhelming juggernaut of the Internet. In the following illustration, we see the learner creating, not only their personal space, but also a personal learning network that they can continue to develop over a lifetime.

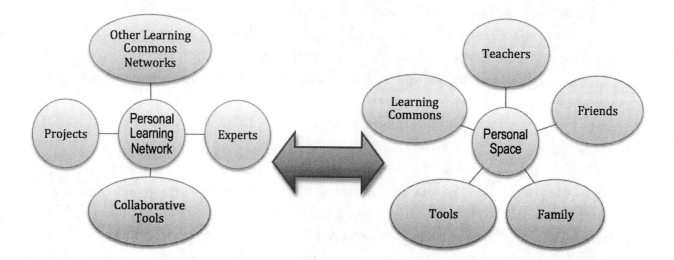

We have noticed other programs such as LiveBinders, Edmoto, and Moodle that have the potential to help learners manage themselves, but those who manage any of these systems have to do so in a way that opens self-management rather than forcible compliance.

At the same time students are becoming, reflective, responsible users of the wired world. Learners must gain the skills and the wisdom to govern their own behavior and identity in digital spaces. They will discover an online digital extension of themselves and explore who they really are. Some studies indicate that behavior in the many emerging environments, at school, at home, or with friends, can be quite different. In chapter seven, Personal Learning Environments, we expand on this concept of learner control of their own information spaces.

Professionals are there to guide the development of positive characteristics such as responsibility, congeniality, and other ethical behaviors. The Kawartha Pine Ridge Board of Education in Ontario, Canada uses the following list of characteristics they want learners to develop in the digital world:

Character Makes a Difference:
- *Respect*
- *Responsibility*
- *Honesty*
- *Integrity*
- *Empathy*
- *Fairness*
- *Initiative*

- *Perseverance*
- *Courage*
- *Optimism*

Notice the balance between personal development and academic development in a high tech world when you compare the above character traits with the academic expectations at the Science Leadership Academy in Philadelphia, PA:

- *Inquiry*
- *Research*
- *Collaboration*
- *Presentation*
- *Reflection*

Adults often feel that the only way to develop such characteristics is through direct teaching. We affirm the need for integrated experiences where learners are doing projects or solving problems in science, social studies, the fine arts or literature. As they encounter ideas, problems, and subject content, the adult coaches consciously help them develop the qualities needed in a technological world. The learners are guided to ask the following questions:

- What familiar tools will I be able to use?

- Which new tools will enhance my learning, and who can help me apply them?

- How do I bring new information to my attention?

- What do I need to know to create, store, and share my learning?

- How will I begin to confront the many voices trying to get my attention?

- Who is saying what to me, for what reasons, when, and for what gain?

- What are the ethical challenges of functioning successfully in digital space? How do I avoid such problems as plagiarism?

- How do I stay safe in digital worlds? How do I maintain my digital footprint?

- How can I use the tools available to me to be better organized, more efficient, and more creative?

- How will I update the skills I now possess?

- How can I use the social networking skills I already have to enhance my academic success?

Confronting such questions while constructing knowledge and personal expertise helps learners prepare to function in the new, real world of technology and to become competitive in that world. They build skills, attitudes, and responsibilities to help them be successful digital citizens. Some adults, however, often view liberation into such a world as a licence for children and teens to get into and to cause mischief. They often fear the worst,thus, their tendency to try to build systems to protect students and construct barriers to perceived predators. The problem is that it is very difficult to put up walls that are impenetrable. Many young people see such barriers as minor irritations or as challenges to hack the system. In fact, it is very instructive to learn about the history of hacking and viruses in world technology systems.

> **Digging Deeper** We suggest you watch the following TED talk, paying particular attention to the very last sentence the speaker says about a solution.
>
> http://www.ted.com/talks/mikko_hypponen_fighting_viruses_defending_the_net.html?utm_source=newsletter_weekly_2011-07-19&utm_campaign=newsletter_weekly&utm_medium=email

In view of the nefarious schemes ubiquitously present on the Internet, we suggest the alternative approach. In the same way we teach them to survive in the physical world, we guide children and teens in the construction of a positive and productive digital world where they have the wisdom to protect themselves and to survive its problems.
The U.S. Federal Trade Commission, through its OnGuardOnline.gov initiative, has recently published a guide for kids and teens with the slogan: *Stop. Think. Click.*, with its seven practices for safer computing:

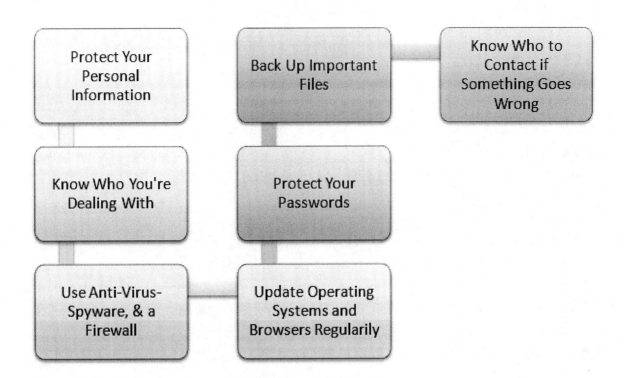

We want and need young people who are participating in the use of technology to enhance their lives. Harnessing their skills in a positive effort helps everyone. It is the difference between lying awake at night trying to figure out ways to confront and defeat the latest abuse of school networks, and the lying awake excited about the latest advances and creativity being constructed by everyone.

Will our grandchildren grow up knowing how to pluck the answer to any question out of the air, summon their social networks to assist them personally or professionally, organize political movements and markets online? Will they collaborate to solve problems, participate in online discussions as a form of civic engagement, share, teach and learn to their benefit and that of everyone else? Or will they grow up knowing that the online world is a bewildering puzzle to which they have few clues, a dangerous neighborhood where their identities can be stolen, a morass of spam and porn, misinformation and disinformation, urban legends, hoaxes, and scams? I have collected evidence over the past several decades that suggests the humanity or toxicity of next year's digital culture depends to a very large degree on what we know, learn, and teach each other about how to use the one billion Internet accounts and four billion mobile phones available today. Howard Rheingold (2009)

One of the best ideas we have encountered to empower students and the technology culture of the school is to have a Tech Squad operating from the Learning Commons. A technology club of students under the direction of the teacher librarian or the teacher technologist learns about devices, software, Web 2.0 tools, the best of the best tools, and knowing whatever they can know about technology and education. These students fan out throughout the school to serve as experts in classes and to staff the expert bar in the Learning Commons. This group can teach a new technology application to an entire school in a week. They establish the school culture of "I will help you, you will help me, and we will all succeed together". They serve as the advisory team for establishing school and district technology policies. They have both opportunity, and feel trusted, to lead the entire school in the power of technology to boost learning.

Activity
Take Action: Establish your own Tech Squad. Here are some examples to help you get started.
California Mouse Squad initiative at: http://ca.mousesquad.org/
An elementary story at:
http://ww2.gazette.net/stories/041008/laurnew125035_32359.shtml
Murray Hill Academy example: http://www.mhacademy.net/mouse-squard

buffyjhamilton Buffy Hamilton
Happy moment: one of my juniors is now my resident expert on embedding Glogsters and Google Forms; he's helping classmates.
2 hours ago

Empowering the Teacher

The major question teachers face is how technology can help each of the learners in their care advance toward excellence. Until technology becomes a real extension of the teacher rather than just equipment or networks to battle, that question remains unanswered. Each teacher in the school is provided with opportunities to use technology in ways that improve their own performance and job satisfaction. To do this, each teacher asks the question, "What is the impact of technology on my teaching?" Based on the possibilities for improvement, the technology leadership team provides the support necessary to make those possibilities a reality.. In the following diagram, we provide a list of ways that technology can boost teaching effectiveness:

- Enhancing teaching strategies
- Maximizing learning opportunities
- Managing learning
- Growing and developing personally and professionally

How can Technology Impact Teaching?

Enhancing Teaching Strategies	Maximizing Learning Opportunities	Management of Learning	Personal Growth and Development
• Improved presentations • Monitoring results as teaching progresses • New methods of presentation beyond the lecture • Extended possibilities for differentiation • Opportunities to collaborate with teaching collegues • Access to experts both near and far	• Instant communication with learners and caregivers • More options in the kinds of choices I can provide learners • Both synchronous and asynchronous • Time to reflect before responding • Empowerment through valued voice • On demand and repeatable	• Paperless communication, assignments, and grading • A variety of ways to assess, document and analyze learning • Efficient assessment practices • Track student attendance and progress	• Online professional development • Participation in action research studies across subjects and schools • Instant access to professional literature • Connections to professionanl learning communitities in the school and beyond

The Learning Commons is the laboratory where the faculty and staff learn and develop their skills in embedding technology to boost learning and achievement. Classes, short courses, and students manning the expert bar, provide support to those seeking to improve their skills. Collaborative experimentation with teacher learners and Learning Commons staff not only originate and are refined in the Commons, but are also demonstrated to other faculty observers who wish to improve the role of technology in their own classrooms. Collaborative experimentation and creative new uses of technologies emerge as the flowchart below illustrates.

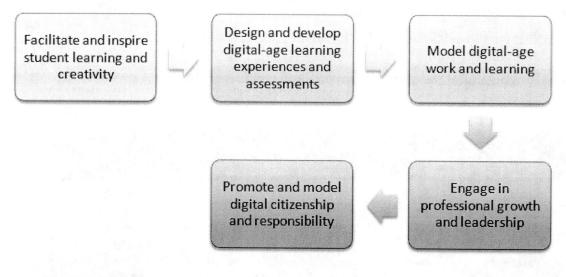

Digging Deeper

Sometimes, the major problem is to just get started without a major outlay of funds. Try the suggestions in this article: "Doing More with Less (and Other Practical Educational Technology Tidbits)" at:

http://www.edutopia.org/blog/education-technology-advice-adam-bellow

You can also follow up on Adam Bello's other useful site at:

http://edutecher.net/library.php

Systems and Networks that Support Learning and Experimentation

Because the Learning Commons is a learning laboratory, teacher technologists continually experiment with networks, open source applications, and Internet access to facilitate rather than restrict learning. We strive to create a read, think, write, reflect, web filled with personal learning spaces and networks. These networks are never static; they are ever evolving test beds of innovation. Access and responsibility is tested in the Commons and then introduced to the students and the school as a whole. Both students and teachers test and experiment with new software applications for recommendation on a wider scale.

Building an instructional network requires that the system itself be a teaching and learning resource constructed not only by teacher technologists and teacher librarians, but by the users themselves. We no longer think of completing the construction of a physical network, rather the network becomes organic, a perpetual beta. It is true that as the uses of the network evolve, dysfunction occurs, causing disruption and frustration. However that is the nature and challenge of progress.

Much can be done by creating a help center in the Learning Commons that becomes a sharing center for teachers, students, and caregivers at home as illustrated here:

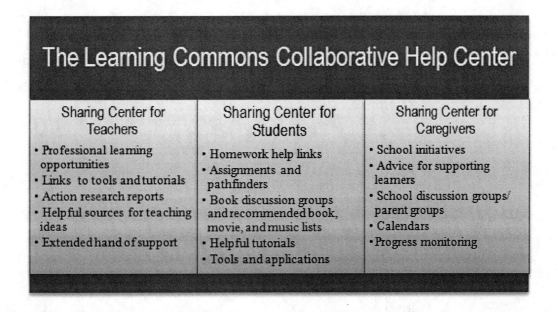

Safety concerns coupled with the threats of legal challenges often are used as barriers to the opening of instructional networks. In a client-side organization, the learners will help construct the safety nets and review them on a regular basis. The adults not only coach young people how to stay safe crossing the street, on the playground, or in the neighborhoods, they do so in virtual space. Thus, the adults leave nothing to chance as they educate, educate, and educate. They realize that unguided interaction will surely result in likely catastrophe. There is no such thing as a totally safe physical or virtual space, but there are many ways to handle the problems encountered.

The school library website becomes the collaborative Virtual Learning Commons help center, with drag and drop applications, resources, RSS feed recommendations, and other helps that can be brought on to the student's or teacher's personal information space. It is also the space for conversation, communication, and collective knowledge building.

Challenge Help to build an 'idea bank'

Teacher librarians and teacher technologists can take advantage of the International Virtual Learning Commons Idea Bank to help transform their library an/or technology one-way websites into a more "Wikipedia" type collaborative.

See the idea bank at: https://sites.google.com/site/internationalvlcideas/

The Virtual Learning Commons has open and closed areas of access to the general public on a need to know/participate basis. One of the challenges of building systems is the undue pressure by commercial organizations to sell expensive systems and packages based on the Microsoft model to school districts or schools. If a client side system is to be built and supported, then great care needs to be taken in the selection and implementation of packages that may or may not be what users would embrace and use. Such purchasing decisions should be within the province of the Technology Leadership Team as will be described later.

Another major change in systems is the trend to moving from local servers and closed systems to utilizing the benefits of cloud computing.

> **Digging Deeper** For a quick overview of cloud computing with the expert, Derek Wenmoth, watch:
> http://blip.tv/core-ed/ten-trends-episode-6-cloud-computing-5235605

Such a major shift from local control to off-site control has been difficult for many tech directors, but the affordability and realizability of cloud solutions have been gaining major popularity. Instead of services and staff to manage local networks, resources can be pointed toward areas such as increasing bandwidth.

Building the Systems Around Learning Rather Than Around Technologies

The number of digital tools now available seem overwhelming at times. Hundreds of webinars, blogs, websites, and presentations focus on a new tool or tools and how they can be used with learners. After sitting in such a session, it is easy to be overwhelmed and uncertain where to begin. See **Bright Ideas to Build On** toward the end of this chapter for some of the best sources to keep you on track.

In the face of a plethora of tools, we recommend flipping the emphasis to the kinds of learning boosts we need with various learners and classes, and then finding the tool or tools that will help accomplish that learning need.

Types of Learning Boosts from Technology

Learning How to Learn
1. Brainstorming
2. Question building

3. Gathering and organizing quality information
4. Reading engagement
5. Analysis and synthesis of information and ideas
6. Collaborative writing and editing
7. Collaborative visualization, mind mapping
8. Presenting, publishing and communicating
9. Reflection and metacognition
10. Collaborative knowledge building; collaborative intelligence
11. Best learning how to learn tools

Motivation
12. Novelty
13. Real world
14. Relevant
15. Experimenting with and playing problem posing and problem solving simulations
16. Global projects, appreciation and understanding of other cultures
17. Best motivational tools

Creativity and Content Creation
18. Building/composing, creating, and using many tools and presentation venues
19. Digital storytelling, growth in oral communication
20. Creativity tools and innovation because of those tools
21. Presenting, publishing, and communicating
22. Collaborative and individual writing
23. Experimentation, and testing ideas
24. Best creativity and content creation tools

Efficiency
25. Tools that save time for individuals and groups
26. Organizational tools that help everyone get the job done
27. Opportunity to learn, review, and collaborate in real time
28. Best efficiency tools?

Deep Understanding of Content Knowledge
29. Collaborative visualization; mind mapping
30. Multimedia experiences not possible in a non-tech world
31. Idea and concept sharing beyond the school
32. Growth in content knowledge, the major ideas of the various disciplines, what we know and are able to do
33. Best tools to deepen understanding of content knowledge

Assessing What We Really Value

34. Deep understanding
35. Learning how to learn
36. Critical thinking
37. Creative thinking
38. Habits of mind
39. College and career readiness
40. Common Core Standards and other standards we value
41. Formative and summative assessment
42. Best assessing "What We Really Value" Tools

Teaching Strategies, Techniques and Organization

43. Differentiation
44. Digital Presentations
45. Going paperless
46. Tracking and managing
47. Management systems for courses, grading
48. Environments such as Google Apps for Education, Moodle
49. Online coaching, homework help
50. Best Teaching Strategies, Techniques and Organization Tools

Challenge How do we use such a list?

Example # 1. Collaborative writing and editing - Try Google Documents. They can be used both by individuals and groups of students working on the same document. View these videos for samples:
http://www.youtube.com/watch?v=hq8GihqslWs
or
http://www.youtube.com/watch?v=A7y7NafWXeM
or
http://www.youtube.com/watch?v=LKcy9UAz7Lw

A Google Document has many excellent features and also some drawbacks. This tool does not provide grammar or dictionary look-up, but it does provide a way another person can comment, like this:

reader.david

Should students use for fee tools such as Microsoft Word alongside Google documents?

Comment Cancel

Now, how does the Learning Commons make staff aware of the potential? Let's say teachers have a short professional development session in the Experimental Learning Center about collaborative writing.

- They could learn the basic functions of Google Documents, and then each could experiment with their students and a Tech Squad member in a real lesson.
- They could then come back together to discuss the results, show examples, talk about problems, talk about how to help groups of students produce a better result, analyze the quality of the results they got in the time available, and offer suggestions to each other given by the students themselves and the adult coaches as well.
- They would then go back and try again and again until the benefits of collaborative writing were making a difference in the process of writing as well as the product.

Example # 2 Collaborative mind mapping

Instruct your Tech Squad to research available free mind mapping tools. Connect them to experts such as Richard Byrne of *Free Technology for Teachers*. His favorite list of mind mapping tools can be accessed at: http://www.freetech4teachers.com/2011/07/seven-tools-for-creating-mind-maps-and.html?utm_source=feedburner&utm_medium=feed&utm_campaign=Feed%3 A+freetech4teachers%2FcGEY+%28Free+Technology+for+Teachers%29 The Tech Squad could test all of them and make recommendations to the faculty and other students as to the best and most reliable tools, and offer short training sessions on their use for specific needs.

Collaborative Technologies

A true innovation in education is the ability to have multiple students or adults work in real time on a document, a project, a drawing, or a spreadsheet. As described above, Google has led the way with their Google Docs tools. Now, a growing number of Web 2.0 tools for collaboration are available. These tools provide an opportunity for individuals to develop personal expertise and to contribute that expertise to the development of collaborative intelligence in real time. The teacher and other adults can watch this happen in real time, can monitor who is contributing what with what level of expertise, and can coach a group in real time. There is no better way to do both formative and summative assessment and to provide ongoing differentiation.

Digging Deeper

The following video describes the creation of a Google Form to conduct a survey. What it does not show is the spreadsheet where the data ends up: http://www.youtube.com/watch?v=DZEjmxTvR4k

Using the same tool, students can collect data or ideas from their research, enter these into the form, and then the entire class can do analysis and synthesis of the collected material. The resulting collaborative thinking is an incredible experience to watch, guide, participate in, and assess.

View these presentation slides of a real collaborative writing experiment: http://www.slideshare.net/lpahomov/iste-2011-using-google-docs-to-improve-student-writing

buffyjhamilton Buffy Hamilton
why I love social media: collaborating with one of my teachers for a new project via Facebook chat tonight :-)
18 minutes ago

Technology and Learning Virtually

The ideas and principles of the Learning Commons apply in virtual spaces just as they do in physical spaces. More and more opportunities exist for learners to take part of their coursework, or all of it, through virtual learning networks. These virtual courses should be a part of the Learning Commons activities and should receive support and collaboration from the mentor teachers and specialists in the school just as regular classes do. Virtual schools should have their own virtual Learning Commons as described in this book. Teacher technologists and teacher librarians build the Commons as a collaborative among teachers and learners to allow both synchronous and asynchronous delivery. The aim is for anytime, anywhere, any device, access.

Assistive Technologies

Everyone needs assistive technologies. We all require an Internet connection to see e-mail, the human eye cannot see viruses without electron microscopes, the visually impaired require audio assistance, and GPS helps us to navigate in unknown territory. Since everyone needs assistive devices, the stigma of help for a few disappears. Cost is not always the major factor, but a range of choices for the learner is essential. The primary understanding is that everyone helps everyone else achieve by overcoming whatever barriers exist. When assistance becomes a normal part of the learning environment, everyone benefits.

With all the interest in technology, in the latest devices, trends, and initiatives, the concentration should always be focused on how technology fosters better learning. Not all is well just because a school or district invests in technology. For example, read the following article by K. Walsh, *Technology is an Enabler Not a Magic Wand*, and its link to an important New York Times article to consider more deeply just how technology is being used and how it is actually increasing what we really value.

http://www.emergingedtech.com/2011/09/education-technology-is-an-enabler-not-a-magic-wand/

The Technology Leadership Team

School administrators need to establish a leadership team to guide the school's technological systems, the applications, and the impact of technology on learning. This professional learning community has representatives from both adult and student users. Collectively they hold a shared vision as they advise the administration on implementation opportunities, problems, and budgets, and then assess the impact of technology on the school as a whole. Teams which seem to be making the most impact are teams that combine technology and library programs into a collaborative Learning Commons approach. We are impressed with teams, across North America, which intertwine and support technology with learning through inquiry approaches and information skill instruction within district wide systems.

BRIGHT Ideas to Build On
Keep up to date with major tech trends and consider how they can empower both teacher and student learners.

- Tools and tutorials From Ed Technology Guy: http://educationaltechnologyguy.blogspot.com/2011/04/google-for-educators-resources-for.html

- Cool Tools for Schools: http://cooltoolsforschools.wikispaces.com/Tools+at+a+glance

- New Tools Workshop: http://newtoolsworkshop.wikispaces.com/

- Web Tools 4U2 Use: http://webtools4u2use.wikispaces.com/

- Handbook of Emerging Technologies for Learning: http://ltc.umanitoba.ca/wikis/etl/index.php/Handbook_of_Emerging_Technologies_for_Learning

- Free Technology for Teachers blog by Richard Byrne:
  http://www.freetech4teachers.com/

- TechSets: People Supporting Technology in Schools
  http://www.techsets.org/

- Converge Magazine: http://www.convergemag.com/

- Building Professional Learning Networks (PLN) by Kim Cofino:
  http://www.slideshare.net/mscofino/the-21st-century-educator

- An article to inspire: *The Virtual Library: Have We Put the Cart Before the Horse* by Anita Brooks Kirkland
  http://clatoolbox.ca/casl/slicv29n2/292brookskirkland.html

- The 21st Century Fluency Project blog: http://www.fluency21.com/

- Get lots of ideas from the EDTE.CH blog:
  http://edte.ch/blog/?page_id=424

- Make learners aware of their digital footprint:
  http://www.iste.org/connect/iste-connects/blog-detail/10-01-21/A_Teaching_Moment_Introducing_Students_to_their_Cyber-selves.aspx

- Discover interactive info graphics:
  http://www.yaleclimatemediaforum.org/2011/02/making-the-complicated-clear-integrated-graphics-make-data-visual/

Scenarios Demonstrating Technology for Learning

The Tech Team One computer teacher we know assembled a "cadre of student geeks" in her computer club. Every few weeks, the club met to learn a new application or jointly share troubleshooting for applications already in use around the school. This teacher advertised to the faculty that if they had any trouble, they could call on any member of the techiclub. A few tried it, though some teachers were reluctant because a student might uncover the teacher's own incompetence. However, after a month or so, the news got around the faculty that the tech club was a stunning success. It was a tipping point from fear of technology to the attitude, "you teach me, I'll teach you, and we will all succeed together." Such an attitudinal change in one area may be the stimulus toward a collaborative attitude in other areas, turning an isolated and competitive faculty into a collegial Professional Learning Community.

Reinventing What We Already Own Jeff Brown, the Instructional Leadership Consultant for Technology and Learning Resources, of the Kawartha Pine Ridge Board of Education, Peterborough, Ontario, Canada, regularly uses videoconferencing systems to facilitate administrative meetings, school board meetings, classroom enrichment, and collaborations with classes and individuals around the world. When Jeff encountered a deaf student, who is in a wheel chair and isolated because few around him can sign, he decided to use the existing technology to link deaf students from around the province together. Using a computer based video conferencing system, this student now meets with other deaf students every Monday to discuss personal and curriculum based topics. For them it is a chance to speak in a real time conversation, and have their thoughts heard and their ideas valued among peers. The individuals in this community talk together in American Sign Language, and new community has been born. The smiles on the faces, the depth of discussion, and the development of personal connections have been enabled by the technology. The student, who had lost his hearing over time, has experienced a rebirth in his citizenship in society based on his access to technology and innovative thinking.

Connectivity Entitlement Agreement (CEA) In support of access to the powerful learning tools on the Read Think Write Web, learners need to have guidelines within which to work. Typically these rules are laid out in Acceptable Use Policies, which outline the limitations of use, and the consequences of any contravention of the policy. These documents are command/control and protection based. Some learners then test the effectiveness of the security measures on the networks that these punitive documents are established to protect. Savvy learners often treat these restrictive documents like a red flag as they have no vested interest in the network. In response to this, the Kawartha Pine Ridge District School Board in Ontario, Canada is developing a Connectivity Entitlement Agreement (CEA). The CEA is designed in such a way as to outline the relationship of the learners in the school board with the network resources offered by the board to augment learning. Individuals are extended access to resources within a wired world. The mindset shift here is, as a member of a greater learning community, each member has rights to use the network and also has the responsibility to maintain its functionality to honor the rights of others. In this way the learners have a vested interest in the continued operability of their link to the world.

Over to You Discuss with your group and the authors:

• How do we as schools and districts move into the safe but open Web 2.0 instructional computing environment?

• What is the impact on achievement and engagement when learners discover the power of transformative technologies? As this happens, what happens to the way teachers teach?

References

- Federal Trade Commission. "Stop. Think. Click. 7 Practices for Safer Computing". *OnGuardOnline.gov.* pueblo.gsa.gov/cic_text/computers/**stopthink**/**click**.htm

- Partnership for 21st Century Skills. *The Intellectual and Policy Foundations of the 21st Century Skills Framework.* 5-6. http://www.21stcenturyskills.org/route21/images/stories/epapers/skills_foundations_final.pdf

- Rheingold, Howard. 2009. "21st Century Literacies". Blog Post. http://blog.sfgate.com/rheingold/2009/04/10/21st-century-literacies/

- Warlick, David. 2011. "Reflections on REDxLondon: the Education Revolution". *2¢ Worth.* Blog Post. September 18, 2011. http://davidwarlick.com/2cents/?p=3230

Resources

Foundational Ideas

- Educational Testing Service. 2001. *Digital Transformations: A Framework for ICT Literacy. A Report of the International ICT Literacy Panel.* Princeton, NJ: ETS. http://www.ets.org/Media/Tests/Information_and_Communication_Technology_Literacy/ictreport.pdf . A major theoretical document that has formed the foundation for the creation of an Information and Communications Technology assessment by ETS.

- Jenkins, Henry et al. 2007. *Confronting the Challenge of Participatory Culture: Media Education for the 21st Century.* MacArthur Foundation White Paper. http://www.projectnml.org/files/working/NMLWhitePaper.pdf

- Partnership for 21st Century Skills. *The Intellectual and Policy Foundations of the 21st Century Skills Framework.*

http://www.21stcenturyskills.org/route21/images/stories/epapers/skills_foundations_final.pdf   A white paper arguing the intellectual foundation of technology and learning.

Professional Documents

- American Association of School Librarians. 2007. *Standards for the 21st-Century Learner.* Chicago, IL: American Library Association.
  http://www.ala.org/aasl/standards
  A vision document that integrates technology into the inquiry process.

- "Children and Electronic Media". 2008. *The Future of Children.* 18 no. 1 Spring 2008. Princeton University-Brookings Institute,
  http://ccf.tc.columbia.edu/pdf/Children%20and%20Electronic%20Media_Spring%2008.pdf

- International Society for Technology in Education. 2007. *National Educational Technology Standards for Students* 2nd edition. Washington, DC: International Society for Technology in Education. http://www.iste.org/standards.aspx

- International Society for Technology in Education. 2008. *National Educational Technology Standards for Teachers* 2nd edition. Washington, DC: International Society for Technology in Education. http://www.iste.org/standards.aspx

- Partnership for 21st Century Skills. *Route 21.*
  http://www.21stcenturyskills.org/route21/
  A model of what skills young people need to have and be able to do to be competitive globally.

Professional Organizations

- The International Society for Technology in Education (ISTE) with its NETS standards and annual NECC conference provides a great deal of guidance for technology programs. http://www.iste.org/welcome.aspx

- Most jurisdictions have a professional organization connected to technology with an accompanying annual conference.

- Check out opportunities at local and national organizations to exhibit technological projects and creations like science fair competitions. http://www.futureofchildren.org/usr_doc/Media_08_01.pdf

Other Resources

- Blos, Suzie and Jane Krauss. 2007. *Reinventing Project-Based Learning.* Washington, DC: International Society for Technology in Education.

- Christensen, Clayton M., Michael B. Horn, and Curtis W. Johnson. 2008. *Disrupting Class: How Disruptive Innovation Will Change the Way the World Learns.* New York: McGraw-Hill.

- Churches, Andrew, Lee Crockett, and Ian Jukes. 2010. *The Digital Diet: Today's Digital Tools in Small Bytes.* Thousand Oaks CA: Corwin Press.

- Crane, Beverley E. 2009. *Using WEB 2.0 tools in the K-12 classroom.* New York: Neil-Schuman.

- *Digiteen: A web page for a digital citizenship group project between Qatar Academy, Westwood Schools in Camilla, Georgia USA and Vienna International School in Vienna, Austria.* At: http://digiteen.wikispaces.com/

- *Educational Media and Technology Yearbook.* Annual. Westport, CT: Libraries Unlimited.

- Hendron, John G. 2008. *RSS for Educators: Blogs, Newsfeeds, Podcasts, and Wikis in the Classroom.* Washington, DC: International Society for Technology in Education.

- Johnson, L., Adams, S., and Haywood, K. 2011. *The NMC Horizon Report: 2011 K-12 Edition.* Austin, TX: The New Media Consortium. http://www.nmc.org/pdf/2011-Horizon-Report-K12.pdf

- Jonassen, David H. et al. 2007. *Meaningful Learning with Technology,* 3rd edition. Upper Saddle River, NJ: Prentice-Hall.

- Jukes, Ian, Ted McCain, and Lee Crockett. 2010. *Understanding the Digital Generation: Teaching and Learning in the New Digital Landscape.* Thousand Oaks CA: Corwin Press.

- Kolb, Liz. 2008. *Toys to Tools: Connecting Student Cell Phones to Education.* Washington, DC: International Society for Technology in Education.

- Li, Charlene and Josh Bernoff. 2008. *Groundswell: Winning in a World Transformed by Social Technologies.* Boston, MA: Harvard Business Press.

- National Education Association in collaboration with the American Federation of Teachers. 2008. *Access, Adequacy and Equity in Education Technology: Results of a Survey of America's Teachers and Support Professionals on Technology in Public Schools and Classrooms.* http://sc08.sc-education.org/conference/k12/sat/stem/08gainsandgapsedtech.pdf

- Nevin, Roger, Micah Melton, and David V. Loertscher. 2010. *Google Apps for Education: Building Knowledge in a Safe and Free Environment.* Salt Lake City UT: Hi Willow Research & Publishing.

- November, Alan. 2009. *Empowering Students with Technology,* Second Edition. Thousand Oaks CA: Corwin Press.

- November, Alan. 2008. *Web Literacy for Educators.* Thousand Oaks, CA: Corwin Press.

- Pitler, Howard et al. 2007. *Using Technology with Classroom Instruction That Works.* Alexandria, VA: Association for Supervision and Curriculum Development.

- Richtel, Matt. 2011. "Grading the Digital School: In Classroom of Future, Stagnant Scores". The New York Times. (September 3 2011). http://www.nytimes.com/2011/09/04/technology/technology-in-schools-faces-questions-on-value.html?_r=3

- Rose, David and Anne Meyer. 2002. *Teaching Every Student in the Digital Age.* Alexandria, VA: Association for Supervision and Curriculum Development.

- Simonson, Michael, et al. 2008. *Teaching and Learning at a Distance: Foundations of Distance Education* 4th edition. Upper Saddle River, NJ: Prentice-Hall.

- Spector, J. Michael and Philip A. Harris. 2007. *Handbook of Research on Educational Communications and Technology*. New York: Routledge.

- Tapscott, Don and Anthony D. Williams. 2008. *Wikinomics: How Mass Collaboration Changes Everything*. Expanded Edition. New York: Portfolio Books (Penguin Group).

- Trolley, Barbara C. and Constance Hanel. 2010. *Cyber kids, Cyber Bullying, Cyber Balance*. Thousand Oaks CA: Corwin Press.

- Warlick, David. 2007. *Classroom Blogging* 2nd edition. Lulu.com. www.lulu.com

Blogs
- Barseghian, Tina. *MindShift*. http://mindshift.kqed.org/

- Hamilton, Buffy. *The Unquiet Librarian*. http://theunquietlibrarian.wordpress.com/

- Heppell, Stephen. *Stephen Heppell's Weblog*. http://www.heppell.net/weblog/stephen/

- Jukes, Ian. *The Committed Sardine*. http://web.mac.com/iajukes/thecommittedsardine/BLOG/BLOG.html

- McKenzie, Jamie. *From Now On: the Educational Technology Journal*. http://fno.org/

- November, Alan. *November Learning* http://novemberlearning.com/index.php?option=com_frontpage&Itemid=1

- Valenza, Joyce. *NeverEndingSearch*. http://blog.schoollibraryjournal.com/neverendingsearch

- Warlick, David. *2¢ Worth: Teaching & Learning in the New Information Landscape*. http://davidwarlick.com/2cents/

Chapter 6

Collaboration
and the Learning Commons

Why must schools succeed with collaboration?
Even though the stereotype of poor decision-making by committee still persists, new attention in the past decade has been drawn by a plethora of authors (particularly in the business sector) to the advantages of teaming, collaborative intelligence, and group problem solving. As Steven Johnson has shown in his book, *Where Good Ideas Come From*, idea sharing in the "coffee house" has resulted in many of the great inventions over time.
View his TED Talk at: http://www.youtube.com/watch?v=0af00UcTO-c

And from the education sector, Michael Fullan and Heidi Hayes Jacobs provide food for thought as we explore the need to foster a collaborative learning culture in schools.

The We We Solution: "When teachers within a school collaborate, they begin to think not just about "my classroom' but also about "our school." Michael Fullan (2008)

"Rather than being victimized by our program structures, we should be creating new types of learning environments for a new time and for various types of teaching and learning. **Not to do so is a declaration not to learn."** Heidi Hayes Jacobs (2010, 79)

———————— ❋ ————————

The establishment of the Learning Commons as a collaborative community of learners opens the door for the reinvention of instruction and learning experiences and, consequently, for effective school improvement. In the Learning Commons we experience many types and layers of collaboration, with everyone working together to analyze and improve teaching and learning for all. Teachers and administrators work on specific facets of school improvement and safety. Students work with other students and teachers on solving problems, building knowledge, and creating together. The broader school community works within the Learning Commons to support learning and local initiatives. All work done together is supported by the rich physical and virtual resources and technologies of the Commons.

With a Learning Commons approach, teaching partnerships and inviting collaborative work spaces replace lone teachers boxed in individual classrooms. This environment provides individual teachers with the freedom to take risks, try new strategies and truly innovate when they realize the security of supportive specialists and other teachers.

The isolated classroom and the pressure on classroom teachers to cover material in preparation for standardized testing have created an almost impenetrable barrier for specialists in the school. Many of these specialists have a mandate to collaborate with teachers to demonstrate, for instance, the power of the integration of technology, of information, of career exploration, or of visual arts. However they often find the classroom door bolted shut.

For example, intervention by the teacher librarian has a long and successful history of improving student achievement. Research has consistently shown that in schools where the teacher librarian and the classroom teacher collaborate to design, teach and assess learning experiences together, student test scores are consistently higher. Lance and Loertscher (2004) Based on that experience, the Learning Commons provides a 'tipping point' for building successful collaborative teams.

In spite of the barriers, many careers and businesses thrive on the use of teams and the building of collaborative intelligence; the idea that two heads are better than one. In education, we posit that a functional learning team which asks critical collective questions of learners has a powerful impact on both deep understanding and on building learning how to learn skills as shown below.

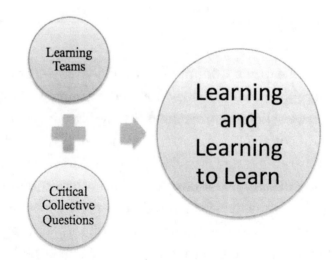

Building Collaborative Physical and Virtual Learning Environments

Collaboration is a key consideration when transforming existing school libraries, computer labs, and existing school library websites into facilities that support a Learning Commons approach. Key elements to strive for are flexibility of spaces, connectivity, and the active participation of users in the transformation process to ensure their needs are met. Spaces in which to celebrate learning accomplishments, to share cultural events, to plan new projects, to encourage and support innovation and creativity are also priorities in such a transformation.

Web 2.0 tools to facilitate and encourage collaboration have the potential to open up many new doors for teachers and students. For teachers, these tools can fundamentally change instructional design as learning partnerships replace teacher isolation. As facilitators of learning, teachers have the tools to collaboratively construct, teach, and assess learning as well as to archive learning experiences in order to examine progress over time. By working together using these tools, teachers can turn a fairly good learning experience into an exceptional one without having to plan a face to face meeting to do it. Refer to Chapter 3, Knowledge Building in the Learning Commons for more detail on the design of virtual centres for collaboratively planning, instructing and working on units of study.

For students, the benefits of collaboration in virtual spaces are priceless. The 'Always on' benefits are huge with regard to student engagement and relevance. Regardless of their location or the time of day, learners can be connected, on task, and involved in constructing, creating and communicating their new knowledge. Many teachers report that students who are usually reluctant to share their ideas in class, suddenly find a voice in online discussions. Teachers also report advantages for assessment because of the tracking capabilities of Web 2.0 tools. See activities in Chapter 7, Building the Learning Commons as a Client Side Organization , for inspiration to initiate the design of collaborative environments.

Resource TIP
See *Building the Learning Commons: A Guide for School Administrators and Learning Leadership Teams.* Learning Commons Press, 2010, for rubrics and planning templates. (http://lmcsource.com)

Empowering the Learner in the Commons

In an established Learning Commons, students can be found working with partners or in groups on projects, coaching others, reading to buddies, planning with staff, consulting experts, and networking by utilizing evolving technologies in both the the Physical and Virtual Commons. All day, every day, through collaborative work and play, students are learning and honing needed skills for school and for life. The following are sample indicators of collaboration that would be observed:

Collaboration in the Learning Commons - Indicators of Learner Success

Doing
- Group work
- Literature circles
- Information circles
- Discussion, debate
- Peer evaluations
- Group reflection
- Coaching peers
- Active listening

Learning to Learn
- Networking
- Communicating
- Problem solving
- Decision making
- Flexibility
- Responsibility
- Inquiry

Knowing and Understanding
- Sharing expertise
- Collaborative knowledge building
- Learning by teaching
- Developing multiple perspectives
- Developing points of view
- Empathizing with others
- Conceptualizing big ideas
- Sharing with diverse audiences

> **Children Learn through Social Interaction with Others**
> Children are constantly learning through interaction with others around them. The experience of learning through interaction is called social construction............
> There is a delicate balance between learning through social interaction and constructing for oneself. Traditional research assignments were commonly done as independent work. Collaborating with classmates affords the opportunity to help students think things through. While we acknowledge the importance of collaborating, some group projects foster very little individual learning. Caution needs to be taken to ensure that group activity enables deep individual learning through social interaction. Guided Inquiry considers the students engaged in inquiry a community of learners. This community offers opportunities for interaction with others that promote learning and an audience for sharing what has been learned. Kulthau, Maniotes, and Caspari (2007, 28)

Empowering the Teacher in the Commons

High-level collaboration means that the classroom teacher and one or more specialists co-teach a learning experience. This means that together they:

- Combine the goals and objectives of both/all partners' curricula for the learning experience.
- Jointly create and conduct assessment, both formative and summative.
- Plan and then co-teach the learning activities.
- Conduct a high-level "so what" activity that extends learning.
- Reflect together on their successes and challenges.
- Report their results and impact on learners.
- Plan for further collaborations as a part of evidence-based practice.

Such collaborative and co-taught learning experiences might happen face to face, in online knowledge building centers, or in blended experiences.

The goal of a true collaboration is to demonstrate powerful results. "Collectively, teachers and specialists have been able to achieve better results than if they had taught separately. By combining their creativity and expertise, they have rediscovered the joy of teaching. Together, they have had more success reaching every learner". Dana and Yendol-Hoppey (2008, 28).

Other levels of collaboration, such as cooperation, support, encouragement, and the sharing of good ideas across the faculty, across grade levels and among departments are practiced in the Learning Commons. The potential for integrated and interdisciplinary instruction means greater efficiencies as more curriculum will be addressed in less time. Transference of knowledge and skills from one discipline to another leaves time to go deeper and uncover big ideas and concepts. The result is a healthy learning community, a functional whole, a school that is achieving its mission.

> **Discussion Point** Watch the following video and then have a discussion with your peers on how to create collaborative teams in your school.
> http://www.ascd.org/ascd-express/vol6/619-video.aspx

Benefits of Collaboration as the Heart of the Learning Commons

Collaboration and team work are major components of both the social and business worlds. Web 2.0 technologies have given birth to huge collaborative projects (folksonomies) such as Wikipedia, LibraryThing, Flickr, and Google Apps for Education. These projects build knowledge bases which are tagged by many and searchable by everyone. Collaborative teams which solve problems have increasingly become the norm in the business world. Accounts of such collaborations and guides to their process are numerous in the popular literature as indicated in the following books:

- *Where Good Ideas Come From* by Steven Johnson. Riverhead, 2010
- *Here Comes Everybody: The Power of Organizing Without Organizations*
- *We are Smarter than Me: How to Unleash the Power of Crowds in Your Business* by Clay Shirky. Penguin, 2009.
- *The Wisdom of Crowds* by James Surowiecki. Anchor, 2005.
- *Wikinomics: How Mass Collaboration Changes Everything* by Don Tapscott. Portfolio Trade, 2010.
- *Group Genius* by Keith Sawyer. Basic Books, 2008.
- *Crowdsourcing: Why the Power of the Crowd is Driving the Future of Business* by Jeff Howe. Crown Business, 2009.
- *Developing Group Genius: Getting the Most out of Group Decision-Making* by John E. Kolstoe. George Ronald Publishers, 1995
- *Linked: The New Science of Networks* by Albert-Laszlo Barabasi and Jennifer Frangos. Kindle Edition. 2002.
- *Convergence Culture: Where Old and New Media Collide* by Henry Jenkins. NYU Press, 2008.

The benefits of collaboration are well known in the learning communities where they exist and are touted in the professional literature. Yet, these benefits are elusive to many, particularly when test score pressures create a competitive rather than collaborative environment or where traditional methods have become entrenched over time. The literature of leadership in school reform places the challenge of change squarely on the shoulders of the administrators of the school who must begin with a vision and use sound principles in the building of a school leadership team. The leadership team of the Learning Commons adopts these well-known practices of successful professional learning communities.

Discussion Point
Dana and Yendol-Hoppey list the following ten essential elements of healthy inquiry-oriented Professional Learning Communities:
1. A vision that creates momentum for their work.
2. Build trust among group members.
3. Pay attention to the ways power can influence group dynamics.
4. Understand and embrace collaboration.
5. Encourage, recognize, and appreciate diversity within the group.
6. Promote the development of critical friends.
7. Hold the group accountable for and document learning.
8. Understand change and acknowledge the discomfort it may bring to some PLC members.
9. Have a comprehensive view of what constitutes data, and are willing to consider all forms and types of data throughout their PLC work.
10. Work with building administrators.
    Dana and Yendol-Hoppey (2008, 21-47)

Take Action - Using this list of essential elements, what benefits are likely to emerge and should be documented? The following visual lists a few; make a list of your own.

The Learning Commons as Collaboration Central

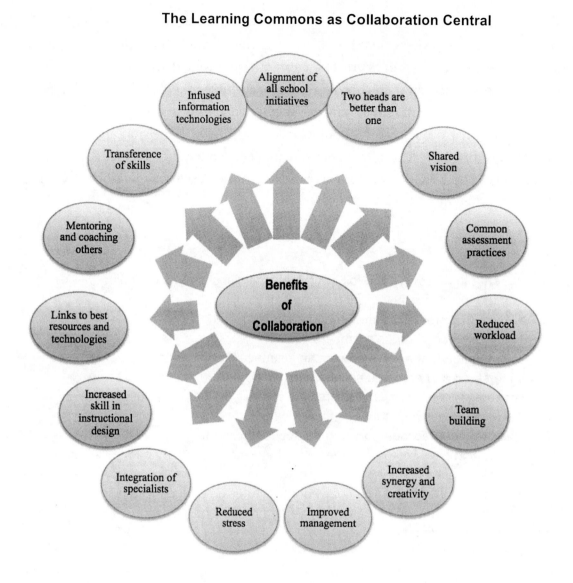

The collaborative dynamic in the Learning Commons is readily apparent. The learning environment has been purposefully designed to welcome and support the needed interactions of students and teachers. The results are purposeful collaborations and the building of enthusiastic learning communities.

Learning together is the mantra of the Learning Commons. Some examples of collaboration are:

- A group of teachers meeting with the teacher librarian to plan a learning unit.(Both face to face and virtual)
- Groups of learners collaboratively creating written documents, presentations, and spreadsheets as thoughtful pieces of group thinking.

- Learners from several classes planning for a visiting expert with the assistance of a guidance counselor.
- A group of learners and community leaders meeting online to plan events for Black History month.
- Learners, teacher librarians, and teacher technologists in two different school districts collaborating on developing a Healthy Lifestyle campaign.
- The reading coach meeting with grade level representatives to set in motion the state literature choice voting program for the next year.

> **Take Action: Transform the Library Website into a Collaborative Conversation and Work Space**
> The Virtual Learning Commons, as it replaces the traditional library website, is a place where everyone is building, experimenting, doing and exhibiting.....But the real value of the VLC lies in the development and implementation of real world projects and high think assignments that make use of collaborative knowledge building centers to deepen understanding and develop new literacies.
> Koechlin, Rosenfeld & Loertscher (2010, 31)

The Learning Commons Partnership Teams

The number of leadership teams needed in any one school will vary. In this book we have suggested that the Learning Leadership Team, the Learning Literacy Team, the Organizational Leadership Team, and the Technology Leadership Team are key groups to the building and the propelling of the Learning Commons to provide improved learning for all. We suggest that all teams should work through the frameworks established in the Experimental Commons and the rich resources and support of the Open Commons to conduct the important work they do for the benefit of all teachers and students. The consistency of working through the same channels will help align real progress that can be analyzed and sustained. Principals and other school leaders can find and track all initiatives in one place as opposed to hunting down isolated and often factious 'start and stop' programs all over the school.

Regardless of the mandate, all collaborative learning teams need to work together with a set of collective inquiry questions critical to the common vision of improving learning for all. For example, DuFour, DuFour and Eaker have developed the following guiding questions:
- What is it our students must learn?
- What is the best way to sequence their learning?

- What are the most effective strategies to use in teaching this essential content?
- How will we know when they have learned it?
- How will we respond when they don't learn?
- What will we do when they already know it?
- What can we learn from each other to enhance our effectiveness?

  DuFour, Du Four and Eaker (2006, 8)

Systems and Networks that Support Learning and Experimentation

Collaboration is one of the most discussed ideas in the professional literature but often the least practiced. As authors, we have heard from teacher librarians a plethora of reasons why it does not happen:

- Collaboration is not taught to preservice teachers.
- Tradition has one teacher in a closed classroom.
- Teachers don't know how to collaborate.
- Scheduled classes allow no time to collaborate.
- The principal does not encourage it.
- Teachers treat specialists such as the teacher librarian as support personnel rather than as colleagues.
- Teachers feel that if they collaborate, others will discover their weaknesses.
- Tradition: "I have always done it this way. Just leave me alone. I have too much to cover."
- Collaboration takes up too much valuable time.

Kuhlthau, Maniotes, and Caspari provide a similar list of inhibitors but also suggest enablers:

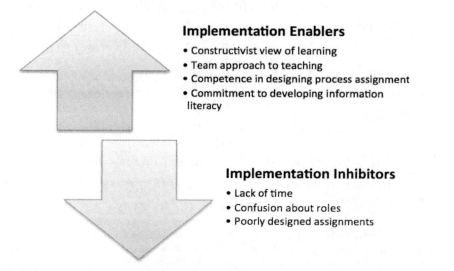

Implementation Enablers

- Constructivist view of learning
- Team approach to teaching
- Competence in designing process assignment
- Commitment to developing information literacy

Implementation Inhibitors

- Lack of time
- Confusion about roles
- Poorly designed assignments

Kuhlthau, Maniotes, and Caspari (2007, 51-52)

Obviously, a system that stimulates collaboration is a leadership issue that begins with the principal and the school's leadership teams. Negatives can be turned into positives with a set of well-known strategies that will be the center of focus for the school leadership teams to confront directly. Replace:

- Dysfunction with purpose
- Isolation with teaming
- Locked doors with an open doors
- Specialists shunned to specialist inclusion
- Rigidity with realistic flexibility
- Habits and predispositions with transformation

The list of resources at the end of this chapter provides direction in this transformation.

BRIGHT IDEAS to Build On
Pathways to Sustainable Collaboration

Sustainable Collaboration begins with people. Making a major change toward a Learning Commons requires vision and support from the administrators at the helm. They select and then support the specialists who are not only comfortable in collaborative roles but can demonstrate and share those abilities. In turn, these professionals challenge the classroom teachers to experiment together, refine, assess, rethink, and keep improving. This usually happens in one of three ways:

- The visionary administrator hires a a staff willing and experienced at collaboration
- A major professional development initiative discourages isolation and introduces, trains, and then nurtures a major change toward a collaborative culture.
- The Learning Commons leadership team entices a few teachers to experiment, demonstrate, and recruit others over a period of time.

The authors have watched all three of the above patterns produce more long-range results in a school culture. The change to a Learning Commons happens in both the physical and the virtual space of the school. Many will find that collaboration in virtual space is easier than in the face to face world. Thus, it may begin there. For example, if the teacher librarian creates a collaborative knowledge building center for a particular learning experience using a collaborative structure such as Google Sites, the fact that several specialists are built into the "room" just presumes that collaboration is natural rather than forced. Alongside the classroom teacher of a social studies experience, the reading specialist may be giving tips on reading complex texts or original documents, the teacher librarian may be assisting students in evaluating the information they are locating, and a teacher technologist may be monitoring a collaborative blog and helping students use the tool to build collaborative intelligence. The result is a vast improvement over a single adult just handing out assignments and deadlines. The idea that multiple adults are coaching online transfers easily into a live work session as students progress through project based learning. Numerous collaborative unit examples can be found at http://www.schoollearningcommons.info under the Knowledge Building Centers tab.

If teachers are unfamiliar with working in a truly collaborative environment, then they need to experience that environment at the same time as they are learning how to structure and scaffold such experiences for their students. Much of the instructional coaching literature recommends that a specialist come into the classroom and model a desired teaching behavior. We recommend that prior to this, participants are guided through a real collaborative experience. For example, an actual knowledge building center site is set up to investigate inquiry learning. Together with coaches, teachers investigate the elements of inquiry while experiencing it as adults. Everyone in the session is talking, working, investigating, creating, reporting, concluding and finally reflecting upon what they know about inquiry after inquiring together. Then, using that experience as a model, the specialist coaches can guide a novice through a planning experience for a typical unit of instruction and then co-teach that unit alongside the teacher in a real classroom. During the professional development workshop, experienced teachers can be matched with novices so that the learning time is shortened and a sense of "I can do this" emerges. As collaborative learning experiences happen in various classrooms, the teams can report their successes and challenges in a follow-up faculty meeting. The result might be a learning fair in which students from various classes across the school demonstrate to parents the results of these learning projects. An example of a day and a half professional development workshop with a middle school faculty and specialists in Norman Oklahoma can be seen at: https://sites.google.com/site/longfellownorman/home

The next question is whether students know how to collaborate and flourish in collaborative environments. Many bring collaborative skills from their backgrounds. They may have teams as they play World of Warcraft or have a buddy in the high stakes thinking game, Portal 2. They may have experience in sports where team skills matter. They may be part of an initiative on Facebook or other social media. They may have families or belong to organizations where work or service projects may have given them collaborative experience. We hope every one of these skills will contribute to the success of a Learning Commons, but we also recognize that we cannot presume that group work will be effective and will automatically succeed. Great collaborative skills begin with personal expertise that can then be shared effectively with a group. The growing number of collaborative technologies available are great tools to use for teaching students how to build upon each other's strengths. Using Google documents to write collaboratively, building a Google presentation together, and creating a collaborative project on a Google site are great training grounds for everyone. In projects, we teach, coach, and point out to students what individual and collective work looks and feels like and how it culminates with something no one person could have produced individually. It is a matter of establishing a collaborative culture as the norm and as a natural extension of our social networking skills.

Some of the best growth comes with the design of projects. For example, students in one school can be doing a collaborative project with students somewhere else in the world. We may be testing ideas and trying to answer questions using data from international astronomical projects. We may be comparing techniques for going green across schools in the country or internationally. We might be working with a local community agency to implement safety issues, environmental problems, homelessness, supporting local food banks. Such real world projects where students can develop both passion and collaborative skills enrich the visions of the adult coaches.

Scenarios to Spark Collaborative Innovations

- **Movement and Learner Collaboration:** A classroom teacher faced a group of middle schoolers, many of whom were English learners and came from various ethnic backgrounds. Noting the lack of trust for any cooperative learning, the teacher happened to mention this problem to the teacher librarian. The teacher librarian recommended that the PE teacher become involved because of the new standards for physical education recently published by National Association for Sport and Physical Education (NASP). In a planning meeting together, the classroom teacher, the PE teacher, and the teacher librarian decided to do a prelude movement exercise with the learners before the teacher and the teacher librarian presented the collaborative project. All three teachers joined the learners in the gym the first day of the unit where the PE teacher had the class get on the floor and tie themselves in a large human knot and then figure out how to get out of the knot without letting loose of their hands. Their experiment with the learners made it possible to approach learner collaboration for the first time. (Watch the entire video at: http://www.edutopia.org/new-physical-education-movement-video)

- **A Day in the Life of:** The year-end tests were over. Two weeks remained in the school year. The students were chomping for vacation; the teachers were left wondering how to survive the bored and restless. In the last professional learning community meeting, everyone faced the grim reality of babysitting. The technology specialist rose to the occasion and suggested that the entire school do a "Day in the Life of" project. The teacher librarian seconded the motion; other specialists said they'd help and in fifteen minutes, dread was replaced with creativity and excitement. Calls to the community went out instantly and a massive brainstorming session with adults and the students ensued. Oral histories, podcasts, photo essays, research, video tours, and any other media that could be mustered were used. A full day of interviews was conducted followed by days of group refinement of projects. On the next to the last day of school there was an evening community program and a docent directed tour of the neighborhood via a gallery walk. The last day was devoted to class reflections: what do we now know, what should happen to all our documentation, what problems did we notice in our community that need to be solved, what needs to be celebrated, how? In a fifteen-minute secret, reflective meeting of the specialists, the feeling was unanimous that the locked doors of the classroom had crumbled.

- **On the Right Foot:** When the principals in the district were asked for their plans for staff development, one principal set forth the idea that every new teacher to the building should have one less class to teach the first semester. Instead of the class, the new teachers would have their release time at the same period of the day and would meet once a week with the teacher librarian and the technology specialist with the balance of the days used to build units of instruction and receive other training they needed. The resulting collaboration was incredibly successful and began to affect teacher retention immediately.

- **Spotlight:** The principal wanted to highlight a successful instructional practice, linked to research, during the monthly faculty meetings. She did not want to turn the presentation into a political reward system, so she called in the technology specialist and the teacher librarian and asked them to assist. They were to observe an instructional practice during the month and make a five-minute presentation, but not identify the teacher observed. This pair of specialists decided to make it a flashy, glitzy, and humorous, but pithy comment on quality teaching and learning, particularly collaborative experiences. What they found was that after the presentation, several teachers thought they were the ones being spotlighted. It was a pleasant beginning to a meeting usually packed with administrivia. Gradually collaboration increased, and teaching and learning became more exciting and more meaningful.

- **Study, Study, Study:** With only two weeks left before final exam, a couple of students who like to study together decided to check out the school library website (the Virtual Learning Commons) to see if anything was there to help them. They were surprised to find a great deal of support; links to study tips, and essay writing tips, as well as subject specific links. They rediscovered all the projects they had done this year in the library as well as the accompanying Pathfinders and the links to project wikis and blogs. Reviewing the collaborative project sites gave the students an idea and they immediately started to explore how to set up a virtual study group space. Within a few minutes, they were all set and ready to invite others into their Exam Think Space.

Over to You
- How will collaborative learning experiences prepare students for their future in the 21st Century?
- How can schools build on the successful collaborative experiences in school libraries to create school wide Professional Learning Communities?
- What are the present roadblocks to collaboration and how can we overcome them?
- How will collaboration help teachers redesign and implement more effective teaching and learning strategies?
- What can I do become a better collaborator?
- How can I contribute to the collaborative culture in my school?

References

- Dana, Nancy Fichtman, and Diane Yendol-Hoppey. 2008. *The Reflective Educator's Guide to Professional Development: Coaching Inquiry-Oriented Learning Communities*. Thousand Oaks, CA: Corwin Press.

- DuFour, Rebecca, Richard DuFour and Robert Eaker. 2006. *Professional Learning Communities at Work Plan Book*. Bloomington, IN: Solution Tree.

- Fullan, Michael. 2008. *The Six Secrets of Change: What the Best Leaders Do to Help Their Organizations Survive and Thrive*. 2008. San Francisco. CA: Jossey-Bass.

- Hayes Jacobs, Heidi. 2010. *Curriculum 21: Essential Education for a Changing World*. Alexandria, VA: Association for Supervision & Curriculum Development.

- Koechlin, Carol, Esther Rosenfeld, and David V. Loertscher. 2010. *Building a Learning Commons: aGuide for School Administrators and Learning Leadership Teams*. Salt Lake City, UT: Hi Willow Research & Publishing.

- Kuhlthau, Carol, Leslie K. Maniotes, and Ann K. Caspari. 2007 *Guided Inquiry – Learning in the 21st Century*. Westport, CT: Libraries Unlimited.

- Lance, Keith Curry and David V. Loertscher. 2004. *Powering Achievement*. Salt Lake City, UT: Hi Willow Research & Publishing. See also additional research studies from the Colorado State Library at: http://lrs.org

Resources

Foundational Ideas

- DuFour, Richard, Robert Eaker, and Rebecca Dufour, eds. 2005. *On Common Ground: the Power of Professional Learning Communities*. Bloomington, IN: Solution Tree.

- DuFour, Richard, Rebecca DuFour, Robert Eaker, and Thomas Many. 2010. *Learning by Doing: A Handbook for Professional Learning Communities at Work*, 2nd edition. Bloomington, IN: Solution Tree.

Professional Organizations

- Association for Supervision and Curriculum Development (ASCD). http://ascd.org

Professional Resources

- Adcock, Donald C. and Patricia Montiel-Overall. 2007. *Collaboration*. Chicago, IL: American Library Association.

- Bishop, Kay. 2011. *Connecting Libraries with Classrooms: The Curricular Roles of the Media Specialist*, 2nd edition. Santa Barbara, CA: Linworth.

- Blankstein, Alan M., Paul D. Houston, and Robert W. Cole. 2007. *Sustaining Professional Learning Communities*. Thousand Oaks, CA: Corwin Press.

- Conderman, Greg, Val Bresnahan, and Theresa Pedersen. 2009. *Purposeful Co-Teaching: Real Cases and Effective Strategies*. Thousand Oaks, CA: Corwin Press.

- Darling-Hammond, Linda, Brigid Barron, et al. 2008. *Powerful Learning: What We Know About Teaching for Understanding*. San Francisco, CA: Jossey-Bass.

- Frey, Nancy, Douglas Fisher, and Sandi Everlove. 2009. *Productive Group Work: How to Engage Students, Build Teamwork, and Promote Understanding*. Alexandria, VA: Association for Supervision and Curriculum Development.

- Fullan, Michael, Peter Hill, and Carmel Crevola. 2006. *Breakthough*. Thousand Oaks, CA: Corwin Press.

- Fullan, Michael. 2008. *The Six Secrets of Change: What the Best Leaders Do to Help Their Organizations Survive and Thrive*. San Francisco, CA: Jossey-Bass.

- Gregory, Gayle H. and Lin Kuzmich. 2007. *Teacher Teams that Get Results: 61 Strategies for Sustaining and Renewing Professional Learning Communities*. Thousand Oaks, CA: Corwin Press.

- Harada, Violet H., Carolyn H. Kirio, and Sandra H. Yamamoto. 2008. *Collaborating for Project-based Learning in Grades 9-12*. Santa Barbara, CA: Linworth.

- Hord, Shirley M. and William A. Sommers. 2008. *Leading Professional Learning Communities: Voices From Research and Practice*. Thousand Oaks, CA: Corwin Press.

- Knight, Jim, ed. 2009. *Coaching: Approaches and Perspectives*. Thousand Oaks, CA: Corwin Press.

- Kuhlthau, Carol, Leslie K. Maniotes and Ann K. Caspari. 2007 *Guided Inquiry – Learning in the 21st Century*. Westport, CT: Libraries Unlimited.

- Lance, Keith and David V. Loertscher. 2005. *Powering Achievement* , 3rd edition. Salt Lake City, UT: Hi-Willow Research and Publishing.

- Marzano, Robert J. 2009. *On Excellence in Teaching*. Bloomington, IN: Solution Tree.

- Prensky, Marc. 2010. *Teaching Digital Natives: Partnering for Real Learning.* Thousand Oaks, CA: Corwin Press.

- Todd, Ross J. 2008. "Collaboration: From Myth to Reality: Let's Get Down to Business. Just Do It!". *School Library Media Activities Monthly* 24 no. 7 (March 2008): 54-58.

- Villa, Richard A., Jacqueline S. Thousand, and Ann I. Nevin. 2008. *A Guide to Co-Teaching: Practical Tips for Facilitating Student Learning.* Thousand Oaks, CA: Corwin Press.

- Wild, Monique D., Amanda S. Mayeaux, and Kathryn P. Edmonds. 2008. *TeamWork: Setting the Standard for Collaborative Teaching, Grades 5-9.* Portland, ME: Stenhouse Publishers.

- Williams, R. Bruce. 2008. *More than 50 Ways to Build Team Consensus.* Thousand Oaks, CA: Corwin Press.

- Zmuda, Allison, and Violet H. Harada. 2008. *Librarians as Learning Specialists : Meeting the Learning Imperative for the 21st Century.* Westport, CT: Libraries Unlimited.

Other Resources

- Cameron, Greg, Monette McIver, and Roger Goddard. 2008. "A Different Kind of Community," *Changing Schools*, Winter, 2008. Download at: http://www.mcrel.org/product/339. The only thing missing from this essay is the role that specialists could have as an integral part of a collaborative faculty working to improve their school.

- Library Research Service http://lrs.org/ is a source for evidence linking library media programs to student achievement.

Chapter 7

Personal Learning Environments
In the Learning Commons

How do we ensure that learners and adults can build and manage their own learning environment?

- Watch this young person's example of her personal learning network: http://www.youtube.com/watch?v=YEls3tq5wIY
- Then, watch Will Richardson's introduction to a PLN at: http://www.youtube.com/watch?v=mghGV37TeK8

Personal learning environments (PLEs) are often described as systems for enabling self-directed and group-based learning, designed around each user's goals, with great capacity for flexibility and customization. PLEs are conceived as drawing on a variety of discrete tools, chosen by the learner, which can be connected or used in concert in a transparent way. While the concept of PLEs is still quite fluid, it does seem to be clear that a PLE is not simply a technology but an approach or process that is individualized by design, and thus different from person to person. It involves sociological and philosophical considerations and cannot be packaged, passed out, and handed around as a cell phone or tablet computer could. Widespread adoption of PLEs, once the tools and approaches are clearer, will almost certainly also require a shift in attitudes toward technology, teaching, and learning. (The NMC Horizon Report: 2011 K-12 Edition)

The sheer volume of information available today renders it impossible for everyone to know all there is to know on specific topics of interest. It is in fact becoming increasingly difficult at times to find reliable, relevant data. This is a problem caused by the Internet and the seemingly endless number of tools available to store and share data. Although there is a promise of 'super' organization and distribution of information in projected Web 3.0 revelations, we need to right now empower learners, and the adults who coach them, to take control of their learning. We can do this by helping them shape their personalized environments. Every learner needs a virtual space of their own which is dedicated to helping them access, manage, and understand information and to helping them contribute to their knowledge building environment.

In the Learning Commons, a Personal Learning Environment (PLE) is critical to building capacity for learning to learn. Both students and educators are coached and supported in constructing, managing, and utilizing their PLE to the fullest potential. The Learning Commons takes responsibility for building and maintaining flexible physical and virtual environments conducive to the best learning for all types of clients and their needs. However, a PLE is different. It is a specific world designed by the user to best meet their individualized information, learning, social, and recreational needs. Individuals and groups can actually build on the rich networks, resources, and tools already established in the Learning Commons to extend their own learning universe.

Thus PLEs are driven by a need to make sense of the vast world of information and ideas and take advantage of technologies and tools available. In addition, they tap into the expertise of others in order to learn, to build knowledge, to create, to collaborate, and to share within their specified community and the broader learning environment.

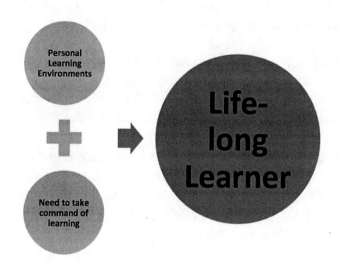

Let's break down the concept.

Personal – It's all about the interests and the needs of each learner. Tools and resources and contacts all need to be selected by the learner or the PLE will have no relevance.

Learning – It's all about learning and that learning should be self-directed. The learner needs to be in control, test ideas, collaborate, create, make mistakes, and fix them and keep on learning. This approach holds true for both formal and informal learning.

Environment - It's all about creating a safe but empowering learning space. The role of the Learning Commons is to ensure that everyone has access to the best tools, resources, skills, and supports to work and play and learn. It is about creating a culture of learning by fostering habits of mind conducive to learning how to learn. These habits include curiosity, a desire to make sense of the world, empathy for others, value of self, the need to take charge, and a sense of community.

To further define the personal learning environment, study the following model that divides the PLE into three distinct stages of development. Each phase empowers the learner to manage specific aspects of their learning potential. Each phase is a critical component of ensuring success. When put together, the result is powerful. Strengthened by continuous reflection and goal setting, the PLE sets up learning for life.

The Structure of a Digital Personal Learning Environment

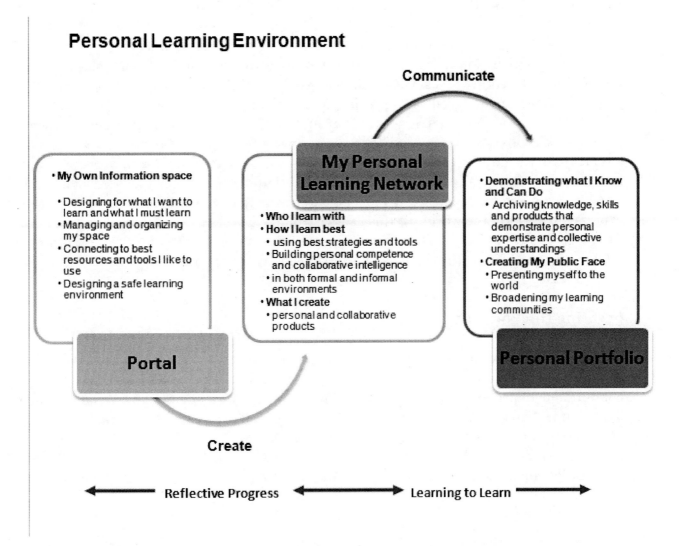

Building the Portal

Portal construction tools continue to appear and are getting more sophisticated over time. Perhaps the easiest one to begin with for kids, teens, and even adults is iGoogle or the Start Page in Google Apps for Education. It takes very little time to understand what is happening when using these tools. Then as awareness of more complex software emerges, the idea of coming into command of one's own information world is set. We are embracing what we wish to spend our time learning and rejecting everything else. And, if we want to go out into the larger world, we can go there as we please. We teach and learn how to create our own "filters" realizing that no wall is foolproof, but intruders are blocked for the most part and our skill in information management grows to meet our changing needs and interests. For schooling, we will want links to our teachers, the school Learning Commons, and anything else connected to our academic world. For other interests, we will invite selected information and people into our space.

Constructing and Using the Personal Learning Network

In the personal learning network or PLN, we are doing our work, connecting, producing, and creating both as a individual and in collaborative groups. The PLN is the place we are developing 21st Century Skills. We are listening, connecting to experts, hanging out our work for inspection and feedback, growing, and evolving. It is the place for formal schooling, but as importantly, it goes far beyond the classroom as we purposefully explore interests, passions, abilities , or just try to keep up in a field in which we are already an 'expert'. Will Richardson and Rob Mancabelli, in their book *Personal Learning Networks*, suggest a few of the many tools that help us connect and share. These include Diigo, Google Reader, and Blogger. These tools help keep us organized and provide a chance to express ourselves to the world. To this list, we would suggest any of the collaborative Google tools such as Google Documents, Google Draw, Google Presentations, and other tools such as Mindomo that help us mind map what we know personally or collaboratively.

Creating the Portfolio

Whether in formal or informal learning, sharing our work to develop a bank of our own personal and collaborative expertise is an essential part of the current connected world. For our bank of products, we select those that we want to be made public. We hang out our personal shingle. We come into command of our public face, knowing that prospective employers or opportunities come to those who get noticed. Tools such as Google Sites, YouTube, blogs, wikis, and the Creative Commons are simple tools to push our best feet forward. We become digital curators (collectors and organizers), who exhibit our work to the public.

Digging Deeper
One interesting article that addresses digital curation is "How Can Web 2.0 Curation Tools Be Used in the Classroom?", at
http://mindshift.kqed.org/2011/08/how-can-web-2-0-curation-tools-be-used-in-the-classroom/
A good example of curation for a specific purpose is *Technology Integration*, curated by Robin Sellers at http://www.scoop.it/t/technology-integration
Finally, check out the public face of Eric Sheninger, Principal of New Milford High School, NJ at: http://ericsheninger.com/esheninger/videos

Physical Personal Learning Environments

The Physical Learning Commons offers many qualities that enable individual, small groups, and large groups to quickly assemble a personal learning environment to meet their specific needs. Spaces are flexible, furnishings are easily moveable, and technology devices are as portable as possible so that individuals and groups can set up special stations for their personalized work. Access to all learning resources, networking potential from stations to others, productivity tools that encourage creativity, and a variety of communication possibilities make the Learning Commons the 'go to' place for personalizing physical learning environments.

PLEs Build 21st Century Skills

Learners are building skills for the future as they work in their own PLE. The following attributes are common to both physical and virtual personal learning environments:

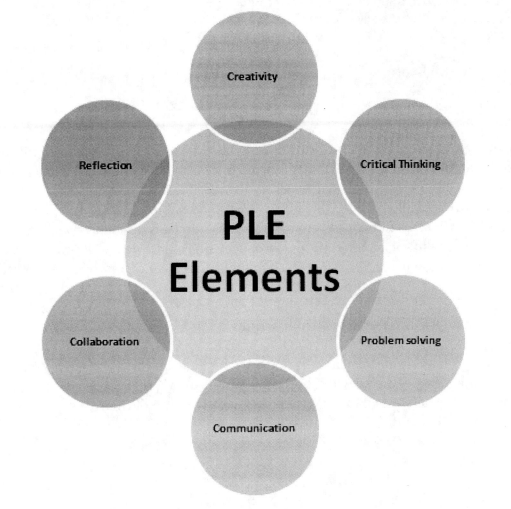

Many in the business world already proclaim the benefits of attention to the learning environment and the need to support personalized spaces for work. The above attributes are highly valued today and will be in jobs of the future. One of the most sought after capabilities is creativity. Those individuals who know how to play with ideas, information, and knowledge in order to innovate or create something new will be valuable employees and citizens of tomorrow. Everything about the Learning Commons is a stimulus for creative thought and activity. For example, the flexible spaces allow for impromptu drama extensions to a great picture book. Learners are taught presentation skills and then invited to play with multimedia tools to design the best way to communicate their discoveries and ideas. The virtual spaces of the Commons are rich with links and tutorials for Web 2.0 applications to encourage teachers to develop creative learning experiences for students.

The following video portrays a business story of building environments that reap all of the above attributes. However, the big gain portrayed is creativity in the workplace. http://creativity-online.com/work/tedxu-the-daydreamers-dillema/24306

Empowering the Learner

A PLE enables learners to build on their own strengths and experiences. Every student comes to school with established knowledge building worlds. Regardless of demographics, economics, or ability, everyone has skills, ideas, and dreams built outside of school. The influence of these personal worlds is very individual, and consequently the visual below will look very different for every learner. Helping students transfer expertise from their worlds of play, home life, culture, and personal interest to the academic world is that much easier in a networked environment. When learners realize that their personal expertise in social networking, computer skills, knowledge of music or of gaming have relevance to their academic world, then educators have an opportunity to broaden the influence they have in the academic sphere. The Learning Commons helps students build personal learning environments that enable them to organize and manage both their personal worlds and their academic worlds.

The following illustration delineates various pieces and aspects of a learner's world that might become a part of an individual's PLE. Learners, using their own preferences, should experiment with such a visual before they start construction of their PLE.

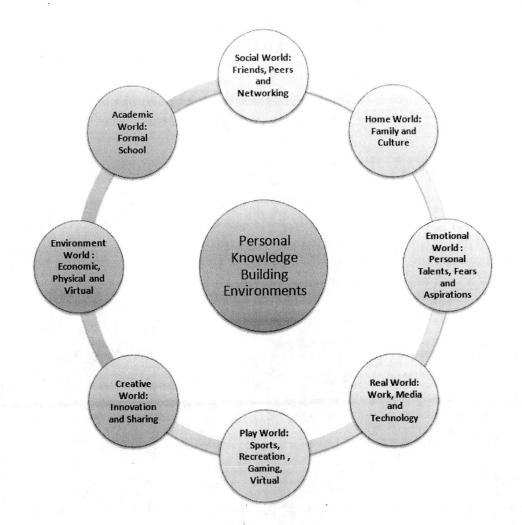

Within the portal and networked spaces of a PLE, students are encouraged to gather and organize links to resources, tools, friends, and experts that will help them expand all their interests both inside and outside of school. It is hoped that learners will discover that often there will be opportunity for connectivity between personal interests and their formal school life. Within their Personal Portfolio students will store and organize their photos, stories, projects, and works in progress. They will also decide how, when, and where to responsibly share with others their success, their ideas, and their creations so that they maintain a healthy constructive public profile. The thoughtful intentional design and construction of a PLE requires planning and know how, but inventiveness and creativity will keep the PLE fresh and exciting.

Reflection Point
As an adult reading this book, reflect on your own personal learning environment. Looking at the two models above, how "in command" of your own world of information and technology are you? How well are you organized? What improvements could and should you make? What tools could you use to boost not only your organizational skills but also your productivity?

Personal Learning environments help learners discover how they learn best. This calls for metacognition and goal setting. Design reflective tools and strategies to help students and teachers assess the effectiveness of their PLE. The article, "7 Things You Should Know About...Personal Learning Environments", at http://net.educause.edu/ir/library/pdf/ELI7049.pdf will provide some background.

Personal Learning Environments in the Learning Commons - Indicators of Learner Success

Personal Learning Environments are not just a good idea for learners and ther adult coaches. They should also have an outcome that pushes everyone toward mature habits in the information and technology world we currently inhabit. The diagram below provides some assessment points of what we might really value.

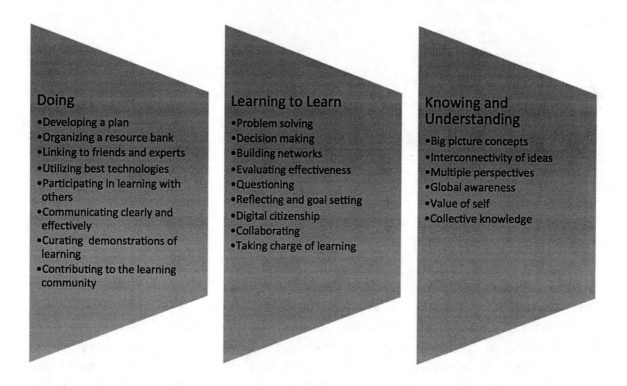

Doing
• Developing a plan
• Organizing a resource bank
• Linking to friends and experts
• Utilizing best technologies
• Participating in learning with others
• Communicating clearly and effectively
• Curating demonstrations of learning
• Contributing to the learning community

Learning to Learn
• Problem solving
• Decision making
• Building networks
• Evaluating effectiveness
• Questioning
• Reflecting and goal setting
• Digital citizenship
• Collaborating
• Taking charge of learning

Knowing and Understanding
• Big picture concepts
• Interconnectivity of ideas
• Multiple perspectives
• Global awareness
• Value of self
• Collective knowledge

Empowering the Teacher

Resource TIPs
In their book, *Personal Learning Networks: Using the Power of Connections to Transform Education*, Will Richardson and Rob Mancabelli make a powerful case for encouraging the adoption of PLNs for all students. They not only make the case, but discuss the basic tools and how to get started, and then devote a lengthy chapter to the creation of the networked classroom. The book is sprinkled with the experiences of real teachers in real schools who are already transforming their classrooms and the lives of their students.

In *A Gardener's Approach to Learning,* David Warlick explores the world of personal learning networks and offers this significant idea:
In the same way that a garden is a rich and intertwined ecosystem where plants, air, soil, birds and bugs interact to grow and reproduce, today's emerging information landscape is an info-system, where content is produced, published, accessed, consumed, discussed, re-mixed and re-published. To be a "master learner" — to be a teacher — today, you must learn to work the info-system in order to cultivate new knowledge and skills from a continual flow of information. David Warlick (2010)

To be a traditional teacher in the current socially networked world is to hold on to your horse when everyone else is driving an automobile. It is to have a dialup phone when everyone else has a smart phone; or it is to keep listening to cassette tapes when everyone else has an iPod. But technological change is not just about trying to keep up with the latest fashion. It is about a basic change in communicating, thinking, and working. Nicholas Carr, in his book, *The Shallows: What the Internet Is Doing to our Brain,* traces the history of various technologies to show the differences in thinking and working across the ages. For instance, when printed books replaced oral tradition, a new type of literacy was born. He contends that this happens whenever there is a major shift in technology. Nicholas Carr (2011).

So, if teachers wish to keep up with their students, then they need to meet them in their world. That is just one advantage of "keeping up." With each new technology, we learn new ways of improving who we are, what we know, how we live, and how we can use this knowledge to make a difference in our world.

Teachers who adopt the new technologies of their students suddenly learn new ways to develop real learning experiences that take advantage of personal network environments . They learn to build upon social networks in ways that develop personal and collaborative expertise, connections to the real worlds, and ways to make learning dynamic, real, meaningful, and even exciting. This change is about using the tools at hand to engage rather than bore, to boost learning exponentially rather than incrementally. And the only way to learn how that can happen is to jump in to this new swimming pool rather than admire the water from the edge of the pool.

Try out the following activity to begin or improve upon your own personal learning environment.

Here are some sample visuals of PLEs developed by adult learners trying to map out a structure to their learning environment. Explore their visualizations and think about your own learning worlds.

- ○ The Rethinking Learning and Teaching Blog at: http://rethinkinglearning.blogspot.com/2010/12/my-personal-learning-environment-as-i.html
- ○ My Personal Learning Environment using Flickr at: http://www.flickr.com/photos/francescesteve/3039956497/
- ○ J-Learning sample PLD at: http://jcarlos.design2001.com/?p=164
- ○ Michael Grace's PLE template you can model yours at: http://geek.michaelgrace.org/2009/07/my-personal-learning-environment/
- ○ Create your PLE on your own mobile device using these recommendations from the School Technology Action Report, "Education's Guide to Mobile Devices: Everything You Need to Know About Mobile Tech and Your Schools" at: http://www.eschoolnews.com/wp-content/uploads/2011/09/mobile_star.pdf

Now, what does your personal Learning Network look like?
Think about how you are informed:
- Who do you read, watch, listen to, consult?
- Where, when, and how do you gather information and for what purpose?
- Your information tools?
- How you process information?
- How you store your projects, creations, works in progress?
- Who do you share with? How do you contribute to your learning community?

Now create a visual to represent your personal information network.

The Learning Commons as Personal Learning Environment Central

It isn't likely that students will have PLEs until teachers do, thus the work of the Learning Commons is twofold. The first step is to coach staff to build their own PLE s and the second step is to encourage them to teach their students how to manage their own learning environments. But it is also certain, given a vision of what might be, its possibilities, and the whys, that creative techies are likely to take off and begin jamming and mashing up their own ideas for scrutiny.

Systems and Networks that Support Personal Learning Environments

In the early years of high tech, many school districts made the assumption that the district would have to purchase the computers, the networks, the learning management systems, and control everything from a central location in order to "protect" the children and teens. Those expensive systems are in decline, and more open and affordable solutions are emerging. In this YouTube video, a young sprout educates a traditional

teacher about this new world of open personal learning networks:
http://www.youtube.com/watch?v=a9zSd5Gs6Mw

Instead of locking systems down, many school districts and individual schools are joining Google Apps for Education, a free and safe environment that works in the cloud and on many personal devices. Google Apps for Education has over 50 different tools that can be used for knowledge building centers, personal learning environments, enclosed e-mail systems, and the building of portals and portfolios. These systems can be used 24/7 and can be exported to follow the various learners and teachers if they move. Such more open and cost effective systems are coupled with the teaching of digital citizenship in order to meet the challenges of state and federal requirements of safety. It just takes a tech director who is willing to experiment with and willing to participate in the creation of tech systems that actually boost learning rather than simply continuing with a locked down system that prevents many types of learning.

Many districts are opening up networks to staff and students so they can use their own personal mobile devices at school. BYOD (Bring Your Own Device) is popular for professional meetings and conferences. All learners would benefit from the immediacy of having the world in their pocket whenever they need it. If that learner now is empowered by a well organized effective PLE then the the notion of 'anytime, anywhere learning' is realized. However the school networks have to be open enough to function this way. Stephen Abram comments on this topic at:
http://stephenslighthouse.com/2011/09/10/preparation-for-living-in-a-public-world/

BRIGHT Ideas to Build On
- Check out the PLN journey of one perpetual beta principal who understands that effort reaps rewards: http://lynhilt.com/effort-in-reward-out/

- See this example of a group PLN in action: http://edupln.ning.com/

- Experiment with creating a visual resume: http://signup.vizualize.me/74xzi

- See how professional learning environments are changing: http://jeffhurtblog.com/2011/08/25/ten-learning-shifts-for-conferences-events-associations/

Scenarios

Sandra's junior class in World History was at year's end, and over the past month a huge cloud of boredom had infected her classroom. Sandra had recently attended a workshop about personal learning environments and networks and had thought it would be nice to wait until the next school year to try it out. But, on her way home from school, she was listening to a very opinionated news report on the world economy and how it would be so easy and simple to fix everything if only... She wondered what her students thought. The next day, she asked her class what they thought. She was shocked to hear them repeat mostly what they had heard from parents or TV. It was apparent that everyone needed a much broader perspective. She asked how many kids currently had access to the Internet or cell phones, or iPads. Almost all had acquired them sometime during the school year. She asked how many of the students would be in favor of studying the world economy if they could use every device they owned. Every hand was raised. She said she would see what she could do.

At lunch she talked with the teacher librarian, the teacher technologist, the assistant principal, and her department chair who she all corralled around her table. Could she try an experiment? Would they all help? They agreed but were worried about the short notice. Sandra promised that she would get her techie students involved, and that between adults and students they might be able to do something. The assistant principal paved the way through the district tech coordinator and invited the district tech and administrative staff to participate in the experiment.

The class met with the adults in the Learning Commons the next day and it was decided that everyone would build a personal learning network to explore the world economy. Some took North America, others Europe, while some tracked China, India, Australia, and Brazil. Luckily, Sandra had Spanish, Chinese, and French speaking students in the class and or relatives or neighbors from other countries that needed to be studied. From their PLN expertise, they would all form a world congress on global economics.

They were off and running...

A second PLN Scenario is http://weblogg-ed.com/2011/personal-learning-networks-an-excerpt/

Over to You

For those who have yet to develop a PLE for yourself or for your students, we suggest you just get started. Start with a group of young people who can invent their own PLEs together with you. Then share your work on your PLN, get feedback, and keep creating and learning. For everyone else, the journey never seems to end. It is the new normal of being in perpetual beta.

References

- Carr, Nicholas. 2011. *The Shallows: What the Internet Is Doing to our Brain*. New York: W. W. Norton & Company.

- Johnson, L., Adams, S., and Haywood, K. 2011. *The NMC Horizon Report: 2011 K-12 Edition*. Austin, TX: The New Media Consortium. http://www.nmc.org/pdf/2011-Horizon-Report-K12.pdf

- Warlick, David. 2010. *A Gardener's Approach to Learning*. Lulu.com.

Resources

Foundational Ideas

- Richardson, Will and Rob Mancabelli. 2011. *Personal Learning Networks: Using the Power of Connection to Transform Education*. Bloomington, IN: Solution Tree.

Professional Resources

- "7 Things You Should Know About...Personal Learning Environments". 2009. *Educause*. May 2009. http://net.educause.edu/ir/library/pdf/ELI7049.pdf

- Nevin, Roger, Micah Melton, and David V. Loertscher. 2011. *Google Apps for Education: Building Knowledge in a Safe and Free Environment*. Salt Lake City, UT: Hi Willow Research and Publishing.

- Waters, Audrey. 2011. "How Can Web 2.0 Curation Tools Be Used in the Classroom?", *Mind/Shift*. August 3, 2011. http://mindshift.kqed.org/2011/08/how-can-web-2-0-curation-tools-be-used-in-the-classroom/

- Williams, Robin T., and David V. Loertscher. 2008. *In Command! Kids and Teens Build and Manage Their Own Information Spaces, and... Learn to Manage Themselves in Those Spaces*. Salt Lake, City UT: Hi Willow Research and Publishing.

- Curation for Learning : how people are curating, utilizing, and sharing information - a digital curation example using Scoop It by Buffy Hamilton http://www.scoop.it/t/curation-for-learning/p/529594589/digital-curation-education-in-practice-catching-up-with-two-former-fellows-gregory-international-journal-of-digital-curation

Chapter 8

Building the Learning Commons
as a Client-Side Organization

Why do educators need to adopt new models?
Before launching into a chapter in which we introduce an organization that is built to elevate each learner, we urge the reader to consider the need for new education models as explained by Sir Ken Robinson in his TED Talk, **Bring on the Revolution** at: http://www.youtube.com/watch?v=r9LelXa3U_I or, his animated talk **Changing Education Paradigms** at: http://www.youtube.com/watch?v=zDZFcDGpL4U

Creating a Learning Commons can be both an evolutionary and a revolutionary organizational transformation. It might be triggered by a change in staff, a grant opportunity, a change in administration, or even an Ah Ha! moment in a professional learning community conversation. Using any catalyst, the conversation centers on the transformation from an "organization centered" concept into a client side model where both students and teachers win. It is the difference between the "If you build it, they will come" model to the "If *they* build it, they will use it" model. It transforms students from bored users to engaged and productive learners, and teachers from masters to learners and coaches.

Beginning with the concept of the Open Commons and the Experimental Learning Center, a combination of learning tools and learning sciences contributes to a fresh and exciting learning environment. Central to this concept is the notion of world-class excellence. The Learning Commons is, as much as possible, a product of informed client input. Shadow leadership and coaching help clients move from their own, often minimal, expectations toward more ambitious visions for themselves.

To be successful, this initiative will require participants to "buy-in" and will require collaborative vision building that capitalizes on the strengths of both the adults and students. Such a change places the client first and should not be a short-term solution, but rather a long-term sustainability model. The vision is one of a "perpetual beta" idea where change keeps pace with forces today and inevitable future evolution. To the learners, this means that the school not only gives them the support and tools to learn but also empowers them to capitalize on their interests and abilities. For the teachers, the opportunities offered by this organization allow them to keep improving as they enjoy the benefits of job embedded professional development.

> **"It Simply Isn't the 20th Century Any More Is It? So Why Would We Teach as Though It Was?"** Listen to Stephen Heppell discuss this statement at http://dotsub.com/view/91dc77e9-89f9-4178-a102-f5f93e4b6aef .
> Then check out New Learning Spaces on Heppell's website www.heppell.net

Creating an Organization That Empowers the Learner

What kind of organization empowers the learner rather than corralling everyone into the same user mode? What sort of configuration defies the one-size-fits-all mentality? The organizational team of the Learning Commons should brainstorm ideas that push from regimentation to opportunity. A sample list might include:

Empower		Regiment
Totally flexible spaces in the Learning Commons	vs	Fixed space configuration
User preferred devices	vs	Prescribed connective devices
Access to elastic print and digital resources	vs	Only static or owned materials /resource collections
Multiple professionals, support personnel, and volunteers	vs	Single adult consultant
Accessible yet safe instructional computer systems; cloud computing	vs	Limited, (inadequate), and tightly controlled networks
Learner-constructed information spaces - the Virtual Learning Commons	vs	Central library web sites as one-way communication systems
Flexible calendars	vs	Rigidly scheduled classes
Open checkout all day as needed, and rotating classroom collections	vs	1-2 books per week at preset times
Experimentation in the Experimental Learning Center	vs	Prescribed professional development

In any of these transitions, learners need to be involved in the design and in its ongoing development. Insight into many key ideas will come from student experiences in social networking and their familiarity with current trends in music, movies, messaging systems, and television. *Involvement, choice, engagement,* and *differentiation* are all terms that will be considered as policies and procedures develop. Care must be taken to build systems for various types of learners with different ability levels, learning styles, languages, and cultural backgrounds.

> **Discussion Point** While there is some skepticism that schools cannot transform themselves, as is the message in the following video, we are confident about the creation of a learning society within the school.
> http://www.youtube.com/watch?v=X8lourogdrM Are you as confident about your organization?

Creating an Organization that Empowers the Teacher

The legendary idea of academic freedom (when the door closes, I do what I darn well please) coupled with intense pressure to raise each learner to a minimal level of achievement has isolated the classroom teacher and contributed to the high dropout rates of not only teens but also their instructors. Numerous autobiographical accounts of the overwhelming challenge, particularly for the first year teacher, bring to mind Frank McCourt's memoir, *Teacher Man*, as he faces, alone, the overwhelming task of making a difference. "Just close the door. No help, sorry. Just keep them under control." Faced with overwhelming odds, few teachers can share a success story as depicted in the film *Freedom Writers*, or in the book *Educating Esme*.

The Learning Commons, as the center of school improvement, offers a lifeline from the frustration often expressed in the teachers' lounge. Administrators will focus the entire faculty on excellence as they lead the initiative of continuous experimentation and improvement. "You are not alone. Here's a lifeline. We are all on the journey together."

The first year teacher is an obvious place to begin in the creation of the Experimental Learning Center. Here, new teachers are introduced to their lifelines: the materials, the resources, the systems, and the specialists that will become their safety net. Panic, negativity, and stress are counterbalanced with collegial understanding, sharing, and encouragement.

Alongside first year teachers, the more experienced teachers who possess attributes of flexibility and creativity will be likely first candidates for the activities featured in the

Experimental Learning Center. As success is achieved with this group, and as evidence of improved achievement surfaces, others will climb aboard.

The Learning Commons as Organization Central

The new vision of the Learning Commons sets the library as a hub of activity in the school – a magnet for a range of teaching professionals to connect with students and to extend their own professional learning and practice. The teacher-librarian is a facilitator in this setting, coaching other professionals, connecting them with each other and with resources. The library's virtual space can be as much of a hub as the physical space, where resources, technology, user-focused design and innovative teaching practices mingle to

---

How can we move traditional libraries and labs to a Learning Commons client-side approach? Sometimes, simple trial and error will help spur needed changes. At other times, action research, testimonials, or best practices will direct progress.

Discussion Point Consider this video explanation of the role of trial and error: http://www.ted.com/talks/tim_harford.html?utm_source=newsletter_weekly_2011-07-19&utm_campaign=newsletter_weekly&utm_medium=email How can your own Learning Commons accept the fact that failure happens, and then move on?

Traditional approaches to every aspect of the previous library and computer laboratory need to be re-examined. Often what is required is that we do a mirror image vision of what has normally been the case, a 180 degree rethinking. The graphic below identifies the various component parts of the Learning Commons organizational elements followed by a brief description of each of those elements.

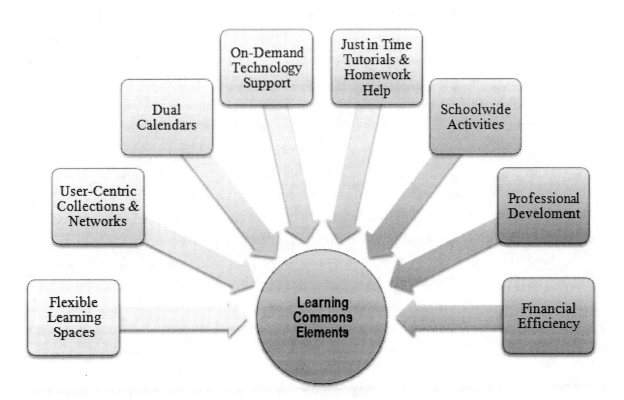

- **Flexible Learning Spaces** Take a look at your current physical spaces in the library and computer lab. What's flexible that could be adjusted any time of the day for individual or group work and creativity? If it doesn't move, does it really belong? Is the room filled with immovable book shelves or banks of computers? How many flexible learning spaces can be created at any one time on demand? Are there performance spaces? A space planning tool that might help is http://classroom.4teachers.org/

  Now consider the virtual library space. Is it a one way street with only information streaming out to clients? School Library websites are traditionally repositories of digital data. They need to be transformed into collaborative multi-way spaces in which to work, learn, create, play, and celebrate just like in the physical commons.

Activity
Take Action - Designing Collaborative Physical Spaces in the Learning Commons
Take Action - Designing Collaborative Virtual Spaces in the Learning Commons
(Worksheets found at the end of this chapter)

- **User-Centric Collections** Both teachers and learners participate in the growth and development of resources. High quality information resources are not free as is often supposed. Ample budgets provide access to copyrighted materials. Combined with the best of the free resources, the collection is available 24/7/365 to all users. These resources include online databases, on demand instructional videos, books, and the tutorials needed to utilize those resources. Materials spanning various reading levels, cultures, interest levels, and genres are sufficient to surround both the learner and teacher with a plethora of choices. Physical items such as books rotate from the Learning Commons into the classrooms and into the homes of learners all year around. The concept of ownership of resources often is replaced by "access to," meaning that collections are elastic in nature rather than static. In-house collections are linked to collections from all over the world such as art museums, great libraries, government sources, and document repositories. The Learning Commons contains the formats, the genres, the types of media, and the devices needed to use the resources wherever and whenever the user needs them. Digital and physical collections will evolve at the preferences of the users.

  > **Resource TIP** To stimulate discussion of new ways to provide access to information, consult David Loertscher and Laura Wimberly's book, *Collection Development Using the Collection Mapping Technique*, available through http://lmcsource.com

- **Dual Learning Commons Calendars** The Open Commons and the Experimental Learning Center are each governed by separate but interrelated calendars. All specialists and assigned administrators are scheduled through the Experimental Learning Center as needed. This includes the teacher librarian whose first responsibility is to the improvement of instruction rather than to tending and managing the Open Commons. For the most part, the Open Commons is the province of support personnel under the direction of the teacher librarian. This could be said of any specialist in the building who has a facility to supervise as well as a teaching and consultative role to the faculty at large. Specialists can also be calendared virtually as well as in person. For example, a teacher technologist might be scheduled in the ELC three periods a day and teach in another space the rest of the day. The more flexible the calendar, the more the various specialists are able to collaborate to maximize both the classroom teacher's agenda and their own in their effort to raise achievement.

- **On-Demand Technology Assistance.** Effective instructional computing systems require that the users have access to various types of hardware and software that assist them in learning. While we can equip learners with numerous devices and systems, regular tune-ups are needed to keep the various systems operational. Such tune-ups are the responsibility of everyone. I help you; you help me; and we all keep it running and operational. Instead of one-size-fits-all protocols, everyone is developing expertise to deal with and handle problems that arise. Cadres of learners and teachers are trained to address problems and then are expected to spread their knowledge. Both faculty and cadre members staff the expert bar in the Open Commons to assist individuals or small groups struggling with technology or software. These mini-experts are recognized in their various classes as sources of information and help. Disaffected students are often enticed by this role and become more connected to the learning community. Hackers can turn around to be systems designers and troubleshooters. Such assistance extends from the Learning Commons into the classrooms and also into the homes.

- **Just-in-Time Tutorial and Homework Help** The idea that, "if I am stuck, there is usually someone around to help whether during school hours or after hours," is a sign that client side practices are working. Help centers for doing homework both in person and via technology are very common. However, help for technology, software use, and the various literacies such as information literacy are not common. Everyone participates in building the help center section of the Learning Commons website home page, which can then be drawn upon by individual learners as needed. The idea that there is one expert in the school who provides timely assistance is unthinkable and undoable by even the most organized. Engaging everyone to help everyone else promotes collaboration across the entire learning community. For example:
    - A team of students can devise a quick tutorial for students on how to use iGoogle to build their own information space.
    - Help links are established on common problems when searching the Internet and on ways to get exactly what one needs when searching.
    - Pathfinders or LiGuides are collaboratively created to help everyone in the class quickly find the right information for a particular assignment.

- **School-wide Activities** The Learning Commons is a great place to center all school-wide initiatives ranging from reading promotions, fund raisers for the entire school, accreditation projects, to grant writing activities and implementation. As in business and industry, teams which have a finite life can be formed for each of the various initiatives and can be reconstituted as opportunities arise. This is particularly true in the Virtual Learning Commons where everyone is contributing to a Wikipedia-type, live school yearbook-type culture.

- **Just-in-Time Professional Development** As the center of professional development, action research, and other experimentation, the Experimental Learning Center (ELC) becomes the center for school improvement. Programs for first year teachers, curricular changes, outside consultant programs, professional learning community meetings and activities, and any other training programs emanate from the Learning Commons and are scheduled on the ELC calendar. Because the Learning Commons is the center of resources and technology, it is a natural place to integrate the potential of information and information technology into whatever training is being proposed, experimented with, or pushed out into various classrooms or departments. The ELC is often like a fishbowl where visitors may observe, critique, interact, examine, and test before various programs radiate out into the school as a whole.

- **Financial Efficiency** The Learning Commons is the place to maximize spending power, a place where competition is centered, and commercial vendor monopolies are resisted. Instead learners, teachers, teacher librarians, and teacher technologists advocate for, select, implement, and hold accountable the very best resources and technologies that are required to support every learner.

How much does it cost to provide the materials and technological devices for each learner? Budget an allocation to equip each learner with a tech device each year including its updates, repair, and replacement. Add to this the cost of materials such as books, videos, online databases, and subscriptions to e-resources such as digital books, podcasts, or other materials accessible via digital devices. Begin by budgeting the equivalent of an average textbook per student per year and follow the impact of those expenditures on individual learners and their usage patterns. Some schools now expect learners to come to school equipped with a preferred digital device. In these cases, school budgets are concentrated on bandwidth, accessibility, and quality information and multimedia resources. As well, the trend toward cloud computing and systems such as Google Apps for Education provide major cost savings over commercial content management systems. The question is, How can we do more with less? Or, How can we expand the use of what we already have access to? And, are there open source systems, or systems already popular with students that we could use?

Dream Big and Be Brave
The rate of technological advancement is increasing exponentially. When designing schools, don't let today's reality limit tomorrow's possibilities. See the book, *The Third Teacher,* and its website http://www.thethirdteacher.com/

The Learning Commons Partnership Teams

Leadership in the Learning Commons is team-based rather than centralized in a single individual. Each school begins with the functions desirable in the Learning Commons and then organizes the various leadership teams to carry out those program elements. We recommend four partnership teams that have responsibility for the entire Learning Commons program, although each school would create its own leadership team configuration:

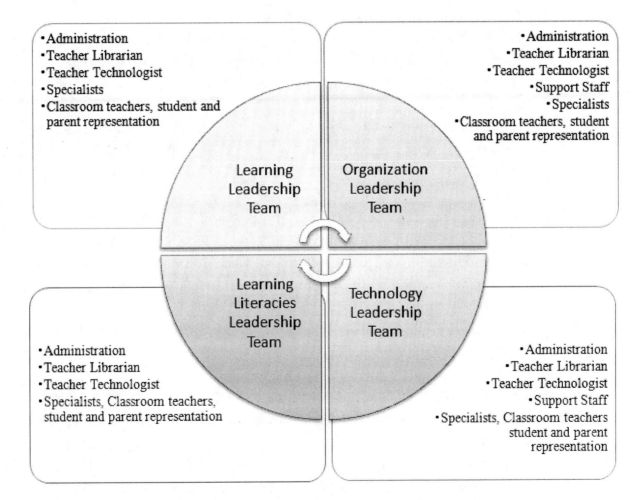

- **The Organization Leadership Team** The lead teachers are a full-time teacher-librarian and a full-time teacher technologist who act as coordinators. As the professional staff of the Learning Commons, they apply their personal strengths and specialist training to the ignition of collaborative and experimental learning programs. These professionals understand and create a client side organization rather than a command and control operation. In addition, they have the time and administrative support to bring vital programming into fruition. They spend the majority of their time building, teaching, and assessing learning experiences and experimental programs as co-teachers with the classroom instructors. For example:

- The Learning Commons teacher technologist concentrates on instructional computing rather than on administrative functions.
- The teacher librarian concentrates on collaboration and instruction as opposed to focusing on the functioning of the Open Commons.
- Specialists such as reading coaches, counselors, learning specialists, art, music, PE, or other specialists have scheduled time in the Learning Commons in order to make an impact across the school
- All the specialists function as a professional learning community under the direction of the administrator charged with instructional excellence.
- As a group, these professionals plan, work, and assess their impact on teaching and learning.
- Student representatives are included on all leadership teams (not just the Geeks or gifted students, but the average and struggling students have a voice).

- **The Technology Leadership Team** The group of professionals, administrators and learners charged with leadership of technology, guide, vision, implement, budget for, and together create the technological environment of both the physical Learning Commons and its virtual counterpart. Consider using the ISTE standards for technology coaches as a guide for planning and staff development at: http://www.iste.org/Libraries/NETS_Refresh_Toolkit/NETS_for_Technology_Coaches.sflb.ashx

- **The Learning Literacies Leadership Team** This team focuses its efforts on the skill levels needed to propel each learner to success. Reading skills, information, media, cultural, critical, visual, digital literacy and other emergent literacies are the province of their attention. Learning how to learn beyond minimal levels is seen as the mission of the entire faculty, albeit the specialization of various professionals.

- **Learning Leadership Team** This team concentrates its efforts on building excellence in teaching and learning both in the Learning Commons and throughout the school. They worry about the learners' depth of understanding, as well as what they know and are able to do. They are particularly concerned with the range of professional development, the action research, and the various learning initiatives of the entire school as they help implement the plan for sustainable school improvement.

- **Learning Commons Specialist Staff** All specialists in the school including administration, subject specific specialists such as art, music, or physical education teachers, teacher technologists, teacher librarians, counsellors, and even school nurses constitute the specialist staff of the Learning Commons. One might consider these professionals as the Professional Learning Community of experts who rise up from compartmental departments to influence the direction of the entire learning community. They drive the Experimental Learning Center of the Learning Commons. whether they are housed there physically or virtually for a part or a full day. These specialists are calendared to partner with classroom teachers, and learning activities are planned, taught, and assessed jointly with one or more of these specialists. As professionals, they have the opportunity to infuse and integrate their specialty into the school curriculum as they work in their own subject areas. Examples might include the following:

  o The school nurse may partner with the social studies teacher on a unit about drug abuse.
  o A teacher librarian integrates information literacy with various subject specific research projects.
  o The teacher technologist assists students in the creation of virtual field trips around their city or across the world.
  o The reading coach and the teacher librarian facilitate virtual book clubs that cross grade levels and school boundaries, as they seek to increase the amount of reading and the love of reading.
  o The music teacher infuses music across the curriculum in addition to directing a band, orchestra, or choir.
  o The counsellor integrates career studies into every subject or discipline in order to stimulate a vision of career opportunities and how to prepare for them.
  o The math teacher partners with the geography teacher for units involving graphing for climate and population studies.

Specific Roles and Responsibilities in the Learning Commons

- **Administrative Leadership** The administrator of the school who is charged with instructional improvement is a vital player in the planning and implementation of a vibrant and functioning Learning Commons. Providing leadership in person or virtually, this administrative leader understands the central role of an information-rich and technology-rich instructional environment and makes the Experimental Learning Center the focal point of school improvement.

- **Support Staff** Support personnel include technicians, clerical assistants, and any other assistants who work in the Learning Commons or computer laboratory. These support persons take on the major responsibility of the "warehouse" under the guidance of the teacher technologist and teacher librarian who are concentrating the bulk of their time on improving instruction. Support personnel may have credentials such as certificates in technology or have had short courses in the operational functions of the Open Commons. They keep networks up and running, collections circulating, handle the calendars of the Open Commons and the computer lab for scheduled classes and the free flow of individuals, small groups, and classes that do not require the services of the professionals. In addition to their knowledge and expertise, these personnel are very organized, friendly, service-oriented, and are problem solvers. They understand and are able to implement client-side policies established by the professionals in order to make the Learning Commons attractive to both students and teachers alike. Every Open Commons has the equivalent of a full-time support person in addition to the full-time teaching professionals. Larger schools will require multiple support personnel to keep the traffic of the center scheduled, productive, and satisfied.

Below, we highlight the roles and preparation of various specialists. All specialists have preparation as teachers first, adding their specialties on top. This prepares them not only to be good teachers in their own right, but to enhance learning across the learning community rather than teach in their specialty alone.

- **The Teacher Librarian** All teacher librarians are master teachers in their own right and embrace co-teaching with others all across the school. Their knowledge of curriculum, instructional design, learning science, and leadership is enhanced by the discipline of library and information science where they add knowledge about information theory, information systems, multimedia resources, collection building, and a host of other issues dealing with information in a high tech world.

They are also comfortable learning any new technological system and software needed to be fluent in these new systems alongside the best of their users. As information specialists they are valuable resources to learners and teachers, and as specialist teachers they combine their expertise to provide needed instructional interventions and differentiated teaching and learning support. They are people persons who understand a client side organization as opposed to the command and control structure that has been the management model in the past. They invest in supervision of the support staff of the Learning Commons but ensure that the majority of their own time is devoted to teaching and learning rather than to fine-tuning the warehouse function of the Open Commons.

- **The Teacher Technologist** Like the teacher librarian, teacher technologists are teachers first. Their principal education as an instructional designer and a great teacher trumps their concerns for equipment, networks, and software. They are visionaries who match up the various available technologies to enhance learning, and they are always looking for new applications that will boost achievement of the learners. As teachers, they model the integrated use of technology as they co-teach with classroom teachers and partner with teacher librarians in the push toward excellence. They supervise the technical support staff who keep the systems, networks, equipment and software running and reliable 24/7. The majority of their day is spent co-teaching rather than fixing machines or troubleshooting problems. Their interactions with learners make not only the geeks approach them but also the mainstream learners and, in particular, those who do not have access to technology in the home. They stress access, access, access as they teach learners to construct their own information spaces, personal learning networks, while blending social networking skills into their academic opportunities.

- **The Teacher Librarian/Teacher Technologist** In smaller schools, where separate positions for both the teacher librarian and the teacher technologist do not exist, a teacher with both sets of expertise is selected. This may be a teacher technologist who has taken coursework in library and information science or a teacher librarian who has excellent instructional technology knowledge These professionals have the best backgrounds of both worlds as they focus their efforts on co-teaching with the faculty and building client-side organizational elements.

The Realities of Learning Commons Staffing

To merely declare the reinvention of the school library and computer laboratory does not make it so. For the past half century, schools have struggled to have both professionals and support staffing in their libraries and more recently in computer labs. States and provinces across North America provide uneven support for professionals and specialists depending on what staffing they view as essential to make a school and learning community function. Financial exigencies in a district or board put pressures on administrators to target either the size of the specialist staff, the number of classroom teachers, or both. An overview across the years points out clues to what hasn't worked. The research studies done by Keith Curry Lance and Ross Todd (with summaries available in *School Libraries Work!, School Library Impact Studies, Powering Achievement,* and *We Boost Achievement),* are very clear when it comes to assessing impact of the library and of the computer lab on the school. In both areas, the lack of either professional or support personnel in these two centers negates much or most of their impact on teaching and learning. Support personnel alone do not have the expertise to make a difference in teaching and learning because they concentrate their attention on organizational or technical matters. Likewise, professionals without support personnel get tied to organizational systems that distract from their real work. The result has been little impact for dollars expended with the conclusion being that neither the library or computer labs earn their keep. It is as if the school was to buy a school bus without wheels and then wonder why kids are not getting to school.

- **The Qualities of the Learning Commons Professionals** Like all other organizations, success depends on the people pushing the vision of the organization. Well-meaning and visionary plans are either spoiled or implemented based on the day to day actions of both professionals and support personnel. Making a radical change from command and control to client side requires leadership, flexibility, risk taking, persistence, and hard work. Administrators are advised to select professionals with the qualities necessary to become learner centered, and who will be catalysts for change. Rigidity founded in tradition has no place in the current changing world.

  Resource TIP For helpful interview questions when considering new personnel for the Learning Commons staff, see pages 38 -42 of *Building a Learning Commons: A Guide for School Administrators and Learning Leadership Teams,* available through http://lmcsource.com.

Systems and Networks that Support the Learning Commons Organization

- **On-Demand Networks** The Learning Commons is the place to begin wireless networking for expected future computing devices. It becomes the "Starbucks" access center of the school with this service extending out into the rest of the school as funding permits. The capacity of this instructional computing network is sufficient to handle the traffic and the volume of materials that need to be delivered. An example is network capability in delivering two way audio and video. As learners create their own materials, the networks must be capable of handling these productions and storing them for further use.

- **On-Demand User Friendly Support** Every learner and teacher deserves prompt, friendly, and supportive assistance in order to realize the goal of transparent technology in the support of teaching and learning.

BRIGHT Ideas to Build On

Ask teachers how you are doing supporting their needs.
- Here is a sample. http://www.surveymonkey.com/s/KZQFPWP
  Ask teachers what else they need.
- An example from British Columbia: ***Bridging the gap between High School and Post Secondary*** - view the film on page 8 of this study http://www2.uregina.ca/wilu2011/wp-content/uploads/2011/06/WILU-T8-Sigalet-Grassroots-1.98MB.pdf
- An example from California http://tlresearchupdate.csla.net/2011/04/national-survey-of-college-preparedness.html

Ask students how well the library works for them
- An example from Blythewood Middle School LMC https://spreadsheets.google.com/viewform?hl=en&formkey=dFVvdDM2Mk44emRmdkF0MIA3X181dnc6MQ#gid=0
  Ask students what else they need.
- Summer reading Requests http://highlandlc.wikispaces.com/ReadingListRequestForm
- EReader Pilot Project http://highlandlc.wikispaces.com/eReaderSurvey
- ***Take the Taste Test –Ask a Student*** (Building a Learning Commons page 68) https://spreadsheets.google.com/spreadsheet/viewform?formkey=dGo5MmdSNGpNeU9WVWg2OUY5dUNNZXc6MQ

https://spreadsheets.google.com/spreadsheet/ccc?key=0Ap3yb3UOI0Ycd
Go5MmdSNGpNeU9WVWg2OUY5dUNNZXc&hl=en_US#gid=0

Invite teachers and students to help build collections and other resources

- ○ Students submit book reviews.
  http://roelibrary.wikispaces.com/Create+a+Book+Review
- ○ Ask teachers and students to help build Pathfinders for units.
  http://springfieldpathfinders.wikispaces.com/home

Work with community organizations

- ○ Read *People for Education* recommendations
  http://www.peopleforeducation.com/annualreport11/libraries

Activity #1

Take Action Designing Collaborative Physical Spaces in the Learning Commons

- **Draw a sketch of your present library facility.**

- **Consider the features criteria of the Physical Commons**
- Flexibility (furniture and schedule)
- Wireless capability
- Networking places and spaces
- Productivity spaces and tools
- Comfortable and stimulating spaces
- Books and computers don't get in the way
- Supports for professional development
- Equitable access
- Attention to differentiation
- Celebration of learning
- Exemplary learning experiences – relevant and real world
- Individual, small group, and large group spaces
- A Cultural center – Listening Lunches
- Centre for Professional Learning Teams
- Experimentation and Creativity

- **Ponder the Possibilities**
  - ○ Try to locate others in your local area who have redesigned their physical spaces for ideas.
  - ○ Check issues of *Teacher Librarian* to find articles about design and examples of teacher librarians who have redesigned their spaces.
  - ○ Assemble a group of interested teacher Librarians, faculty, parents, administrators and students and present them with a vision of the characteristics you are looking for and have them work in teams to draw up and submit ideas that would cost very little money or some

money, and other ideas would be major renovation or building projects involving larger expenditures.

- **Time for 180° Thinking**
  - ○ Apply the above criteria and brainstormed ideas to your original sketch and reinvent your physical library spaces.
  - ○ Share with a small group and keep on reinventing!

Activity #2

Take Action **Designing Collaborative Virtual Spaces in the Learning Commons and then design and build your own VLC. Here are some recommended steps.**

- **Consult the International Virtual Learning Commons Idea Bank at:** https://sites.google.com/site/internationalvlcideas/ What ideas could you contribute to the bank so that you can withdraw from it?

  Now as you begin, select and design the various characteristics you will construct in your VLC. Here are some characteristics to consider. The Idea Bank has others.

- **Learning to Learn:** Learning advice, tutorials, research organizers, search tools and strategies, pathfinders, services, links to OPAC and databases, central portal etc.

- **Building Reading Engagement:** Reading programs, blogs, book clubs, book reviews, surveys, virtual book reports, author links and interviews

- **Knowledge Creation:** Collaborative working, learning, and communicating spaces - Wikis, KBCs, Moodle, blogs, global projects,

- **Celebration of Learning:** Archive, museum, year book, photos, videos, projects

- **School Improvement:** Collaborative planning spaces, Professional Learning spaces, assessments and tracking of Learning Commons initiatives

- **Web Design:** Clarity, visual organization and appeal, accessibility, navigation, user friendliness

- **Ponder the possibilities.........**
  - How do we create a virtual giant conversation about teaching and learning?

- What do our students need?
- What do our teachers need?
- Who else will benefit from a VLC?
- How can the VLC advance 21st Century teaching and learning?
- How can the VLC contribute to school improvement?

- **Time for 180° Thinking.** Apply these criteria to your original sketch and reinvent your virtual library spaces. Share with a small group and keep on reinventing

Scenarios of Organizational Restructuring in Action

- **The Radical Shift:** When the leadership team of a school district, admittedly affluent, decided to implement one on one computing and equip every teacher with a plethora of technology, they realized that few of the current teaching staff had the expertise or the background to use the technological tools that were being provided. In a district-wide professional development session, the leadership team announced the radical change and also announced that every opportunity would be afforded the faculty, over a two-year period, to acquire the needed expertise. After the first year of immersion and facing the second year of major progress, the revolution was well under way, but some faculty, uncomfortable with the shift sought employment elsewhere. (Based on an actual interview with the superintendent by one of the authors).

- **A Teacher Librarian Makes the Shift:** Difficult financial times in one school district forced a teacher librarian to be employed half time in two different schools. In an interview with this teacher librarian two years after the change, she related the following story: At first she was heartbroken about not having the opportunity to be full time and in control of a single school library. A major positive was that each of the two buildings would have a full time support person there all day every day. The teacher librarian asked herself, "What is it that I do that makes the most impact on teaching and learning?" She decided that it was not the day to day operation of the facility, but the planning, co-teaching, and assessment of learning activities. Since the support personnel were quite competent, she turned over the calendars of the libraries to them. Then she created a second calendar for her clients. She announced to both faculties that she would be available to partner with them on learning experiences. Based on her reputation, the faculty at both schools began to sign up on her calendar. She created a flexible schedule so that sometimes, she was full time at one site and other weeks, full time at the other depending on the demands of the various learning experiences that were in progress. At first, there was limited demand for

156

her time, but as the year progressed, more and more teachers and grade level teams were requesting her collaboration. By the end of the second year, she was concerned about her own burn out. But, in retrospect, she had learned that the administrivia, such a part of her former job, had not been missed, and that the enormous satisfaction of watching and leading a push for teaching and learning excellence was paying huge dividends. She was looking forward to going back full time as teacher librarian in one of the schools, but with a whole new vision of what this experience had taught her about priorities. (based on an actual interview)

- **When Coaches Discover a New Role:** In a large urban school district, a literacy coach and a newly appointed teacher librarian decided to pursue a master's degree in library and information science together. When they discovered in the instructional design course that they had to carry out an exemplary unit with a classroom teacher in their school or face failure in the class, they first discussed the possibilities. They discovered that they had one thing in common, with both of them were having difficulty getting into individual classrooms because teachers were saying that there was no time to do anything except prepare their students for standardized tests. Selecting a prospective client, they invited the teacher to have lunch with them. They pleaded their case. Feeling sorry for her colleagues facing this obligatory "assignment," the teacher agreed. The resulting unit was so successful that the team reported: "We felt as if the joy of teaching was back in education!" (based on a log of the assignment to the professor. P.S. They got an A.)

- **Getting Started:** The teacher technologist and the teacher librarian met to discuss ways they could better integrate their agendas into the school so that teaching and learning would be positively affected. Feeling that a shift to a Learning Commons concept might be too radical, they proposed a first step to the principal -- that professional development be conducted in the library. They cleared a space for larger groups and arranged for a conference room. Access to technology in these spaces was exemplary and there was easy access to the print resources. The two specialists arranged their own calendars so they would be available for as many sessions as possible. They began to experience increased acceptance of their professional ideas for the integration of technology and print. In March of the school year, they proposed to the principal that the official organization of the Experimental Learning Center take place. A summer action research workshop later, they were under way. After the staff had the action research PD, everyone was ready to open the Experimental Learning Commons and test all school initiatives here.

- **Living Textbooks:** The skyrocketing price of textbooks for every discipline, for every learner, was the tipping point for change in a large secondary school. Administration demanded a more cost efficient method of information delivery. A committee of specialist teachers, classroom teachers, and students was immediately charged with the problem. During an early brainstorming session a teacher remarked to the group how much he appreciated the Pathfinders the teacher librarian had prepared for his units this term. Others piped up with similar comments. A student on the committee demonstrated how she used I Google pages to keep up-to-date. Then came the big Aha! Subject teams and students are now busy working with Learning Commons specialists to prepare Pathfinders with RSS feeds of up-to-the-minute, subject specific data which they plan to feed into student I Google pages. Administrators are happy with the savings and have agreed to allocate much of the textbook budget to purchasing needed databases and e-books.

Over to You Discuss with your group and with the authors:
- What organizational features do you already have that lead the way toward the client side structure?

- How will this new structure save the school money?

- How will we measure the effectiveness of the new Learning Commons?

References

- Brooks-Kirkland, Anita. 2009. "The Virtual Library as a Learning Hub". *School Libraries in Canada* 27 no. 3.(Fall, 2009). http://clatoolbox.ca/casl/slicv27n3/273brookskirkland.html

- McCourt, Frank. 2005. *Teacher Man: a Memoir*. New York: Scribners.

Resources

Professional Resources:

- Carr, JoAnn, ed. 2008. *Leadership for Excellence: Insights of National School Library Media Program of the Year Award Winners*. Chicago, IL: American Library Association.

- The Freedom Writers, with Erin Gruwell. 2001. *The Freedom Writers Diary: How a Teacher and 150 Teens Used Writing to Change Themselves and the World Around Them.* New York: Broadway Books.

- *Freedom Writers.* 2007. Movie. DVD. Paramount Pictures.

- Heppell, Stephen. *Learning Places and Spaces - virtual and actual.* http://rubble.heppell.net/places/

- Knight, Jim, ed. 2008. *Coaching: Approaches and Perspectives.* Thousand Oaks CA: Corwin Press.

- Koechlin, Carol, Esther Rosenfeld, and David V. Loertscher. 2010. *Building a Learning Commons: a Guide for School Administrators and Learning Leadership Teams.* Salt Lake City, UT: Hi Willow Research and Publishing.

- Lance, Keith Curry and David V. Loertscher. 2005. *Powering Achievement: School Library Media Programs Make a Difference: The Evidence,* 3rd ed. Salt Lake City, UT: Hi Willow Research and Publishing.

- Library Research Service. 2011. *School Library Impact Studies.* http://www.lrs.org/impact.php

- Loertscher, David V. and Ross J. Todd. 2003. *We Boost Achievement: Evidence-Based Practice for School Library Media Specialists.* Salt Lake City,UT: Hi Willow Research and Publishing.

- Loertscher, David. V. and Laura Wimberly. 2010. *Collection Development Using the Collection Mapping Technique.* Salt Lake City, UT: Hi Willow Research and Publishing.

- Marzano, Robert J., Timothy Waters, and Brian A. McNulty. 2005. *School Leadership That Works: From Research to Results.* Alexandria, VA: Association for Supervision and Curriculum Development.

- Marzano, Robert J. 2003. *What Works in Schools: Translating Research into Action.* Alexandria, VA: Association for Supervision and Curriculum Development.

- Nevin, Ann I., Richard A. Villa, and Jacqueline Thousand. 2008. *A Guide to Co-teaching with Paraeducators: Practical Tips for K-12 Educators.* Thousand Oaks CA: Corwin Press.

- O'Donnell Wicklund, Pigozzi, and Peterson Architects Inc, VS Furniture, and Bruce Mau Design. 2010. *The Third Teacher: 79 Ways You Can Use Design to Transform Teaching & Learning.* New York: Abrams Books.

- Raji, Esme. 2001. *Educating Esme: Diary of a Teacher's First Year.* Chapel Hill, NC : Algonquin Books.

- *School Libraries Work!* 3rd edition. Research Foundation Paper. 2008. Scholastic. http://listbuilder.scholastic.com/content/stores/LibraryStore/pages/images/SLW3.pdf

- Tomlinson, Carol Ann, Kay Brimijohn, and Lane Narvaez. 2008. *The Differentiated School: Making Revolutionary Changes in Teaching and Learning.* Alexandria, VA: Association for Supervision and Curriculum Development.

- Waters, Tom and Greg Cameron. 2007. *The Balanced Framework: Connecting Vision with Action.* Denver, CO: Mid-continent Research for Education and Learning.

- Whitaker, Todd. 2002. *What Great Principals Do Differently: Fifteen Things That Matter Most.* Larchmont, NY: Eye on Education.

- Wiggins, Grant and Jay McTighe. 2007. *Schooling by Design: Mission, Action, and Achievement.* Alexandria, VA: Association for Supervision and Curriculum Development.

- Woolls, Blanche. 2008 *The School Library Media Manager,* 4th edition. Westport, CT: Libraries Unlimited.

Professional Organizations

- While the usual educational organizations, particularly those for administrators, have some emphasis on leadership and management, we recommend that an eye toward business management organizations may be of some assistance when looking to how client side structures work and flourish.

Chapter 9

School Improvement
and the Learning Commons

What is the best approach? Improving teaching and learning is a complex process for schools. This video offers a simpler, more personalized approach. The collaborative culture of the Learning Commons supports change and the work of improvement based on 'home grown' research and individual and school needs. http://www.youtube.com/watch?v=IGH5vL2j914

--- ❈ ---

The Learning Commons has the potential to drive the changes needed to bring schools into the future, improve student achievement, and thus sustain whole school improvement. This is not a pie in the sky wish but a reality of change possible when schools embrace the Learning Commons as a whole school approach to educating for the 21st Century. Previous chapters have documented piece by piece the major components and philosophies of teaching, learning, and growing together in the dynamic womb of the Learning Commons. Now we will examine just how we know the Learning Commons can make a difference for schools.

The chemistry that makes a difference in the Learning Commons is distilled from Evidence Based Practice (EBP) being applied by the school community in order to improve teaching and learning. Teachers and learners as well, make informed decisions about improving their performance by considering theories about 'best practice', reading the research ('what the experts say'), as well as by careful assessment of their own experiences. Teachers and students understand and consequently get better and better.

Digging Deeper
Michael Fullan, in a recent article, states that "….the big difference between effective and ineffective schools systems, and all organizations for that matter, is the collective or shared depth of understanding among members about the nature of their work." Michael Fullan (2011, 4). Explore Fullan's article at: http://www.michaelfullan.ca/Articles_11/11_July_Fullan_Learning_is_the_Work.pdf

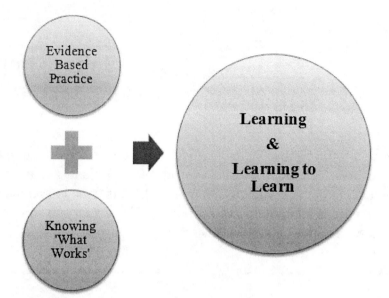

In an Evidence Based Practice approach, for every experience in the Learning Commons clients ask themselves, what worked, what didn't, and why. They continue to use their experiences to improve performance and to advocate for needed resources, staffing, and changes in systems. The guesswork is then removed from teaching and learning because decisions related to both are made based on results.

Discussion Ross Todd (2006) has established three core beliefs that are critical to the success of applying Evidence Based Practice in the Learning Commons: *Difference, Intervention*, and *Transformation*. What kinds of evidence could you gather/document in your library program that meet these three core beliefs?

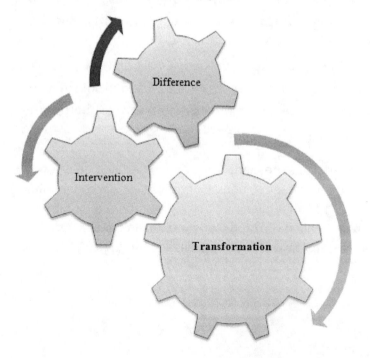

Difference The provision of information and information services makes a difference to the lives of people. This means that conducting a learning experience in the midst of an information-rich and technology-rich environment has more potential of making a difference than the same learning experience done in the information-poor environment of the classroom where resources often consist of the textbook and lecture.

Intervention The key role of the teacher-librarian (and other specialists) centers on pedagogical intervention that directly impacts on, and shapes the quality of student learning through their engagement with information. This is based on the concept that two heads are better than one. At every opportunity, the classroom teacher co-teaches with one or more specialists in the school.

Transformation The role of pedagogical intervention is to bring on transformation. Learning takes place, and the lives of our students are transformed. The knowledge, skills, attitudes, and values of learners are shaped and grow through their engagement in the school Learning Commons and its pedagogical interventions. This means that the instructional units and learning activities of the Learning Commons should showcase the very best teaching and learning of the entire school.

Are these three principles happening in the Learning Commons? How do we know? What is being documented? What evidence do we have that the impact of the Learning Commons activities are spiraling out from this hub into the school as a whole? Is there any evidence that the Learning Commons is transforming the entire school into a healthier environment where improvement is sustained?

Certainly, the idea that one measurement, a single test or small set of tests, would be able to accurately assess all that we are interested in building is foolhardy. It is not just a single reading and/or math score that indicates the health of the school or its overall results.

We look, instead, at a variety of evidence as indicators of continuous coordinated progress.

Critical Indicators of Progress in the Learning Commons:

- The sense of **ownership of the Learning Commons** extends to administrators, classroom teachers, students, to the various specialists in the school and outward toward the parents. "It is our space; we want to be a part of it; we contribute to its success; it is a vital part of teaching and learning; it is a symbol of the health of the school environment."

- The adults in the school recognize that the Experimental Learning Center is the **focal point for school improvement**. Everyone understands its role in experimentation, professional development, and its central role in the push for excellence.

- The Learning Commons is the **cultural center of the school** with constant learning, demonstrations, performances, awards, and projects as it becomes the physical and virtual school yearbook.

- The stream of **exemplary learning experiences** happens so often that multiple examples can be observed both in the physical and the virtual space at any time of day or night.

- We can observe the **power of technology transforming learning experiences**, with student creativity, student engagement, and with individual and collective intelligence growing in both the physical and virtual spaces.

- We are never surprised to see **various configurations** of adults working with full classes, with small groups, or with individuals and succeeding side by side in the same physical or virtual space.

- The Learning Commons **showcases the best** of what we represent as a school community.

- The **leadership team** of the Learning Commons **is making substantial progress**

- **The program of the Learning Commons is held accountable** by
    - Results achieved on individual learning experiences
    - Repertoire of learning experiences across the year
    - Repertoire of learning experiences by teacher and curricular area
    - Usage statistics
    - Evidence Based Practice and other research results
    - Student and teacher Big Thinks

The Learning Commons launches schools on a continuum towards sustainable excellence.

Evidence Based Practice Approaches in the Learning Commons

A rich variety of approaches are encouraged in the Learning Commons with inquiry, collaboration, reflection, and action forming the backbone of each method. The physical and virtual Experimental Learning Commons supports and coaches all of these methods and provides spaces, resources, technologies, and records of achievements. Because of the transparency and centrality of the Learning Commons; administrators can easily observe progress, identify needs, and can often provide capacity building supports on the spot.

Professionals are also learners in the Learning Commons. Just as students need to be encouraged to take control of their own learning, so do the professionals.

Digging Deeper
Explore the New Standards for Professional Learning.
These standards call for a new form of educator learning. The decision to call these Standards for Professional Learning rather than Standards for Professional Development signals the importance of educators taking an active role in their continuous development and places emphasis on their learning. The professional learning that occurs when these standards are fully implemented enrolls educators as active partners in determining the content of their learning, how their learning occurs, and how they evaluate its effectiveness. The standards give educators the information they need to take leadership roles as advocates for and facilitators of effective professional learning and the conditions required for its success. Stephanie Hirsh (2011)
View the overview video at: http://www.learningforward.org/standards/index.cfm

Professional Learning Approaches can include:

Action Research	• projects to explore questions and test out possibilities
Teacher Journaling	• documenting critical moments in learning journeys
Professional Portfolios	• built over time to track teacher growth
Professional Learning Teams	• working on a common goal to improve teaching and learning
Professional Learning Networks	• digital feeds to journals, blogs and other online learning opportunities
Mentoring	• providing advice and support for less experienced teachers
Peer Teaching	• providing in-school embedded professional development or broadcasting to the larger professional community
Walk Through PD	• learning by observing others teach and students work
Showcase	• documenting best practice lessons, student exemplars, sharing and celebrating
Experimentation	• testing out ideas, strategies, technologies and learning by doing
Play	• being creative, innovative, testing ideas, taking risks and having fun with learning
Teacher Big Think	• to ensure metacognition of what works and why • the capping piece of every Evidence Based Practice initiative.

Measures to Gather Evidence

We recommend a variety of measures including triangulation of evidence as a barometer of health. In this system, a variety of simple-to-collect and simple-to-analyze data pieces are collected at the organizational level, the teaching unit level, and the learner level. Examined together they point to the direction for progress toward excellence.

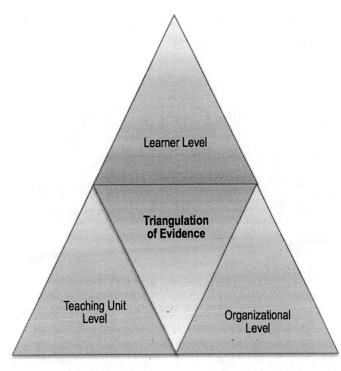

Organization Level evidence includes looking at the facilities, technology, staffing, success of initiatives, results of Professional Learning Communities, the spread of acceptance of the Learning Commons concept, and other whole-building ideas and perspectives.

Teaching Unit Level evidence includes the improvements in instructional design, co-teaching of classroom teachers and specialists, integration of content and 21st century skills, asking whether two heads are really better than one, and considering the impact specialists are having because they are now partnering in instruction rather than delivering their own separate curriculum. Certainly the number of successful collaborative learning experiences by grade level and their diffusion through the faculty is an indicator to watch. A critical measure would be the percentage of learners in a class who meet or exceed unit objectives because of indicators such as the use of knowledge building centers, wise use of technology, and collaboration among adults.

Learner Level evidence looks at individuals and how they thrive in the Learning Commons, their contributions, collaborations, engagement, achievements, assessments, and goal setting. For example, determine the kind of student who excels in the new environment: the gifted?, the mainstream child?, the struggling student? Who is not doing well? Why? Are there patterns among struggling students? How could the Learning Commons program adapt to those needs?

There are many measures that could be taken, and a selection of those that work best is in order. The following lists are a few of the possibilities.

The Challenge: To use measures from all levels to triangulate the view of impact.

Learner Level	Teaching Unit Level	Organizational Level
• Process notes and organizers	• Collaboration logs	• Circulation statistics
• Rubrics and checklists	• Records of debriefing of lessons/units	• Collection mapping
• Presentations and products	• Copies of lessons and units	• Quality of collection (inclusive, curriculum support, print and digital, variety, interests)
• History of contributions in digital projects (wiki, blog)	• Documentation of skills taught over time	• Flexibility of spaces
• Reflection/learning logs	• Workshops designed to help teach and integrate information literacy and other skills	• Scheduling calendars
• Self/peer evaluation		• Budget reports
• Research (e)-folders	• Evidence of differentiated instruction	• Annual reports
• Referencing documents		• Student and teacher comments and surveys
• Evidence of goal setting	• Improved teacher confidence in integrating technologies	• Access to physical and 24/7 virtual collection for all
• Student conferencing notes		• Access to computers and other technologies
• Video tape of students working or sharing	• Increased requests for resources, lessons, professional development and other services	• Showcased learning
• Records of mentor or volunteer work	• Involvement of other specialists	• Engaged, eager students and teachers
• Test results and reporting comments	• Repeat collaboration	

Empowering the Learner

Benefits of EBP to learners in the Learning Commons are twofold. To begin with, students receive first class instruction and support because teachers are engaged in making adjustments and changes to their teaching methodology based on real evidence. Secondly, students gain from their own reflective approach to making decisions about how they can best participate and learn in order to achieve optimum results. Metacognition is embedded in the EBP process. Once they begin to take responsibility for their own learning, students analyze what they do and how it works for them, and they then make decisions informed by evidence/results. Students realize that the Learning Commons programs are designed to provide them with the skills and tools to help them excel. As students apply EBP, they are learning how to learn. In the chart below, we list some of the indicators that show that learners are consciously applying EBP to their own growth. Look at the AASL's *Standards for the 21st Century Learner* (2007) for dispositions that every learner should acquire in order to be successful.

Evidence Based Practice in the Learning Commons: Indicators of Student Progress

Doing	Learning to Learn	Knowing and Understanding
• Designing graphic organizers • Testing ideas with others • Experimenting with presentation techniques • Trying out new software and hardware • Trying different note making strategies • Keeping a learning portfolio • Recording reflections on learning	• Responsibility and ownership of learning • Reflection • Collaborative knowledge building • Problem solving • Decision making • Critical thinking • Risk taking • Constructivist learning	• Metacognition of learning process • Determing personal strengths • Setting goals and planning for improvement • Applying knowledge of brain based learning • Transferring learning to new or different situations • Making informed decisions about strategies and technologies to use • Taking action based on personal research, discoveries, and conclusions

How are these qualities measured? In a client-side organization, the learners shoulder the responsibility for self-assessment rather than assuming that adult evaluators will do it for them. Learners' attitudes thus move from assuming victimization to taking control of their learning success. The role of the professionals in the Learning Commons is to facilitate and coach learners in how to gather and analyze evidence of their own growth. The following diagram illustrates the desired growth mindset.

I can demonstrate what I know, can do, and deeply understand to myself and others by:

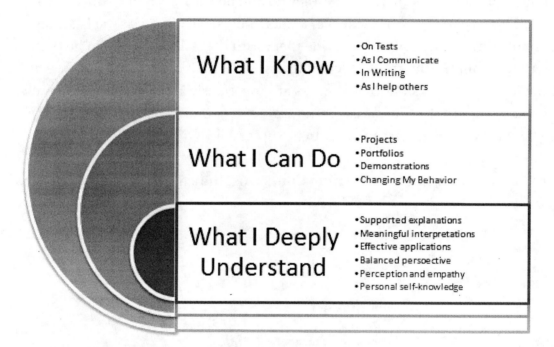

I can demonstrate that I am learning how to learn by:

The professionals will assist learners in developing strategies for gathering evidence to demonstrate their learning. They will show students how to use these measures to set goals for improvement.

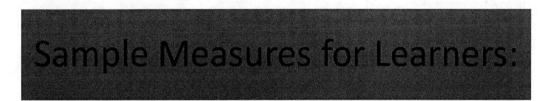

Sample Measures for Learners:

- Analyzing my performance on formative and summative tests.
- Tracking the amount read for pleasure and for topics I am studying.
- Logging a research project in order to valuate my journey and suggest improvements.
- Defense of the quality of information I used for my report/paper/project.
- Self-assessment of products and projects I create.
- Logging my contributions to groups, the classroom, and the school.
- Survey feedback to teachers and specialists about learning units connected to the Learning Commons.
- Rating my progress in taking command of my own learning. Am I on the path to excellence?

Empowering the Teacher

Teachers have the support of the teacher librarian and other specialists in the Learning Commons to help them determine what evidence to gather, how to analyze the data, and then how to apply their findings in order to improve teaching and learning. Becoming a reflective practitioner is a process of discovery. Several methods of EBP are suggested for maximum results:

At the Learner Level
- Formative and summative tests
- Monitoring of learner self-assessment
- Consideration of the percent of learners who meet, exceed, and struggle with expectations for collaborative units with specialists in the Learning Commons. How does this percent compare with results when teaching alone?
- The results for learners in action research projects in the Experimental Learning Center.

At the Teaching Unit Level
- Analysis of journals/notes/teaching plans kept for collaborative units and action research studies. Are two heads better than one?
- Analysis of the characteristics of learners who benefit the most and least from learning units co-taught in the Learning Commons.
- Identification of strategies that have positive results.

At the Organization Level
- The number/quality of collaborative and action research projects by teacher, by grade level, by department level, and by the entire faculty
- Access to technology and to rotating materials in classrooms during the day.
- Access to technology and materials extending 24/7/365.
- Access to specialists, Learning Commons availability, and Experimental Learning Center availability.

When data flows into the various leadership teams of the school from learners, teachers, and specialists, a number of benefits accrue to the teachers, the leadership teams, and the conversations of various professional learning communities. We list a few of these below. Individual teachers will have other items to add from their personal experiences, so we encourage you to make your own lists.

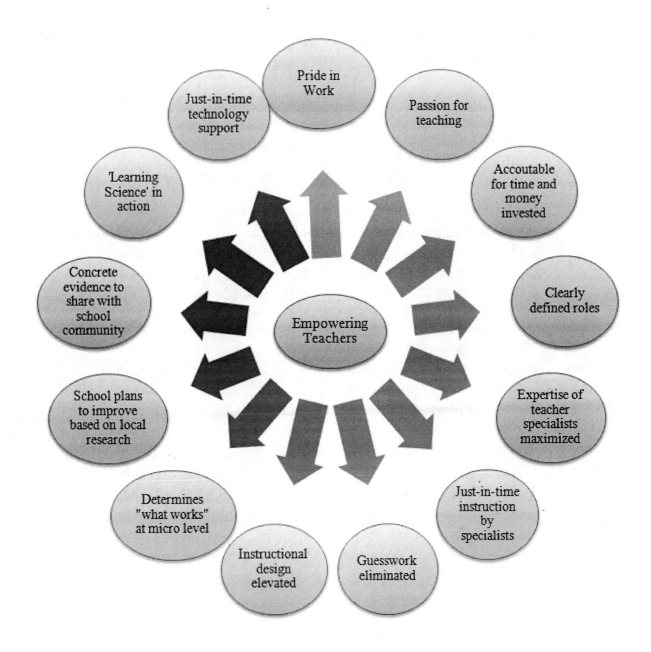

Empowering the Specialists

All of the specialists in the school take a reflective approach to their contributions to teaching and learning. When they are co-teaching in the Learning Commons and the Experimental Learning Center they are constantly testing the notion that two heads are better than one, but they are also interested in the impact of integrating their own curriculum responsibilities and best practice specialties into learning units. For example, the teacher librarian is testing the idea that information literacy instruction is more effective when integrated into learning activities as just-in-time intervention rather than if it is taught separately. Likewise, learning to work in a wiki environment is better integrated into a real learning experience rather than in a contrived one since learning to work in a wiki needs authenticity in order to engage learners.

> **Challenge** Invite specialists to document the difference they make in the school using the following framework.

5 Key Things Specialists Do Every Day to Make a Difference:
- Collaborate with teachers to build, co-teach, and assess solid and engaging learning experiences.
- Analyze the data from learner assessments to keep improving collaborative efforts. Ask whether we are pushing every learner toward excellence.
- Teach integrated skills that match their specialty. For example, information literacy (teacher librarians). For example, targeting specific reading skills as learners are doing research (reading coaches).
- Motivate learners to read more (yes, this is every specialist's responsibility).
- Work with the leadership teams on continuous school improvement.

The Learning Commons as Evidence Based Practice Central

By triangulating or taking into account data from various sources, the school leadership teams and professional learning communities make decisions and adjust policies based on evidence rather than by whim or by well-meaning dictates. It is all a part of learning what practice works in our school with our students, with our parents, and in our community in the advance towards sustainable excellence.

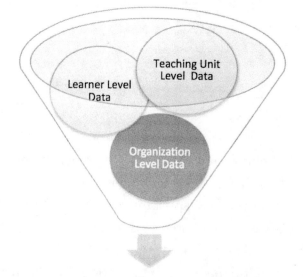

Decisions and Policy Changes

Action Research as the Focus of the Experimental Learning Commons

Action Research is different from scientific research in one major way. Action Research happens in the real world where variables cannot be controlled, as one would be able to do in a laboratory experiment. Action research happens in real classrooms with real learners, or in this case ,in an actual Experimental Learning Center. It takes the best theories of education and research results, and applies them to a local situation. As they embark on Action Research, practitioners ask themselves questions such as: Does this idea work in my inner-city school? Does this strategy work in a school where ten different languages are spoken? How can I differentiate strategies for my special needs students? The steps of action research are well known:

- Begin with a research question.
- Decide on a methodology/strategy to test the question.
- Conduct the research/collect the data.
- Analyze the data.
- Draw conclusions.
- Ask: So what?
- Report the results
- What's next?

Joseph Senese (2000) reminds us that our emphasis is on "how to" teach and "why" teach, not "what" to teach. Examples of action research projects that would be appropriate for the Experimental Learning Commons follow:

- **Impact of Background Knowledge** Robert Marzano's research (2004) encourages teachers to build background knowledge as a prelude to the main event of any topical study. Consider the following scenario. In our school, we have a variety of languages spoken, so we decide to test the idea of spending a bit more time on background building by using a variety of media to see if it makes a difference in the main part of a topical unit. Together, the classroom teacher and the teacher librarian select and allow learners to be exposed to Internet sites, books on the topic, video, pictures, podcasts in various languages – anything that we can find that would introduce a topic to learners ranging from novice to experts who have different language and cultural backgrounds. We decide to spend three class periods with the class in the Experimental Learning Commons as they "consume" the materials we have found and ask them in small groups to create graphic organizers about what they are reading, viewing, and hearing. The class then builds the questions together for the main event of the learning unit, and we continue on as we normally would. We assess the learners along the way and at the end. As a team, we look at the results together. What type of learner seems to have met and exceeded expectations? If there is another class in the school that has studied the same topic but did not spend the time on background building, how do the two groups compare? How did these experiences affect student knowledge of topic related vocabulary? Did the learners seem to be better prepared for the main event? Why? What media and resources seemed to work the best? Why? What did the learners think about this technique to help them master the content better? What would we change the next time? As we present our results to our professional learning community, are we and are they ready to make similar trials in other classrooms and other topics?

- **Eliminate the Cut, Paste, and Plagiarism Behavior of Learners** In *Beyond Bird Units: 18 Models for Teaching in Information-Rich and Technology-Rich Environments*, Loertscher, Koechlin, and Zwaan (2007) postulate that when learners have the habit of just cutting and pasting information from the Internet or other sources and turning it in as their own work, there is a simple solution: change the assignment so that cutting and pasting doesn't work. With a changed assignment, learners have to consume the information, think about it, analyze it, and work with others to massage it, or use it in some way in order to fulfill the task of the assignment. Teachers need to design the assignment so that analysis and synthesis are mandatory.

Consider the following scenario. The teacher librarian and one language arts teacher volunteer to demonstrate this technique to the rest of the faculty in the Experimental Learning Center. They invite visitors at any time during the demonstration and promise to report their project to the faculty as a whole. Learners are doing reports on famous African Americans. In a Google Spreadsheet, they research and post various facts from authoritative information sources about the person's childhood, education, problems faced, challenges faced, defeats, victories, achievements, and tributes paid them from others. Each cell in the spreadsheet contains a sentence or two pulled from the original source together with the citation for that information.

When the spreadsheet has been loaded, the class jigsaws and groups analyze (look for connections, trends, similarities, differences, cause and effect...) each of the categories across people and enter their conclusions in a final right-hand column. After this analysis has been completed, new groups do an analysis of all the characteristics across people and decide on similarities and differences. Then they draw conclusions. Each group then meets with an invited African American Guest to present their findings and discuss "how they overcame." Finally, each leaner writes a personal response about the research journey and the conclusions drawn about people who have overcome any obstacle. The teacher librarian and the classroom teacher then report the major difference made in the learning to the faculty as a whole. Five other classroom teachers volunteer to try similar action research projects and to report back to test whether this type of strategy would be worth full-scale implementation in the school.

The success of such action research projects and the invitation to other teachers to observe the research in the fishbowl of the Experimental Learning Commons requires certain collaborative behaviors on the part of the professionals:
- An openness to collaboration and co-teaching
- The gift of enough time to accomplish the research
- An emphasis on helping every learner achieve excellence
- Recognition by administrators and peers for honesty and risk-taking

A similar list has been developed by Joseph Senese (2000).

Other brief examples of projects and research done to inform the professional learning community might include:
- The teacher-librarian tracks all collaborations and Learning Commons interventions to determine which teachers and classes to target for future work.

- The teacher technologist and the teacher librarian help students develop systems to monitor the use and effectiveness of popular search tools during a collaborative unit with a classroom teacher. Adaptations or enhancements are designed to meet the needs of specific students.

- Teachers and specialists compare the achievement results of special needs students when staff are using a variety of differentiation and 'just-in-time' intervention strategies.

- Learners, specialists, and a classroom teacher, experiment with a new rubric for self-assessment that has been proposed to be used school-wide.

There is a note of caution about Action Research. The research findings of work done with one classroom apply to that classroom only. However, as the same technique is used over and over in the school, patterns will begin to emerge so that the leadership team can make policy with confidence. As we all realize, situations can change and subsequently negate what we know. For example, a school's demographics can change rather rapidly, so that strategies and teaching techniques that were successful previously no longer work as well. Thus, schools need to focus on the current needs of their learners. Professional learning communities always keep this idea in mind as they focus on sustainable, evolutionary, excellence.

The Learning Partnership Teams

All the leadership teams, classroom teachers, and learners are engaged in the collection, analysis and interpretation of Evidence Based Practice data to inform the school improvement plan.

Systems and Networks that Support Evidence Based Practice

To be successful in the pursuit of excellence with a foundation of research and best practice, the entire tone and culture of the school must be pointed in that direction. What works? What research and best practice is out there and being published that we should examine and try? The authors are well aware of the various cycles of education. Old ideas once in favor seem to come around again with new names and new fanfare. New strategies are often dictated without local experimentation or action research. **This may be one of the best arguments for a Learning Commons with a vibrant Experimental Learning Center program.** When the entire faculty realizes that administrators are serious about sustainable school improvement, many barriers fall. Experimentation and risk taking are encouraged and rewarded.

Take Action
Activity 1 School Improvement - What is Your Current Agenda?

- List goals and initiatives that are the current focus for improving the effectiveness of teaching and learning in your school

- Highlight those initiatives that could be affected by inquiry, independent reading, and rich information and technology environments

- In the face of your current school improvement goals, how could the Learning Commons contribute to school improvement?

- Create a report. Make it succinct and visual. This is valuable information to share with your School Improvement Team, the Learning Leadership Team of the Learning Commons, your students, your parents, your district.......

Take another step – How can you use this alignment of school goals and Learning Commons potential to develop goals for the Learning Commons, Budget Proposals and Reports, as well as your Annual Report?

Activity 2 Build Your Advocacy Toolkit

Base it on your school improvement evidence. These articles will help you.

- o "The Evidence-Based Manifesto for School Librarians" by Ross Todd
  http://www.schoollibraryjournal.com/article/CA6545434.html

- o "Seven Strategies to Develop Your Advocacy Toolkit" by Karen Bonanno
  http://www2.curriculum.edu.au/scis/connections/seven_strategies_to_dev
  elop_your_advocacy_toolkit.html

Scenarios to Drive School Improvement

- **Fishbowl Findings** As co-teaching units between specialists and classroom teachers began in the school, the specialists were assigned the task of documenting on a large chart the units they co-taught for each month. During the professional development community meeting each month, the principal would select one of the previous month's units at random. Those involved would give an impromptu five minute report highlighting the percent of learners who met or exceeded unit expectations. The challenges of learners who did not succeed were explained and ideas from the entire faculty were sought for improvement. The principal "salted the audience" the first few times to guarantee that the discussion would be active, humorous, and productive. After that, the faculty settled into an informative and anticipated part of the learning community's meeting. Over time, the conversations became more and more complex and analytical, leading to some questions being developed for action research.

- **Real Time is Key** A teacher librarian in a multicultural school was distressed with the lack of communication in Book Chat, her very well attended lunch club. Students seemed to like being part of the club but were reluctant to share verbally. Suspecting this problem was related to language skills, the teacher librarian met with the ESL teachers, consulted with other teacher librarians, did some research on Web 2.0 environments, and decided to try a wiki to extend the book club experience. Students were excited but slow to start, however after a few weeks the questions and comments started to flow. Once students had gained confidence discussing the novels, the teacher librarian partnered with two other school districts involved in the same book club program to set up video conferencing sessions. Each week students took turns introducing the novel for discussion. An author was invited to join one of the video conferencing sessions and the enthusiasm was infectious. The teacher librarian summed it up nicely in a media release to her school district. "Our students come from such a wide range of cultural backgrounds, and to see them come together as a community on the wiki and then take that step further and watch them find the courage to build new connections with students from other communities has been an enriching experience for all of us." The teacher librarian reviewed the wiki history and archived video to document student growth, and has plans to share this evidence with her staff.

Over to You Discuss with us at: http//schoollearningcommons.pbwiki.com
- What steps could be taken to ease into an evidence based practice organization?
- How can we take a critical incident and apply action research?

References

- Fullan, Michael. 2011. "Learning is the Work". Unpublished Paper. May 2011. http://www.michaelfullan.ca/Articles_11/11_July_Fullan_Learning_is_the_Work.pdf

- Hirsh, Stephanie. 2011. *Standards for Professional Learning*. Dallas, TX: Learning Forward. http://www.learningforward.org/standards/index.cfm

- Loertscher, David V., Carol Koechlin, and Sandi Zwaan. 2007. *Beyond Bird Units: 18 Models for Teaching in Information-Rich and Technology-Rich Environments*. Salt Lake City, UT: Hi Willow Research & Publishing.

- Loertscher, David V. and Ross J. Todd. 2006. *We Boost Achievement*. Salt Lake City, UT: Hi Willow Research & Publishing.

- Marzano, Robert J. 2004. *Classroom Instruction That Works*. Alexandria, VA: Association for Supervision and Curriculum Development.

- Senese, Joseph. 2000. "What Are the Conditions That Sustain Teacher Research?" Research Paper prepared for Session 18.16 at the American Education Research Association meeting in New Orleans, April 24-28, 2000. http://resources.educ.queensu.ca/ar/aera2000/senese.pdf

Resources

Foundational Ideas

- Sawyer, R. Keith, ed. 2005. *The Cambridge Handbook of the Learning Sciences*. New York: Cambridge University Press.

- Popham, W. James. 2008. *Transformative Assessment*. Alexandria, VA: Association for Supervision and Curriculum Development.

Professional Resources

- American Association of School Librarians. 2007. *Standards for the 21st Century Learner*. Chicago, IL: American Library Association. http://www.ala.org/ala/mgrps/divs/aasl/guidelinesandstandards/learningstandards/AASL_LearningStandards.pdf

- Bonanno, Karen. 2011. "Seven Strategies to Develop Your Advocacy Toolkit". *SCIS Connections*. Issue 78 2011. Education Services Australia. http://www2.curriculum.edu.au/scis/connections/seven_strategies_to_develop_your_advocacy_toolkit.html

- Caro-Bruce, Cathy, et al. 2007. *Creating Equitable Classrooms Through Action Research*. Thousand Oaks, CA: Corwin Press.

- Champlin, Connie, David V. Loertscher, and Nancy A.S. Miller. 2008. *Sharing the Evidence: School Library Assessment Tools and Resources.* 2nd edition. Salt Lake City, UT: Hi Willow Research & Publishing.

- Clauset, Karl H., Dale W. Lick, and Charlene U. Murphy. 2008. *Schoolwide Action Research for Professional Learning Communities: Improving Student Learning Through the Whole-Faculty Study Groups Approach.* Thousand Oaks, CA: Corwin Press.

- Costa, Arthur L. 2008. *The School as a Home for the Mind*. Thousand Oaks, CA: Corwin Press.

- *Habits of Mind* http://www.habits-of-mind.net/

- Kelly, M.G. (Peggy) and Jon Haber. 2006. *Resources for Student Assessment*. Washington, DC: International Society for Technology in Education.

- Koechlin, Carol and Sandi Zwaan. 2006. *Build Your Own Information Literate School.* Salt Lake City, UT: Hi Willow Research & Publishing.

- Marzano, Robert J. and Tammy Heflebower. 2011. *Teaching & Assessing 21st Century Skills.* Blooming ton, IN: Solution Tree Press.

- National Staff Development Council. 2011. *Standards for Professional Learning.* Dallas, TX: Learning Forward.
  http://www.learningforward.org/standards/standards.cfm

- Reeves, Douglas B. 2008. *Reframing Teacher Leadership to Improve Your School.* Alexandria, VA: ASCD.

- Todd, Ross J. 2008. "The Evidence-Based Manifesto for School Librarians". *School Library Journal.* April 1 2008.
  http://www.schoollibraryjournal.com/article/CA6545434.html

Other Resources

- *OSLA Toolkit.* http://www.accessola.com/osla/toolkit/intro.html

- *Project Achievement.* http://www.davidvl.org/achieve.html

- *Building Evidence Based Evidence through Action Research*
  http://www2.hawaii.edu/~vharada/vi-Building%20Evidence-12-03-jav.htm

- *Action Research in the Grand Erie District School Board*
  http://www.actionresearch.ca/

Professional Organizations

- CARET Centre for Applied Research in Educational Technology
  http://caret.iste.org/index.cfm?fuseaction=resources

- IES Institute of Educational Sciences http://ies.ed.gov/ncee/wwc/

- American Educational Research Association http://www.aera.net/

- International Association of Learning Sciences http://www.isls.org/index.html

Chapter 10

Connections with People and Ideas
and the Learning Commons

In this chapter, we identify major people and ideas across education that we believe advance the field toward excellence. Then, we make connections between those people and their ideas to propel libraries and computer labs into the very center of school improvement.

The Power of Action Research

Douglas B. Reeves, founder of the Leadership and Learning Center, places action research at the center of school improvement in his book, *Reframing Teacher Leadership to Improve Your School.* He posits that teachers become leaders when they are testing ideas from research in their classrooms and reporting the results on data walls or science-fair type expositions. The key to school improvement, according to Reeves, is using evidence that our practices are effective based on increased learning. This follows up on the ideas in his previous book, *The Learning Leader,* where Reeves categorized the successful teacher as one who succeeds and knows why.

Learning Commons Connections In the context of the Learning Commons, we recommend that the Experimental Learning Center be the center of action research activity that informs the faculty as a whole. There is an atmosphere of collaboration in the achievement of excellence, because everyone expects that this is a place in the school where experimentation is the central focus. It follows that a positive attitude toward continuous school improvement is likely to develop and be sustained through a number of years, even with faculty turnover or student demographic evolution. If the action research combines both the classroom teacher and one or more specialists such as the teacher librarian, then the focus of school improvement values the impact of collaboration among the faculty. Such a focus would go a long way in promoting the idea that everyone has a stake in school improvement, not just isolated teachers in closed classrooms. For example, the action research theme of the school year could be the impact of actual collaborative teaching and learning. This could result in a data wall exhibition for the school board, parent groups, the news media, and presentations at professional conventions or to any other interested audience. What is learned as a group becomes part of the repertoire of teaching strategies for the school.

Instructional Strategies

In their book, *Classroom Instruction That Works: Research-Based Strategies for Increasing Student Achievement*, Marzano, Pickering, and Pollock list nine strategies supported by research that are worth replicating in the classroom. These strategies are:

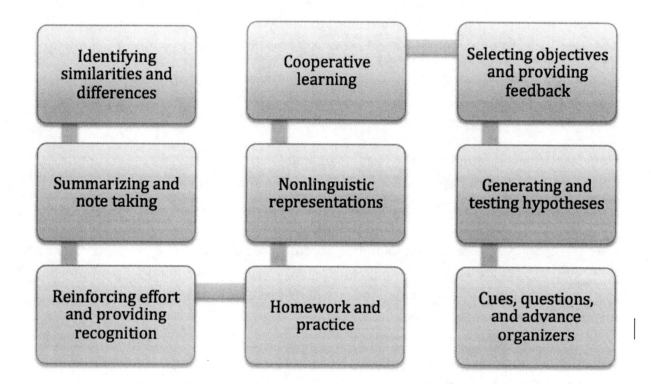

Learning Commons Connections One of the benefits of the movement to base teaching and learning on more scientific principles has been collections of strategies like those above that are supported by research. These and other strategies form the foundational base for all teachers as they mature in their profession. However, teachers need to tailor, test, and reinvent these strategies as generations of learners change and the cultural backgrounds of learners shift. Using the Experimental Learning Center to bring such conversations to the forefront as a collaborative rather than competitive focus seems to us to be a major step in the direction of school improvement.

Michael Fullan, Peter Hill, and Carmel Crevola

In their book, *Breakthrough*, Fullan, Hill, and Crevola propose that three components must form the core of instruction in the school in order to make major changes in education and make them sustainable.

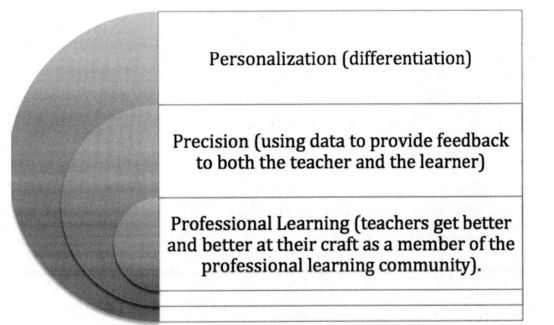

Personalization (differentiation)

Precision (using data to provide feedback to both the teacher and the learner)

Professional Learning (teachers get better and better at their craft as a member of the professional learning community).

They see a systematic effort where these core components are not just discussed, but practiced and applied to the actual learning activities of the classroom.

Learning Commons Connections It is not enough to have a professional development session and then assume that something will automatically change actual classroom practice. When the specialists of the school collaborate with the teachers to co-teach units of instruction, everyone in the building knows that new ideas are being tested in the Experimental Learning Commons. There, all can observe and, there, teaching and learning are examined for excellence and better and better ideas are recommended and tested. Then, the specialists can follow such ideas out into the school as a whole, complete with a feedback system for everyone. Each initiative is tracked and displayed in the Learning Commons , thereby providing a timeline of progress. Thus, diffusion of the initiative, strategy, policy, or operation is tracked on large graphic organizer charts for all to see and discuss. Sustainable school improvement becomes a part of striving for excellence, both in terms of the percent of students who achieved beyond expectations, and in terms of teachers who keep improving.

Bernie Dodge and WebQuests

Bernie Dodge is well known for the inquiry projects, known as WebQuests, that challenge users to complete a quest using Internet resources. Learners are grouped and face some type of problem or challenge. Each learner takes a different role as the group tackles the web-related task, resulting in an authentic project or presentation. For help with creating a new task or with searching the thousands of WebQuests available online, visit http://webquest.org/index.php. To help teachers in the design of real world tasks Dodge has compiled a taxonomy to illustrate the types of tasks that have been developed around this model:

Taxonomy of WebQuest Tasks

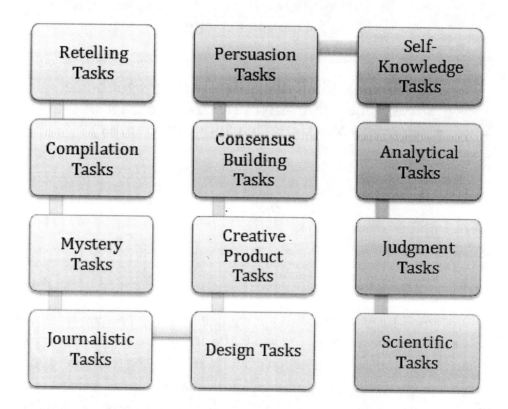

For an explanation of each of the tasks, consult Bernie Dodge's website at: http://webquest.sdsu.edu/taskonomy.html

Learning Commons Connections The various tasks of WebQuests compare in many ways to the think models created by Loertscher, Koechlin and Zwaan and presented in the Knowledge Building chapter of this book. Some of the best characteristics of WebQuests are their focus on engaging tasks, learner collaboration, and collaborative product building. At the conclusion of such learning activities, it is wise to build a culminating "big think" activity where the various teams of learners develop big ideas across the topics studied and also reflect on the journey they had in getting to their destination.

Backwards Design and the Six Facets of Learning:
Grant Wiggins and Jay McTighe

Wiggins and McTighe have made an incredible contribution to teaching and learning through their development and popularization of using backwards design to help learners know, do, and deeply understand. Check out the new edition of their ideas: Wiggins, Grant and Jay McTighe. 2011. *The Understanding by Design Guide to creating High-Quality Units.* ASCD.

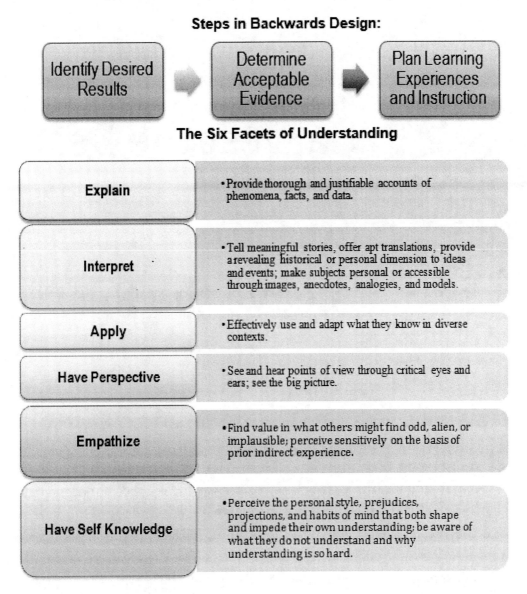

Steps in Backwards Design:

Identify Desired Results ➔ Determine Acceptable Evidence ➔ Plan Learning Experiences and Instruction

The Six Facets of Understanding

Explain	• Provide thorough and justifiable accounts of phenomena, facts, and data.
Interpret	• Tell meaningful stories, offer apt translations, provide a revealing historical or personal dimension to ideas and events; make subjects personal or accessible through images, anecdotes, analogies, and models.
Apply	• Effectively use and adapt what they know in diverse contexts.
Have Perspective	• See and hear points of view through critical eyes and ears; see the big picture.
Empathize	• Find value in what others might find odd, alien, or implausible; perceive sensitively on the basis of prior indirect experience.
Have Self Knowledge	• Perceive the personal style, prejudices, projections, and habits of mind that both shape and impede their own understanding; be aware of what they do not understand and why understanding is so hard.

Learning Commons Connections These elements are the foundational ideas of teaching and learning in the Learning Commons, and are a part of the major ideas being developed and tested in the Experimental Learning Center.

Alan November

In his most recent book, *Web Literacy for Educators*, Alan November discusses his concerns about the quality of Internet derived information that ends up in student projects. He provides a number of suggestions to help learners ascertain who is saying what to them, for what reasons, for what gain, and when it was said. Teachers are encouraged to teach a variety of evaluative strategies, such as investigating who created the website, or looking at the URL extension (whether it is .org, .edu, .com, or .gov). November rejects the notion that we should forbid the use of the Internet just because there is poor information, propaganda, or misleading information. Rather, he believes we need to teach learners to:

Harvest the Best

Leave the Rest

See Alan November's web page at: http://novemberlearning.com/

Learning Commons Connections Since the rise of the Google search engine, the virus of the cut and paste mentality has struck across the world. Teacher librarians have been waging a battle to help learners judge information quality before they embrace it as exactly what they need. In the Open Commons and the Experimental Learning Center, quality information is a foundational expectation, whether the ideas come from the Internet, a book, a database, a newspaper, or an interview. Discernment of quality is a constant, which is not likely to be less important any time soon.

Critical Thinking

The Center for Critical Thinking in Sonoma, California is one of a network of centers for critical thinking. It publishes a variety of miniature guides to various aspects of critical thinking for use by learners and teachers available through their website. One of their excellent models appears below, but one needs to check out the original info graphic to see the mouse-over explanations of each main point.

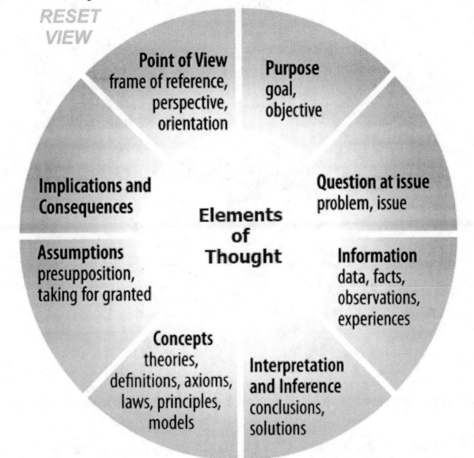

The Critical Thinking Community page is at: http://www.criticalthinking.org/

Learning Commons Connections Critical thinking is a basic element built into learning activities that happen both in the Open Commons and the Experimental Learning Center. These skills are part of the information literacy skills taught by teacher librarians, are part of any excursion on the Internet, and are part of the normal strategy of the classroom teacher. Like other literacies, critical thinking is best integrated into a topical exploration rather than taught as a topic in and of itself. When specialists and classroom teachers build learning activities, critical thinking should be on their checklist for integration planning.

Stephen Krashen

In his books, Stephen Krashen backs up the idea that kids who read widely score high on standardized tests with 100 years of research. As well, according to Krashen, kids who read widely also develop a number of characteristics that push them toward excellence.

The Reading Hypothesis

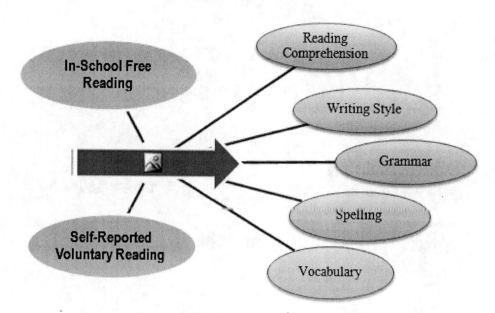

Stephen Krashen (2006, 17)

Further explore Krashen's articles and research at his site: http://www.sdkrashen.com/

Learning Commons Connections There is no stronger idea and support for the reinvention of the school library into a Learning Commons than Krashen's hypothesis. It is here that learners and teachers have a plethora of materials they **want to read**, and access to these materials is far beyond the norm of the past. Now with so much reading being done on the Internet, and with the very best fiction and nonfiction books available in the Learning Commons, there is really no excuse not to embrace the Krashen idea. Reading is not just about developing skills. It is a life-long embrace. Teacher librarians should survey the learners to find out whether they like to read. With any percentage under 100% yes answers, a revolution in the reading program needs to be considered.

David Warlick

David Warlick has a very popular blog, *2 cents Worth,* at http://davidwarlick.com/2cents/ His musings on technology, the people he meets, and the conferences he attends help his readers keep up with the current happenings in the field. Over the last few years Warlick has been experimenting with the development of Personal Learning Networks. He believes that a PLN is a way to manage and make sense of the information ecosystem and there are many paths for achieving this as this visual from his article, "Grow Your Personal Learning Network", represents.

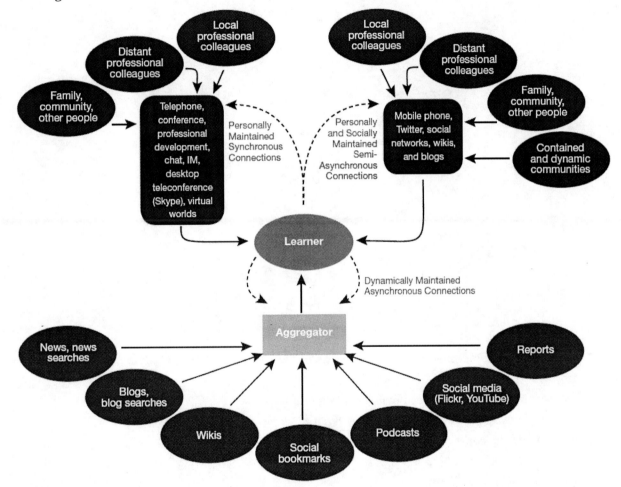

Discover lots more about his work with PLNs from Warlick's wiki http://davidwarlick.com/wiki/pmwiki.php?n=Main.TheArtAmpTechniqueOfCultivatingYourPers onalLearningNetwork

Learning Commons Connections We advocate that all young people learn how to command their own information space, and learn how to govern themselves within this space. Whether through iGoogle pages or some other technology, the idea of being at the mercy of the juggernaut of the Internet is unacceptable. For each of our roles as student, family member, worker, creator, thinker, we must establish various neighborhoods that help us flourish in that role. The nice thing is that we can have as few or many as we please.

Will Richardson

Will Richardson is a visionary about the power of transformative technology, and he teaches us what the real world requires of a new generation of learners. One example is his list of the independent learning skill set students need to acquire in order to live effectively and learn effectively in today's world that is pictured below. Check out his latest book: Richardson, Will. 2011. *Personal Learning Networks: Using the Power of Connection to Transform Education.* Solution Tree Press.

The current educational system creates and nurtures **dependent** *learners. Our students depend on us to:*

- *create the environment in which learning takes place*
- *tell them what they should know, when and why*
- *provide the context for knowing*
- *provide appropriate materials for learning*
- *assess what they know*
- *select appropriate ways to share what they have learned with others*

The new world of learning requires us to teach students to be **independent** *learners, that are not dependent on teachers.* Richardson (2011)

Learning Commons Connections Young people will not automatically assume the command of their own learning unless we as adults coach them to do so. Learners often feel that school is a place where adults are dictating what, how, and when to do tasks. As they begin to participate in taking command of their own learning, they will become more engaged and independent. They will seek more and more relevance to both now and the future. More from Will Richardson can be found at http://willrichardson.com/

The Whole Child Initiative (ASCD)

The official statement from ASCD for their Whole Child Initiative is as follows:

What will prepare each young person to work in careers that have not yet been invented; to think both critically and creatively; and to evaluate massive amounts of information, solve complex problems, and communicate well? Research, practice, and common sense confirm that a whole child approach to education will develop and prepare students for the challenges and opportunities of today and tomorrow. Every school, community, classroom, educator, student, and family has unique challenges and strengths, and has a role to play in ensuring that each student is healthy, safe, engaged, supported, and challenged. ASCD

Whole Child Tenets:

- Each student enters school **healthy** and learns about and practices a healthy lifestyle.

- Each student learns in an environment that is physically and emotionally **safe** for students and adults.

- Each student is actively **engaged** in learning and is connected to the school and broader community.

- Each student has access to personalized learning and is **supported** by qualified, caring adults.

- Each student is **challenged** academically and prepared for success in college or further study and for employment and participation in a global environment.

Schools implementing a whole school approach use **collaboration**, **coordination**, and **integration** to ensure the long term success of the approach. Details and support found at http://www.ascd.org/whole-child.aspx

Learning Commons Connections The Learning Commons is the perfect place to initiate, monitor, test, and make decisions about such initiatives as the Whole Child concerns of ASCD. Too often, such initiatives are dictated by well meaning administrators but never gain the strength needed to permeate the school. The Commons provides a checkpoint for all such shifts in program.

Professional Learning Communities

Rebecca DuFour, Richard DuFour, and Robert Eaker in their book, *Professional Learning Communities at Work Plan Book,* provide three major big ideas about professional learning communities:

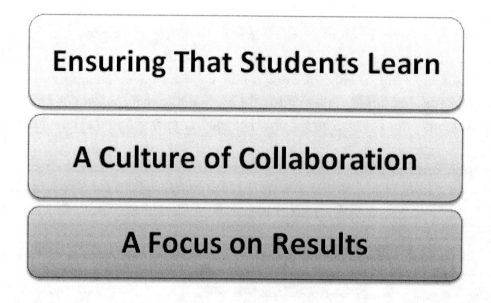

They see the following main shifts in doing business:
· A shift in fundamental purpose
· A shift in the use of assessments
· A shift in response when students don't learn
· A shift in the work of teachers
· A shift in focus
· A shift in school culture
· A shift in professional development

Learning Commons Connections The Learning Commons provides a central non-threatening place in which to center the work of professional learning communities. It becomes the place for serious discussion and experimentation across the faculty so that a sense of excellence permeates the entire school. It is the place we can share, test, succeed or fail together, pick up the pieces, and move forward without stigma. This is essential if any school is to make progress as a learning community. Such communities, however, can lock out the learners. We advocate that to turn client-side, representatives from the various segments of the learning community be involved, from gifted, to mainstream, to struggling.

Habits of Mind

A Habit of Mind is knowing how to behave intelligently when you DON'T know the answer. A Habit of Mind means having a disposition toward behaving intelligently when confronted with problems, the answers to which are not immediately known, and also when confronted with dichotomies, dilemmas, enigmas and uncertainties.

The 16 Habits of Mind identified by Arthur Costa and Bena Kallick in their article, *16 Habits of Mind,* include:

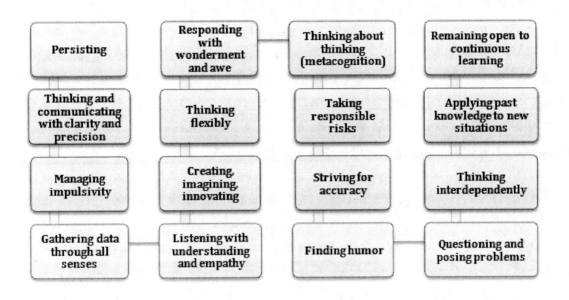

Learning Commons Connections The concept behind Habits of Mind is the that learners should be engaged in their own learning and need to take control and responsibility for their own progress. A pessimist would say that this not the human nature of most kids and teens. We propose that the learning experiences in both the Open Commons and the Experimental Learning Center embrace Habits of Mind. As we observe learners in this fishbowl experience, we ask, what are the strategies that engage students and encourage self-direction and independence? It is this kind of sharing and discussion across the faculty that will enable change.

Stephen Heppell on Technology

To listen to a Stephen Heppell presentation is a real treat because of his vision and his experimentation with how technology can actually change learning. On his blog, we have found his defense of technology as the enabler of learning:

Computers are everyday tools for us all, seen or unseen, but their value in learning is as tools for creativity and learning rather than as machines to develop the curriculum. These tools, in our children's hands, are forever pushing the envelope of expertise that previous technologies excluded them from: they compose and perform music before acquiring any ability to play an instrument, they shoot, edit and stream digital video before any support from media courses, they produce architectural fly-throughs of incredible buildings without any drafting or 2D skills, they make stop frame animations with their plasticine models, they edit and finesse their poetry, they explore surfaces on their visual calculators, swap ideas with scientists on-line about volcanic activity, follow webcam images of Ospreys hatching, track weather by live satellite images, control the robots they have built and generally push rapidly at the boundaries of what might be possible, indeed what was formerly possible, at any age. Little of this was easily achieved in the school classroom ten years ago although the many projects emanating from Ultralab over that decade offered clear enough indicators of what might be possible. The challenge here is to criterion referencing. So often the cry of the teacher that work is better than my degree exhibition piece, reflects a substantial step change in both the age at which a creative act can be enjoyed and the quality of the tools supporting that creativity. Stephen Heppell

Explore Heppell's website for a look into the future of technology and learning spaces. http://www.heppell.net/

Learning Commons Connections In the early stages of technology integration in schools, students quickly realized how to add glitz to a presentation so that it would appear impressive even though it was not necessarily substantive. Rubrics created for all products and presentations should be weighted toward excellence in content and deep understanding rather than toward the clever or polished use of the technology itself. Slick and polished-looking presentations need to also convey compelling messages that elevate the understanding of the audience.

International Baccalaureate Schools

The International Baccalaureate School network (which offers programs for elementary and high school students) was founded in 1968 and has expanded to over 3000 schools in over 140 countries. Their mission is identified on their website as follows:

The International Baccalaureate aims to develop inquiring, knowledgeable and caring young people who help to create a better and more peaceful world through intercultural understanding and respect. To this end the IB works with schools, governments and international organizations to develop challenging programs of international education and rigorous assessment. These programs encourage students across the world to become active, compassionate and lifelong learners who understand that other people, with their differences, can also be right.

According to the *IB Learner Profile Booklet* (2008), IB program learners strive to be:

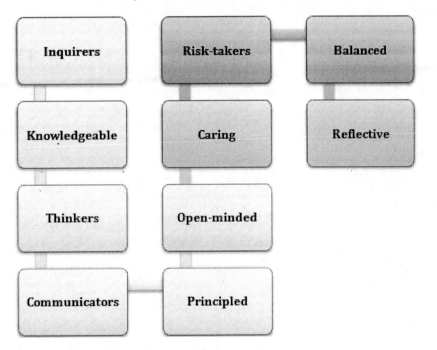

Learning Commons Connections The creators of the International Baccalaureate believe in the centrality of the library as a foundational element to make their ideas work. In practice, our interviews with teacher librarians in IB schools indicate that many of them are left out of the IB planning and implementation. In the revised concept of the Learning Commons, this and other such global initiatives benefit from the connection to information-rich and technology-rich resources as well as to the opportunities for experimentation with this great concept.

Brain Based Learning

Scientific advancements continue to unlock the mysteries of the brain. We know so much more about how the brain works, how we learn, and even why some conditions for learning are better than others. To help us visualize how the brain deals with information, we have combined an Information Processing Model by Patricia Wolfe from her book, *Brain Matters: Translating Research into Classroom Practice*, together with a model from Eric Jensen's book, *Teaching with the Brain in Mind*.

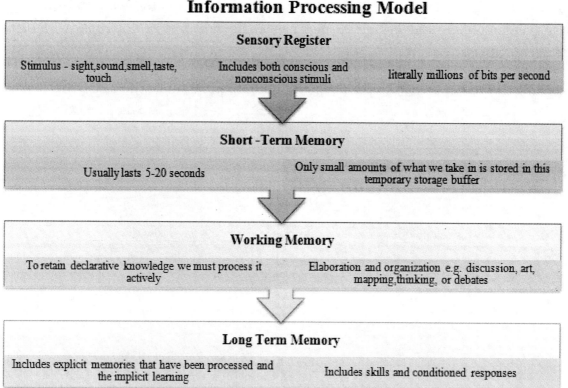

Information Processing Model

Sensory Register

| Stimulus - sight, sound, smell, taste, touch | Includes both conscious and nonconscious stimuli | literally millions of bits per second |

Short-Term Memory

| Usually lasts 5-20 seconds | Only small amounts of what we take in is stored in this temporary storage buffer |

Working Memory

| To retain declarative knowledge we must process it actively | Elaboration and organization e.g. discussion, art, mapping, thinking, or debates |

Long Term Memory

| Includes explicit memories that have been processed and the implicit learning | Includes skills and conditioned responses |

Learning Commons Connections If we know how the brain learns best, why aren't we doing more to design learning to take best advantage of this information? This valuable learning science can realize its potential to enhance learning in the new spaces and places of the Learning Commons. Here, learning strategies and environments can be designed and trialed to create brain compatible experiences. Techniques and technology tools to help learners actively process information must be essential components of every information task to ensure that learners attain deep understanding and long lasting knowing.

Differentiated Instruction

Carol Ann Tomlinson, a leader in this field, tells us that differentiation is acknowledging that kids learn in different ways, and that we need to respond by doing something about that through curriculum and instruction. In her book, *The Differentiated Classroom,* Tomlinson explains that differentiating instruction is not an instructional strategy nor is it a teaching model. It is in fact a way of thinking, an approach to teaching and learning that advocates beginning where students are at, and designing experiences that will better help them to achieve.

In their book *Integrating Differentiated Instruction and Understanding by Design,* Tomlinson and Jay McTighe suggest that teachers first need to establish standards for student achievement and then design many paths of instruction to enable all learners to be successful. To reach desired learning standards, Tomlinson and McTighe encourage teachers to differentiate for students through the following design elements:

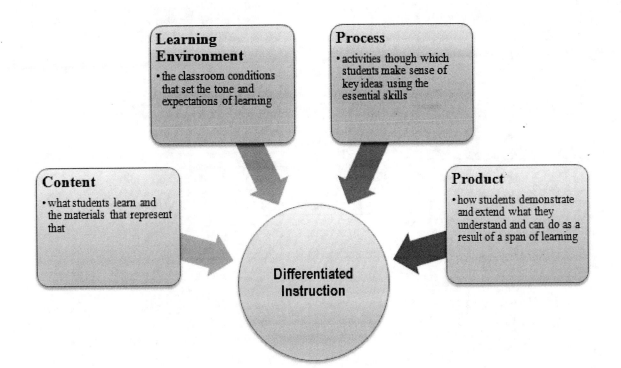

Learning Commons Connections Driven by client-side needs and opportunities, the Learning Commons is the ultra responsive learning space. The teacher librarian and technology specialist help classroom teachers to design differentiated learning with rich resources and technologies and strategies. Working through the Learning Commons, school leadership teams can ensure that the Tomlinson and McTighe's design elements can be infused in all learning experiences.

Multiple Intelligence and Five Minds for the Future

This widely accepted theory has been developed by Howard Gardner, a psychologist, and professor of neuroscience at Harvard University. Over 25 years ago his classic book, *Frames of Mind: Theory of Multiple Intelligences,* made a major impact on the education world. In that book and in later statements, he has identified eight unique intelligences:

- Verbal-Linguistic Intelligence
- Musical-Rhythmic Intelligence
- Logical-Mathematical Intelligence
- Visual-Spatial Intelligence
- Bodily-Kinesthetic Intelligence
- Interpersonal Intelligence
- Intrapersonal Intelligence
- Naturalist Intelligence

Gardner's newest book, *Five Minds for the Future,* outlines the specific cognitive abilities that may well illuminate future directions for 21st century schools.

Five Minds for the Future

The Disciplinary Mind	• The mastery of major schools of thought, including science, mathematics, and history, and of at least one professional craft.
The Synthesizing Mind	• The ability to integrate ideas from different disciplines or spheres into a coherent whole and to communicate that integration to others.
The Creating Mind	• The capacity to uncover and clarify new problems, questions and phenomena.
The Respectful Mind	• Awareness of and appreciation for differences among human beings and human groups.
The Ethical Mind	• Fulfillment of one's responsibilities as a worker and as a citizen.

Learning Commons Connections Gardner provides grounding frameworks for the leadership teams of the Learning Commons who strive for teaching and learning environments where all learners and teachers win.

Guided Inquiry

This theory has been developed by Carol Kuhlthau and Ross Todd at the Center for International Scholarship in School Libraries at Rutgers University and has been expanded in Kuhlthau's book, *Guided Inquiry: Learning in the 21st Century*. It has been defined as follows:

Guided Inquiry means careful planning, close supervision, ongoing assessment and targeted intervention by an instructional team of school librarians and teachers through the inquiry process that gradually leads students toward independent learning. An integrated unit of inquiry is planned and guided by an instructional team of a school librarian and teachers. Its ultimate goal is to develop independent learners who know how to expand their knowledge and expertise through skilled use of a variety of information sources employed both inside and outside of the school. Resources inside the school, such as library materials, databases and other selected sources are supplemented and expanded by public libraries, local community resources, museums, and the Internet. Kuhlthau, Maniotes, and Caspari (2007).

Guided Inquiry is not …	Guided Inquiry is …
Preparation solely for the test	Preparation for lifelong learning
An add-on subject	Integrated into content areas
Isolated information skills	Transferable information concepts
Relying on one textbook	Using a variety of sources
Finding answers to a prescribed question	Involving students in every stage of the learning from planning to the final product
Curriculum without meaning to students	Curriculum connected to student's world
Individual students working exclusively on solitary tasks	A community of learners working together
Solely teacher directed	Students and teachers collaborating
Overemphasis on the end product	Emphasis on the process and product

Learning Commons Connections The constructivist basis of this theory and the belief that learners share responsibility in seeking understanding, supports all work in the Commons. The characteristics of Guided Inquiry are excellent criteria for measuring successful design of learning experiences in the Learning Commons. A collaborative space, designed to facilitate sharing information about the theory and practice of Guided Inquiry is found at: http://guidedinquiry.ning.

Participatory Culture

Recent advancements in technology, and Web 2.0 features in particular, have opened up new collaborative spaces for users. In their paper, *Confronting the Challenges of Participatory Culture: Media Education for the 21st Century*, Henry Jenkins and the other writers proclaim that these advancements have spawned a unique way of creating, sharing and learning. They call it a participatory culture, and identify its characteristics as the following

Characteristics of a Participatory Culture

- relatively low barriers to artistic expression and civic engagement
- strong support for creating and sharing one's creations with others
- some type of informal mentoring whereby what is known by the most experienced is passed along to novices
- members believe that their contributions matter
- members feel some degree of social connection with one another (at the least they care what other people think about what they have created).

The paper maintains that while not every member must contribute, all must believe they are free to contribute when ready and that what they contribute will be appropriately valued. The document also suggests that *participation* is expressed in a variety of forms: affiliations, expressions, collaborative problem solving, and circulation.

Affiliations	Expressions	Collaborative Problem-solving	Circulations
• memberships, formal and informal, in online communities centered around various forms of media, such as Friendster, Facebook, message boards, • metagaming, game clans, or MySpace.	• producing new creative forms, such as digital sampling, skinning and modding, fan videomaking, fan fiction writing, zines, mash-ups	• working together in teams, formal and informal, to complete tasks and develop new knowledge (such as through *Wikipedia*, alternative reality gaming, spoiling).	• shaping the flow of media (such as podcasting, blogging).

Further connections to the work of Henry Jenkins can be found at his blog: http://www.henryjenkins.org/, and in his recent publications, *Convergence Culture* and *Fans, Bloggers and Gamers*.

Learning Commons Connections The emerging participatory culture will find nourishment and inspiration in the client based organization and learning environment in the Learning Commons.

The Current Crisis

An important Canadian report has laid bare many systemic problems for school libraries. This document, *The Crisis in Canada's School Libraries: the Case for Reform and Re-Investment*, commissioned by the Association of Canadian Publishers and Canada Heritage in 2003, has played a critical role in the battle to strengthen school library programs in Canadian schools. Designed with the policy maker in mind, this valuable work provides volumes of evidence, based on research that school library programs have a positive impact on student achievement. One of the unique contributions made in this work is a formal recognition of the impact the school library has on cultural identity, socialization and citizenship. The report, written by Ken Haycock, former director of the School of Library and Information Science at San Jose State University and a champion of school libraries in Canada and everywhere, is a grounded starting point for change. Haycock, together with Brooke Sheldon, has produced a recent publication, *The Portable MLIS: Insights from the Experts,* which provides a broad overview of librarianship.

Learning Commons Connections No change will happen unless all levels of educational institutions and governments recognize the need. This document goes right to the top.

Active Literacy

Active Literacy is about knowing how to work information and ideas dynamically to construct meaning. Today's emphasis on content curriculum has driven the need for learners to have the ability to apply strategic thinking while reading, viewing, listening to all kinds of media, ideas, and information, as well as communicating their new learning. Two leaders in this movement over the years are Stephanie Harvey and Anne Goudvis. Their strategies for working with non-fiction have helped teachers understand that literacy involves working with far more than the novel. Link to their books, podcasts and recent video support at Stenhouse. http://www.stenhouse.com/html/authorbios_32.htm

Another leader in the field of active literacy is Heidi Hayes Jacobs. As well as her recent book, *Active Literacy Across the Curriculum: Strategies for Reading, Writing, Speaking and Listening*, Jacobs is president of Curriculum Designers, Inc. and offers support and professional development for schools in the areas of Interdisciplinary curriculum and curriculum mapping. http://www.curriculumdesigners.com/

Learning Commons Connections The success of knowledge building hinges on the ability of learners to construct meaning in all disciplines. In the Learning Commons learners are not only active consumers, but also active producers of information and ideas.

Administrative Leadership

Through his many publications and presentations, David Booth has broadened definitions of reading and literacy to address the real world of 21st century learners. In a recent second edition of his popular book, *The Literacy Principal,* Booth lays the groundwork for principals and school literacy leadership teams to advance schools to address the new literacies. He acknowledges the critical role teacher librarians and technology play in this process. David Booth is Professor Emeritus in Education at the Ontario Institute for Studies in Education of the University of Toronto where he is Scholar in Residence in the Curriculum, Teaching and Language Department. Further connections to Booth's research can be found at :

- http://www.oise.utoronto.ca/cted/Faculty/David_Booth/index.html
- http://www.edu.gov.on.ca/eng/research/boys_literacy.pdf

Learning Commons Connections The hard work involved in the reinvention of school libraries and computer labs to support school wide action research and improvement requires the leadership and dedication of strong administration.

Sparking the Middle Years

Adolescent learners have their own special set of needs. One of their characteristics is the need for real world relevant learning experiences. Cris Tovani has coined the phrase "fake reading" in her book *I Read It but I don't Get It* and, in a later publication, *Do I Have to Teach Reading?,* has challenged all teachers to consider reading to be their mandate whatever their subject discipline. Further information about her books and videos can be found at Cris Tovani's website http://www.tovanigroup.com/

Adolescents also tend to lose interest in school just at the time when they start to develop the abilities to think and reason at higher levels. In his book, *Puzzle Them First: Motivating Adolescent Readers with Question Finding,* A. Vincent Ciardiello presents a powerful way to make learning relevant and engaging for learners. This book is a goldmine of effective strategies and is a valuable approach to addressing the needs of this special group of learners.

Learning Commons Connections Keeping learning real world, relevant, and engaging becomes easier when the world is at the fingertips of learners and teachers. There is no "fake work" in the Learning Commons.

Literacy and Libraries

Connecting literacy and libraries is not always as intuitive as we would like. There are a myriad of ways to make those connections for schools. Ray Doiron and Marlene Asselin have combined collective minds across Canada to explore this issue in their publication, *Literacy, Libraries and Learning*, and highlight these ideas:

- promoting reading for learning and pleasure;
- improving critical literacy skills when using information from many sources;
- encouraging research methods that respect copyright and lead to original work;
- designing information tasks to help students work effectively with data;
- developing better informational text structures that increase comprehension;
- encouraging the integration of emerging technologies and traditional resources.

Discover more on their wiki at
http://asselindoiron.pbworks.com/w/page/9693252/FrontPage

Learning Commons Connections Whole school literacy is developed, initiated, and celebrated through leadership in the Learning Commons. Improving literacy achievement is an organized and coordinated effort rather than one that is driven by isolated projects.

Effective Student Questioning

For students to fully participate and thrive in this new 'learning age', they must be critical thinkers. Questioning is the base skill that makes all thinking purposeful. **Consequently intuitive questioning techniques are becoming essential learning tools**. Through the lens of effective questions, students learn to be responsible and effective information users.

Questioning skills will help every student succeed with many kinds of information tasks including:

- Exploring a topic for research
- Developing a focus for research
- Accessing information
- Validating information sources
- Designing surveys and interviews
- Processing information
- Thinking critically about information
- Deeper understanding of issues
- Connecting to real world problems and events
- Critical analysis of media texts
- Self analysis and peer review

Questioning is the Answer to Engagement of Learners and Personal Knowledge Building

A practical professional text to kick start staff development on effective student questioning is *Q Tasks: How to empower students to ask questions and care about answers* by Carol Koechlin and Sandi Zwaan. Another valuable resource is the educational journal, *The Question Mark* at www.questioning.org.

Learning Commons Connections Building a school-wide climate conducive to inquiry is a key goal for the Commons. Modeling and testing questioning strategies for all ages and disciplines is natural in this high stimulus environment

Learning to Learn: From Information to Knowledge Creation
Together for Learning: School Libraries and the Emergence of the Learning Commons

The information to knowledge learning journey is at the heart of school library program in the Ontario School Library Association's document, *Together for Learning: School Libraries and the Emergence of the Learning Commons.* Each element of the journey is supported by rational and practical ideas for implementation, thus enabling teacher librarians to design excellent learning experiences.

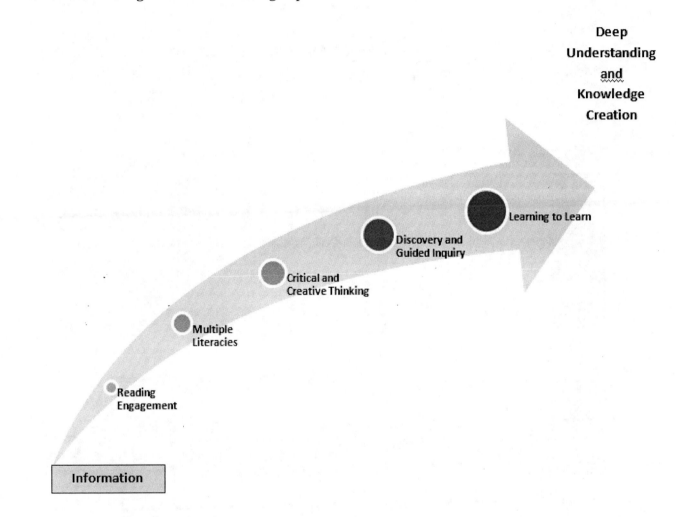

Learning Commons Connections Recognition of the many aspects of knowledge building increases the potential for success. The Ontario School Library Association document provides many more supports for schools transitioning to a Learning Commons approach. Of particular note is a section called *Supporting the Individual in the Learning Commons* on pages 29-33.

Together for Learning :School Libraries and the Emergence of the Learning Commons.
http://www.accessola.com/data/6/rec_docs/677_OLATogetherforLearning.pdf

What did you do in school today?

Beginning with the belief that student voices are crucial to designing successful solutions for student disengagement, the Canadian Education Association (CEA) set out on an exciting research partnership with 17 schools across Canada. Working with the Galileo Educational Network and the Learning Bar, CEA completed the research and published results in a document called, *What did you do in school today?* One of their findings is represented in the graphic below. This visual makes it eminently clear that learner engagement is linked to both the challenge presented and the skill level the student possesses.

Sharon Friesen, a lead researcher in the CEA project, responded to the research findings by developing *What did you do in school today? Teaching Effectiveness: A Framework and Rubric,* a powerful framework and rubric for change in the design of learning experiences.

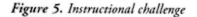

Figure 5. Instructional challenge

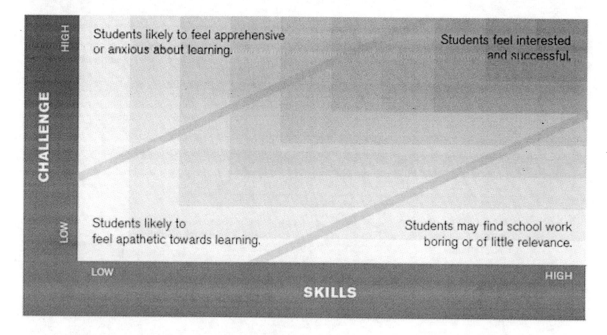

See the full report at http://www.cea-ace.ca/programs-initiatives/wdydist

Learning Commons Connections The client-side and collaborative facets of the Learning Commons, enhanced by a participatory culture and "just in time" skill support makes a perfect pairing with the CEA research initiative. All the stakeholders work together to involve and engage students in meaningful 'high think' learning experiences while strategically providing support on an as needed basis. What a winning combination to meet instructional challenges.

The Six Secrets of Change
Michael Fullan

What the Best Leaders Do To Help Their Organizations Survive and Thrive, is the subtitle of Michael Fullan's book, *Six Secrets of Change.* This work uncovers and simplifies the fundamentals needed in any organization to realize and succeed with change.

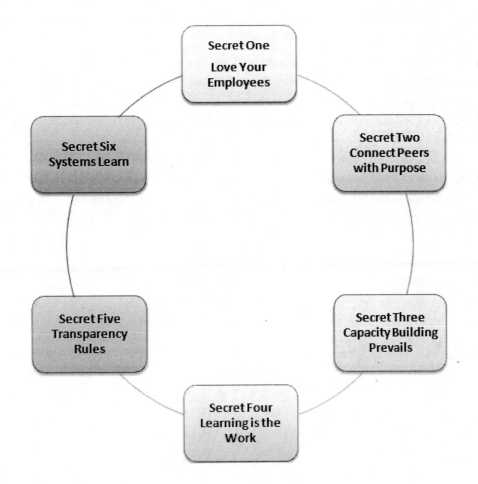

Learning Commons Connections Throughout his book, Fullan weaves examples of the business world and education embracing one change or another. The Learning Commons is a mix of both worlds, thus the big ideas of Fullan's secrets are even more valuable. Teaching partnerships and learning communities of the Learning Commons are validated in his statement, "With purposeful peer interaction, people band together to outperform themselves relative to their own past performance. His ideas of "transparency", "ever learning", "rallying around a higher purpose" and "learning steeped in reflective action" are all valued targets in the Learning Commons.

Discover more works by Michael Fullan at http://www.michaelfullan.ca/index.htm

PLAY: Participatory Learning and You
Project New Media Literacies

The central goal for Project New Media Literacies (Project NML) is identifying and creating educational practices that will prepare teachers and students to become full and active participants in the new digital culture.

According to Project NML, designing and implementing a participatory learning environment fosters:

- *Heightened motivation and new forms of engagement through meaningful play and experimentation.*
- *Learning that feels relevant to students' identities and interests.*
- *Opportunities for creating and solving problems using a variety of media, tools and practices.*
- *Co-configured expertise where educators and students pool their skills and knowledge and share in the tasks of teaching and learning.*
- *An integrated learning system where connections between home, school, community and world are enabled and encouraged.* http://playnml.wikispaces.com/

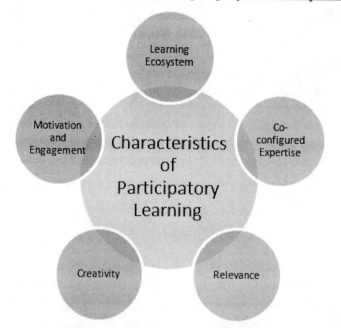

Learning Commons Connections: Opportunities abound for rich 'play to learn' experiences in both the physical and virtual Learning Commons. Everyone is encouraged to experiment with strategies and technologies, bounce ideas with others, play with language, innovate when problem solving as well as other sandbox types of experiences. When teachers and students engage in these collaborative and creative experiences everyone benefits.

More on PLAY by Henry Jenkins

- Shall we Play Part 1 http://henryjenkins.org/2011/05/shall_we_play.html
- Shall we Play Part 2 http://henryjenkins.org/2011/05/shall_we_play_part_two.html

Standards of Professional Learning

Learning Forward, formally known as The National Staff Development Council, has presented seven principles to guide districts in the work they do to advance opportunities and learning for their educators. These standards introduce a new shift in teacher training that gives teachers an active role in their continuous professional learning journeys.

Professional learning that increases educator effectiveness and results for all students:

Learning Communities	• occurs within learning communities committed to continuous improvement, collective responsibility, and goal alignment.
Leadership	• requires skillful leaders who develop capacity, advocate, and create support systems for professional learning.
Resources	• requires prioritizing, monitoring, and coordinating resources for educator learning.
Data Uses	• employs a variety of sources and types of student, educator, and system data to plan, assess, and evaluate professional learning.
Learning Designs	• integrates theories, research, and models of human learning to achieve its intended outcomes.
Implementation	• applies research on change and sustains support for implementation of professional learning for long term change.
Outcomes	• aligns its outcomes with educator performance and student curriculum standards.

Learning Commons Connections Everyone is a learner in the Learning Commons. School improvement means that both teachers and students are getting better and better. Evidence Based Practice and opportunities to experiment with teaching practices, test out new technologies and resources are all supported and tracked in the Learning Commons. See more at http://www.learningforward.org/standards/index.cfm

References

- Association for Supervision and Curriculum Development. *The Whole Child Initiative.* http://www.ascd.org/whole-child.aspx

- Booth, David and Jennifer Rowsell. 2007. *The Literacy Principal: Leading, Supporting, and Assessing Reading and Writing Initiatives,*second edition. Markham, ON: Pembroke Publishers.

- Ciardiello, A. Vincent 2006. *Puzzle Them First: Motivating Adolescent Readers with Question Finding.* Newark, DE: International Reading Association.

- Costa, Art and Bena Kallick . *Describing 16 Habits of Mind.* http://www.instituteforhabitsofmind.com/resources/pdf/16HOM.pdf

- *The Critical Thinking Community* http://www.criticalthinking.org// . Also see the *Online Model for Learning the Elements and Standards of Critical Thinking.* http://www.criticalthinking.org/ctmodel/logic-model1.htm#

- Doiron, Ray and Marlene Asselin. 2005. *Literacy, Libraries and Learning: Using Books and Online Resources to Promote Reading, Writing, and Research.* Markham, ON: Pembroke Publishers.

- Dodge, Bernie. *WebQuest Taskonomy: A Taxonomy of Tasks.* http://webquest.sdsu.edu/taskonomy.html

- Dodge, Bernie. *WebQuest.Org* http://webquest.org/index.php.

- Friesen, Sharon. 2009. *What Did You Do in School Today? Teaching Effectiveness: A Framework and Rubric.* Toronto, ON: Canadian Education Association. http://www.cea-ace.ca/publication/what-did-you-do-school-today-teaching-effectiveness-framework-and-rubric

- Rebecca DuFour, Richard DuFour, and Robert Eaker. 2006. *Professional Learning Communities at Work Plan Book.* Bloomington, IN: Solution Tree.

- Fullan, Michael, Peter Hill, and Carmel Crevola. 2006. *Breakthrough.* Thousand Oaks, CA: Corwin Press.

- Fullan, Michael. 2008. *Six Secrets of Change: What the Best Leaders Do To Help Their Organizations Survive and Thrive.* San Francisco, CA: Jossey-Bass

- Gardner, Howard. 2011. *Frames of Mind: The Theory of Multiple Intelligences,* Third Edition. New York: Basic Books.

- Gardner, Howard. 2009. *Five Minds for the Future.* Boston, MA: Harvard Business School Press

- *Habits of Mind* http://www.habits-of-mind.net/

- Haycock, Ken. 2003. *The Crisis in Canada's School Libraries: the Case for Reform and Re-Investment.* Toronto, ON: Association of Canadian Publishers. http://www.cla.ca/slip/final_haycock_report.pdf

- Haycock, Ken, and Brooke E. Sheldon. 2008. *The Portable MLIS: Insights from the Experts.* Westport, CT: Libraries Unlimited

- Hayes Jacobs, Heidi. 2006. *Active Literacy Across the Curriculum: Strategies for Reading, Writing, Speaking and Listening.* Larchmont, NY: Eye on Education.

- Heppell, Stephen. http://www.heppell.net/weblog/stephen/ . For his current writings, see also *prof stephen heppell: writings* at http://workshop.heppell.mobi/ , and his composite website at http://www.heppell.net/ .

- International Baccalaureate Organization. 2008. *The IB Learner Profile.* http://www.ibo.org/programmes/profile/documents/Learnerprofileguide.pdf

- International Baccalaureate Schools. http://www.ibo.org/ See also *Mission and Strategy* http://www.ibo.org/mission/

- Jenkins, Henry et al. 2007. "Confronting the Challenge of Participatory Culture: Media Education for the 21st Century." MacArthur Foundation White Paper. http://www.projectnml.org/files/working/NMLWhitePaper.pdf

- Jenkins, Henry. 2008. *Convergence Culture: Where Old and New Media Collide,* revised edition. New York: NYU Press.

- Jenkins, Henry. 2006. *Fans, Bloggers, and Gamers: Media Consumers in a Digital Age.* New York: NYU Press.

- Jenkins, Henry. 2011. "Shall We Play? (Part One)". Blog Post. May 13, 2011. http://henryjenkins.org/2011/05/shall_we_play.html and "Shall We Play? (Part Two)". Blog Post. May 17, 2011. http://henryjenkins.org/2011/05/shall_we_play_part_two.html

- Jensen, Eric. *Teaching with the Brain in Mind.* 1998. Alexandria, VA: Association for Supervision and Curriculum Development.

- Koechlin, Carol and Sandi Zwaan. 2006. *Q Tasks: How to Empower Students to Ask Questions and Care About Answers.* Markham, ON: Pembroke Publishers.

- Krashen, Stephen. 2006. *The Power of Reading*, 2nd edition. Westport, CT: Libraries Unlimited.

- Kuhlthau, Carol, Leslie Maniotes, and Ann Caspari. 2007. *Guided Inquiry: Learning in the 21st Century.* Westport, CT: Libraries Unlimited. See also the collaborative space at http://guidedinquiry.ning.com/.

- Robert J. Marzano, Debra J. Pickering, and Jane E. Pollock. 2001. *Classroom Instruction That Works: Research-Based Strategies for Increasing Student Achievement.* Alexandria, VA: Association for Supervision and Curriculum Development.

- November, Alan. 2008. *Web Literacy for Educators.* Thousand Oaks, CA: Corwin Press. See also Alan November's web page at: http://novemberlearning.com/

- Ontario School Library Association. 2010. *Together for Learning: School Libraries and the Emergence of the Learning Commons.* http://www.accessola.com/data/6/rec_docs/677_OLATogetherforLearning.pdf

- Project New Media Literacies http://playnml.wikispaces.com/

- *The Question Mark: an educational journal devoted to questions,questioning, sound intelligence, strategic reading and quality teaching.* www.questioning.org.

- Reeves,Douglas B. 2008. *Reframing Teacher Leadership to Improve Your School.* Alexandria, VA: Association for Supervision and Curriculum Development.

- Reeves,Douglas B. 2006. *The Learning Leader*. Alexandria, VA: Association for Supervision and Curriculum Development.

- Richardson, Will. 2011. "An Introduction to New Internet Literacies for Educators: Blogs, Wikis, RSS, Online Bookmarking." *Will Richardson's Wiki.* http://weblogged.wikispaces.com/New+Internet+Literacies

- Tomlinson, Carol Ann. *The Differentiated Classrom*. 1999. Alexandria, VA: Association for Supervision and Curriculum Development.

- Tomlinson, Carol Ann and McTighe Jay. 2006. *Integrating Differentiated Instruction + Understanding by Design*. Alexandria, VA: Association for Supervision and Curriculum Development.

- Tovani, Cris. 2000. *I Read It, but I Don't Get It: Comprehension Strategies for Adolescent Readers.* Portland, ME: Stenhouse Publishers

- Tovani, Cris.2004. *Do I Have to Teach Reading?* Portland, ME: Stenhouse Publishers

- Warlick, David. 2009. "Grow Your Personal Learning Network: New Technologies Can Keep You Connected and Help You Manage Information Overload". *Learning & Leading with Technology* (March/April 2009) : 12-16. http://landmark-project.com/workshops/handouts/gypln_ll.pdf

- Wiggins, Grant and Jay McTighe. 2005. *Understanding by Design*, expanded 2nd ed. Upper Saddle River, NJ: Pearson Prentice Hall.

- Willms, J. D., Friesen, S. and Milton, P. 2009. *What Did You Do in School Today? Transforming Classrooms Through Social, Academic, and Intellectual Engagement.* (First National Report). Toronto, ON: Canadian Education Association. http://www.cea-ace.ca/programs-initiatives/wdydist

- Wolfe, Patricia. 2001. *Brain Matters: Translating Research into Classroom Practice.* Alexandria, VA: Association for Supervision and Curriculum Development.

Chapter 11

Everyone Wins
in the Learning Commons

In 1938, a depression weary United States desperately needed some new encouragement. It would come from a long-shot horse named Seabiscuit. To trained horse owners, Seabiscuit was a dismal disappointment. But one owner saw in him a spark of potential worth the investment. And then, there was also that has-been jockey the owner spotted – a pair of misfits that just might make a perfect match. It wasn't just the acquisition of both that worked, but the long experimenting and training regimen. That year, Seabiscuit would face the sleek, beautiful, popular, and fast, Triple Crown winner War Admiral. The underdog triumphed. A nation cheered, and Seabiscuit had provided a breath of fresh optimism in a dreary landscape.

We have titled this book, *The New Learning Commons: Where Learners Win,* very intentionally. Faced with bleak news about public education on all sides, with demands for improvement and with assessments that measure only part of what we value, we have journeyed through our own 180 degree thinking. We have pondered about the role of school libraries and computer labs, some of which are outmoded dismal places, and which are in deep decline. We have researched what the education experts and futurists have been saying about learning for the future, and we have studied the work of educators who are really making a difference. We became convinced that each word of the title had to express what we really have envisioned. *New,* because everything needs to be rethought. *Learning,* because libraries as storage spaces and computer labs used for machine skills have to shift. *Commons,* because ownership has to be transferred to clients. *Learners,* because they are the hope of each nation. And *Win,* because global forces make teaching and learning today much more complex and yet stimulating in our 'flat world'.

For all of you who have stuck with us through this journey, we want to end this book with not only a vision of what the winners circle looks like, that blanket of roses signaling triumph, but also the various markers along the track that measure our progress towards the finish line. Our first realization was that no single horse had to win. That as we focus on the learners, everyone in the educational business will win.

The Learning Commons whole school approach to learning for the future offers a vision of success for the entire school community. The mantra of a Learning Commons is learning for all for a lifetime, helping everyone get better and better at whatever they are trying to do. Everyone is a learner, and everyone is a winner.

Learning Commons Winners Circle

Why do so many win as the Learning Commons is envisioned, trained, groomed, practiced and raced? Let's make a checklist around the circle. Add your ideas to ours.

The Learning Commons provides:

Learners

- A sense of command over personal learning
- A central place for both formal and informal learning
- An environment for creating, collaborating, thinking, doing, and enjoying learning
- Resources and coaching to build personal expertise and collaborative intelligence
- Support for projects and other information needs 24/7
- The center of school culture
- Validation of student suggestions and contributions

Classroom Teachers

- A place for collaboration, team teaching, sharing assessment responsibilities, and demonstrating how two heads are better than one
- A stage for the best learning experiences we can create
- An extension of the classrooms
- A place of experimentation, risk taking, failure, and success
- A place to assess knowledge building, critical thinking, learning to learn skills and dispositions
- A haven of support for differentiation, resources, and instruction

Administrators

- The center of school improvement, experimentation, and action research
- A snapshot of the work of the school community
- A showcase of the best of the best learning experiences across the school
- The first stop in a school tour
- The school center of Learning Leadership

Teacher Librarians

- The center of teaching and learning in the school
- Collaboration central both in physical and virtual space
- Access, access, access
- The integration center for information and other learning literacies
- A reading community

Teacher Technologists

- The hot spot n the school for teaching and learning with technology
- Collaboration central both in physical and virtual space
- Access, access, access
- A power boost to learning through technology
- Maximum efficiency and integration of technology and technical expertise

Other Specialists

- A place where their agenda meshes with classroom teacher agendas

- A collaboration central both in physical and virtual space
- Support for differentiation; resources, and instruction
- Professional learning spaces and supports

Support Personnel
- A dynamic center of teaching and learning
- The center for their support roles and contributions
- The one-stop center for connecting and sharing with staff and students
- Network central for all information needs

Parents
- A point of collaboration to build school culture
- Supports to enable an active role in their children's learning
- A 24/7 virtual connection to current school initiatives and activities
- The center of parent initiatives in support of the school

The Process

Getting to the winners circle requires vision, determination, experimentation, and sustainability. The Learning Commons is much more than an updating of the library, more than a merger with the computer lab, more than a library web presence, more than new technology, and much more than changing the name of the facility. When do you start with your transformation? Where do you start? The track ahead is probably already familiar to you:

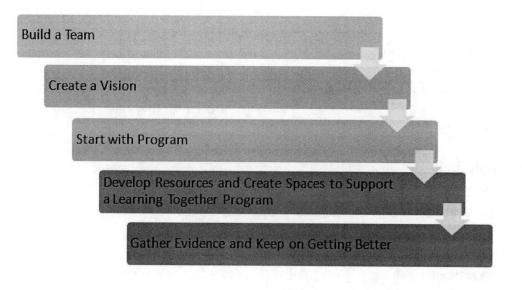

Build a Team

Create a Vision

Start with Program

Develop Resources and Create Spaces to Support a Learning Together Program

Gather Evidence and Keep on Getting Better

Wherever we have seen progress toward the Learning Commons concept, we have seen the essential component of a visionary administrator and 21st Century teacher librarians and teacher technologists at the helm. We counsel administrators to hire the best. We counsel teacher librarians/teacher technologists to build their expertise and then seek a visionary administrator to team with, and then get started, whether there is money or not. Money will be attracted to demonstrated success and outcomes, and these can be achieved in microcosm anywhere and right now.

Register with us in a collaborative support group. Let's talk, share, experiment, explore, stumble, get up, and try again. Join us in the winners circle at:
https://sites.google.com/site/schoollearningcommons/

Digging Deeper
"Libraries aren't going away; old school libraries are going away".
Doug Johnson shares a story on his *Blue Skunk Blog* of evidence gathered by an excited high school teacher librarian, Robin Cicchetti.
http://doug-johnson.squarespace.com/blue-skunk-blog/2010/6/17/close-the-library-guest-post-by-r-cicchetti.html

Bright Ideas to Build On
The following schools and districts are in the midst of transformations and reinventions of school library lab facilities and programs. Explore and learn from these pioneers.

- A Virtual Learning Commons under construction at Markham Middle School
  http://sites.google.com/site/markhamlibrary/

- The Allen Center in New Zealand (Elementary)
  http://allencentre.wikispaces.com/home+page

- Ann Arbor Skyline High School
  http://skyline2.aaps.k12.mi.us/mediacenter/Skyline_Library/Home.html

- Chelmsford High School Learning Commons
  http://www.chelmsford.k12.ma.us/chs/library/index.htm

- Springfield Township High School Virtual Library
  http://www.sdst.org/shs/library/

- Google Apps Project at Adam Scott Collegiate and Vocational Institute
  http://www.adamscott.ca-a.googlepages.com/googleappsproject

- Henry Wise Wood Senior High School's Learning Commons
  http://lc.henrywisewood.ca/

- Earl Haig Secondary School Library http://earlhaig.ca/library/

Video Stories
- "See Sally Research", an inspiring TED Talk by Joyce Valenza
  Shttp://tedxphillyed.com/2011/09/video-post-dr-joyce-valenza-see-sally-research/

- Highly Effective School Librarians - view all 5 videos in the series
  http://www.youtube.com/user/coloradolibraries#p/c/8DD57FDA3F082313/1/Gi8KWFxxACw

- Gwyneth Jones as "The Daring Librarian"
  http://www.youtube.com/watch?v=BX5NXp2BUGc

- Get creative with space at "Shaping Space at The d.school's Environments
  Collaborative" http://vimeo.com/11438598

- Explore more design ideas at "The Library Initiative" of Robin Hood Project
  in New York City http://www.robinhood.org/initiatives/the-l!brary-initiative.aspx

- Get ready for "flash cart" at
  http://www.youtube.com/watch?v=PGTBWLDatas

- View how to make school real in "A short intro to the Studio School" by Geoff
  Mulgan
  http://www.ted.com/talks/geoff_mulgan_a_short_intro_to_the_studio_school.html?utm_source=newsletter_weekly_2011-09-27&utm_campaign=newsletter_weekly&utm_medium=email

Elementary School Journeys Towards a Learning Commons
- Belfast School
  http://media.stream.cbe.ab.ca/media/LearningCommons/BelfastLC.wmv

- Monterey Park School
  <http://media.stream.cbe.ab.ca/media/LearningCommons/ElemLC.wmv>

- Elizabeth Rummel Elementary School
  http://www.youtube.com/watch?v=EpwhQYafNp4

Secondary School Learning Commons Transitions

- Stevenson High School Information and Learning Center in Lincolnshire, Illinois.
  http://www.d125.org/library/default.aspx

- Crescent Heights High School - CHHS Learning Commons Part 1
  http://www.youtube.com/watch?v=lo0gaTzU0qw CHHS Learning Commons Part 2 http://www.youtube.com/watch?v=nVipfjDk6A8&feature=related

District Initiatives

- Waterloo Region District School Board is developing a central Learning Commons http://library.wrdsb.ca/

- The Learning Commons is growing in Calgary
  http://www.innovativelearning.ca/sec-rlc/slib-index.asp

Inspiration

- You Know You're a 21st Century School Librarian When....
  http://informationfluency.wikispaces.com/Categorized+version+of+You+know+you%27re+a+21st+century+school+librarian

- The Best of YouTube for teaching and learning:
  http://www.classroom20.com/profiles/blog/show?id=649749%3ABlogPost%3A177332&page=2

- AASL's Best Websites for Teaching and Learning:
  http://www.ala.org/ala/mgrps/divs/aasl/aboutaasl/bestlist/bestwebsites.cfm

- Review the iCenter approach to discover an Australian version of school libraries of the future. See the *Rethink, Rebuild, Rebrand* slide show by Lynn Hay http://www.slideshare.net/lhay/rethink-rebuild-rebrand-think-icentre
  Also view, her closing keynote at the International Association of School Libraries 2011 conference, *If the Future is Now, What Next?*
  http://www.slideshare.net/lhay/lyn-hays-iasl2011-closing-keynote

Over to You
So What?

Each chapter of this book ends with an *Over to You* invitation to help you explore each section a little deeper and to help you make connections to your own school or district.
Consciously reflect on our suggestions for the Learning Commons, and keep track of new questions as well as connections to other readings and ideas you have as

you work your way through each chapter. Share your ideas on the editable version of each chapter. We also invite you to contribute to the Learning Commons site. https://sites.google.com/site/schoollearningcommons/
Building the Learning Commons philosophy as well as the learning spaces and programs will take the collective minds of all.

As you make your first steps toward change consider these questions:
- What has intrigued you about the reinvention of school libraries and computer labs into a Learning Commons for all?
- What are the benefits for your school community?
- Where would the problems be?
- Where are you now?
- Who are your supporters and how can they help?

What Next?
- Get the word out.
- Review this book with others.
- Analyze the pros and cons.
- Read the research and consider your school strengths.
- Know and understand the process of change.
- Form an inclusive planning team.
- Look at how others are creating a Learning Commons
- Develop an action plan.
- Decide how you will measure success.
- Implement plans, and review, reflect and reinvent as you go.
- Share the process, your problems, and your successes with others.
- Keep getting better together

---

*Today's climate of reform demands that teacher-librarians become advocates for students and teachers. Being an advocate means becoming a change agent and actively and thoughtfully entering the educational conversation. It means having the language and knowledge to move beyond the library and into the wider school community. It requires familiarity with current research on teaching and learning to effectively facilitate the change process. It means carefully listening with an open mind and being responsive to teachers' concerns and questions. It means knowing how and when to communicate and whom to seek out for support. It means learning new skills to achieve the school's vision. Finally, it means being proactive and positive. Although educational change is a journey filled with uncertainty and conflict, it is an immensely rewarding one for students and adult stakeholders. **It is a journey worth leading.***
Harada and Hughes-Hassell (2007)

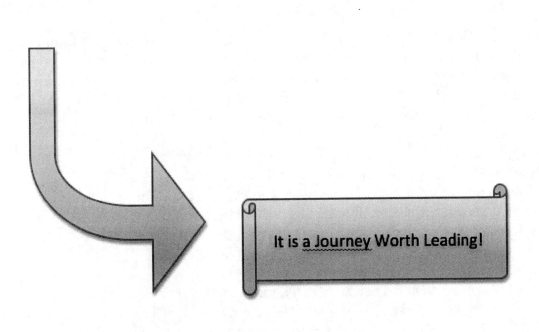

It is a Journey Worth Leading!

References

- Harada, Violet H. and Sandra Hughes-Hassell. 2007. "Facing the Reform Challenge: Teacher-Librarians as Change Agents". *Teacher Librarian* 35 no.2 (December 2007): 8-13.

Resources

- Diggs, Valerie. 2009. "From Library to Learning Commons: a Metamorphosis". *Teacher Librarian* 37 no.4 (April 2009): 32-38. Valerie Diggs of Chelmsford High School in Chelmsford, Massachusetts details her five year journey to transform her library into the band new and very popular Learning Commons.

- Koechlin C., Loertscher D., and Zwaan S. 2007. "The Time is Now: transform your school library into a Learning Commons". *Teacher Librarian* 36 no. 1 (September 2008): 8-14. In this article, teacher librarians are encouraged reinvent their school library and computer labs; listen to clients; build learning partnership teams; infuse the best teaching science; lead the journey in creating a school wide Learning Commons.

- Koechlin, C. 2010. "Leading the Way in the Learning Commons" *Teaching Librarian* 17 no. 2 (2010): 20-23. Discover guiding principles for planning a Learning Commons.

- Loertscher David. 2008. "Flip this Library: School Libraries Need a Revolution," *School Library Journal* (November 2008). http://www.schoollibraryjournal.com/article/CA6610496.html?q=flip+this+library This article challenges the status quo and encourages 180 degree thinking to reinvent the school library into a Learning Commons.

- Martin, L.M., Douglas D. Westmoreland, and Angie Branyon. 2011. "New Design Considerations that Transform the Library into an Indispensible Learning Environment". *Teacher Librarian* 38 no. 5 (June 2011): 15-20. This article describes a more formal transformation of their high school library into a vibrant Learning Commons. Readers will see why Henrico School District was selected as one of the AASL National School Library Programs of the Year.

- Schwelik, Jennifer C. and Theresa M. Frederika. 2011. "INFOhio's 21st Century Learning Commons: Transforming How Educators Use and Think about School Libraries". *Teacher Librarian* 38 no. 5 (June 2011): 21-26. The authors describe how INFOhio created an online professional development environment for K-12 educator. It is an amazing program from a state that continues to lead the profession.

- Waskow, Linda M. 2011. "The Journey from Library Media Center to Learning Commons". *Teacher Librarian* 38 no. 5 (June 2011): 8-14. Waskow recounts her journey transforming the Beaufort, South Carolina Elementary School media center into a lively and inviting Learning Commons and she shows that vision, creativity, imitative, and resourcefulness are worth their weight in gold.

- Cicchetti, Robin. 2010. "Close the Library? Guest Post by Robin Cicchetti". *The Blue Skunk Blog* by Doug Johnson. June 17, 2010. http://doug-johnson.squarespace.com/blue-skunk-blog/2010/6/17/close-the-library-guest-post-by-r-cicchetti.html

Appendix

The following chart is developed to link the articles in the Learning Commons Treasury publication to the appropriate chapters in this book. All the articles were originally published in Teacher Librarian.

Learning Commons: Chapter Connection	Article Title	Author		Pg.
Chapter 1 **The Learning Commons: A Justification**	*The Time is Now: Transform your School Library into a Learning Commons*	C. Koechlin, S. Zwaan, and D. Loertscher	It is time to close the gap between what we know and what we do in schools. We know there is a disconnect between what our students do with technologies inside and outside of school.	3
	Concord-Carlisle Transitions to a Learning Commons	Robin Cicchetti	In 2007 our library was dedicated to books, and it showed... Signage warned, Don't Move Chairs, No Group Work, Don't Talk.	20
	Curriculum, the Library/Learning Commons and the Teacher Librarians: Myths and Realities in the Second Decade	David Loertscher	What needs to be taught to a generation of young people who face incredible global competition? The myths, the realities, and the implications.	37
	Librarians as Learning Specialists: Moving From the Margins to the Mainstream of School Leadership	Allison Zmuda and Violet Harada	The authors believe that our leaders *must* envision the library as integral to students achieving their missions; that the stakes of preparing students for the 21st century world have never been higher.	111
Chapter 3 **Knowledge Building in the Learning Commons**	*The Library is the Place: Knowledge and Thinking, Thinking and Knowledge*	Derek Cabrera and Laura Colosi	It appears by what we assess, that content knowledge is vastly more important that thinking. But is it?	43
	Gifted Readers and Libraries: A Natural Fit	Rebecca Haslam-Odoardi	Can the two even be separated?	77

			Jenna, a fourth grader, thinks the library is the best place in the entire school. The librarian understands that to keep her engaged in reading, Jenna needs books that are challenging and exciting, and that make her think deeper about what she reads.	
Chapter 4 **Learning Literacies and the Learning Commons**	*The Role of the School Library in the Reading Program*	Betty Marcoux and David Loertscher	Learning to read and reading to learn is every bit as important in the 21st century as it has ever been. The ability to read and read well affects every part of our existence and often predicts success throughout life.	49
	Information Literate? Just Turn the Children Loose!	Joy Mounter	Joy describes a process of taking command of one's own learning that is both a remarkable and an essential element of the literacy program of the Learning Commons.	73
	Information and Technology Literacy	Bill Derry	Bill shares the successes and challenges of working together to utilize information technology literacy skills and strategies in daily teaching in his school district.	117
Chapter 5 **Technology and the Learning Commons**	*Achieving Teaching and Learning Excellence With Technology*	Betty Marcoux and David Loertscher	The authors identify roadblocks to learning, diagnose learning problems, and then search for tools and best practices to overcome the problem.	85
	Supporting 21st Century Learning Through Google Apps	Roger Nevin	Roger describes how students and teachers use Google Apps; how it provides a common system that supplies all the	94

			applications they need, under one platform, at no extra cost.	98
	The Effect of Web 2.0 on Teaching and Learning in the 21st Century	Richard Byrne	One classroom teacher's personal success story as he embraced computers and the Internet, piqued the interest of his students, and saw improved results.	
Chapter 6 **Collaboration and the Learning Commons**	*Three Heads are Better than One: The Reading Coach, the classroom teacher, and The Teacher Librarian*	Christopher Lamb, Winnie Porter and Carol Lopez	Through working together, this team was able to ensure that student learning went well beyond what students were asked to do.	122
	Advanced Contemporary Literacy: An Integrated approach to Reading	Sharon Swarner	This school district set out to replace tired novel studies with high thinks and active learning experiences and reaped the benefits.	124
	Technology Leadership: Kelly Czarnecki	TL's Editors	In this interview Kelly shares her insight and ideas about technology, the teaching profession, and teacher librarianship.	120
Chapter 7 **Personal Learning Environments in the Learning Commons**	*Rethinking Collaboration: Transforming Web .o into Real-time Behavior*	Sheila Cooper-Simon	Patterns of interaction must be flexible and evolving constantly, if they are to be relevant. The author is constantly reevaluating what she is doing and how she can improve services in her library.	81
	The Impact of Facebook on our Students	Doug Foderman and Marje Monroe	This article cautions us about many of the negative consequences possible when students use social network sites.	104

Chapter 8	*From Library to Learning Commons: A Metamorphosis*	Valerie Diggs, with editorial comments David Loerstcher	Valerie's account of the transformation, with editorial comments, provides an analysis of how TLs can move to the center of teaching and learning.	13
Building the Learning Commons as a Client-side Organization	*From Book Museum to Learning Commons: Riding the Transformation Train*	Christina Bentheim	Transformation is possible with a strong mission, vision, and goals. If you want change to happen badly enough you have to be the change agent.	31
	WLANS for the 21st Century Library	Cal Calamari	Wireless Local Area Networks are an important component in a Learning Commons. Cal helps us understand what they do, how they do it, and how we can benefit.	101
Chapter 9	*The Learning Commons is Alive and Well in New Zealand*	Peggy Steadman and Greg Carroll	The Learning Commons of the Outram School was designed to provide support for teaching and learning, not simply as a place to store books and hope someone would take them home and read them.	27
School Improvement and the Learning Commons	*Influencing Positive Change: The Vital Behaviors to Turn Schools toward Success*	Vicki Davis	Vicki hypothesizes that six vital behaviors hold the key to positive transformation in schools.	55
	Cultivating Curious Mind: Teaching for Innovation Through Open-Inquiry Learning	Jean Sausele Knodt	The mission of the described open-inquiry lab is to engage innovative thinking in students by opening up, extending, and guiding the inquisitive energy children naturally bring to the table.	66
	Using the library learning commons to reengage disengaged students and make it a student-friendly place	Cynthia Sargeant and Roger Nevin	When disengaged students are called to the library they tend to arrive relaxed and in a more positive frame of mind because there aren't negative	81

Everyone Wins: Differentiation in the School Library	Carol Koechlin and Sandi Zwaan	connotations associated with the library. What does differentiation in look like in the Learning Commons? How can the Learning Commons contribute to the opportunity for differentiation?	60
Creating Personal Learning Through Self Assessment	Jean Donham	Jean explains how self assessment can become a habit of mind that engages learners in metacognition and reflection.	129
Our Instruction Does Matter! Data Collected From Students' Works Cited Speaks Volumes	Sara Pionier and Jennifer Alevy	Collecting and scoring students' works cited pages demonstrated that their role as collaborative, reflective practitioners really did make a difference.	137
The Big Think: Reflecting, Reacting and Realizing Improved Learning	Carol Koechlin and Sandi Zwaan	A Big Think is critical not only to the content learned but also to the learning process for both teachers and learners. Included are nine metacognative strategies.	139

Glossary

Definitions in this glossary refer to the context of use in this document.

AASL – The American Association of School Librarians

action research –assessing and testing the impact of strategies, ideas, practices, or initiatives with actual classes of learners as they work through a new initiative. Findings apply to those particular classes, but patterns do emerge for broader use

active listening – processing what is being said while it is being said vs. "in one ear and out the other"

administrative computing – the computer system in the school and district that handles budgets, attendance, grades, or any other official data; well protected against hackers

analytical thinking – considering information and situations from a variety of perspectives, breaking down, sorting, reorganizing, testing, making connections to empower synthesis

Assistive technologies - Any device that assists you as a human in working in the world of information or in the real world. For example, hearing aids, magnification, search engines, text to speech, etc.

backwards planning – application of three stages when designing a learning experience; identify desired results, determine acceptable evidence and plan learning experiences and instruction

big think - an elevated group activity occurring after the creation of a product (the report, product, poster, or individual presentation) when the unit would traditionally end; all the students combine what they have learned as a group rather than end with the expertise gained by an individual investigation., to answer "So What" and "How is this new knowledge relevant ? e.g., What do we know about the significance of the African American experience; not, what do I know about the African American I studied.

cadres of learners – adult or student groupings of any kind, by skill, need, interest, mixed etc.

calendars of the Learning Commons – two calendars used to schedule operations of the Open Commons and the Experimental Learning Center, both open to clients on an as-need basis as opposed to former practice of scheduling classes once a week for teacher prep periods

client-side organization - the needs and interests of users are paramount in planning, teaching and learning, organization, and resources, rather than putting the needs of the organization first

coach - facilitate learning, create conditions conducive to learning; guide, nudge, prompt, encourage, and respond rather than tell, direct, command, etc.

collaboration – planning, teaching and assessing learning experiences as a pair or group of teachers and specialists vs. teaching alone in an isolated classroom

collaborative knowledge building – working together to construct understanding to build a body of knowledge

collaboration logs – notes kept by classroom teachers and specialists as they co-teach a learning experience; valuable as a documentation of success and challenges, particularly useful as professional learning communities engage in serious discussion of teaching and learning

collection mapping – graphical representation of the strengths and weaknesses of a collection of resources both physical and digital; a quick way to assess the current state of resources and make judgments on the direction the collection should take

collective intelligence – the combined knowledge of a group where everyone has contributed

computer lab – a previous model of the expanded technology services now integrated into the Learning Commons *co-teaching* – team teaching, two or more professionals who work together to plan, teach, coach, and assess progress of a group of learners together

constructivist – a strategy of teaching that requires learners to take a great deal of the responsibility to learn the task and topic at hand

content instruction – teaching of topical knowledge such as mathematics, science, social studies

critical thinking – applying high level thinking and reasoning skills such as analysis, evaluation, and synthesis to develop understanding and facilitate transfer and creation

cross curricular – involving more than one subject or discipline, subject integration, e.g., combining standards from social studies, music, and art in a learning experience

deep understanding- making sense of the big and important ideas; relating to and able to communicate new learning

differentiated instruction – learning experiences designed to ensure success for all students; modifying content, process, environment , and product to empower all learners to achieve

Digital Citizens - users of the world of the Internet who have the ethical stance to understand and practice acceptable behavior on wikis, blogs, and the use of intellectual property during content creation. They understand copyright and attribution of materials and resources they incorporate into their own production. They understand and fight against scams, and other practices designed to tear down vs. support other learners and users of kigital space

digital resources – information and multimedia available via computer to teachers and learners at all hours of the day and night and in any location, whether at school, home, or on vacation. e.g., periodical databases, streaming video, Internet access, computer software and tools, learner-created media, ebooks, digitized textbooks, etc.

elastic collections – access to, resources, rather than ownership of ; the "collection" of materials available to teachers and learners ebbs and flows as demands are placed upon it

empathy – seeing and understanding another person's feelings and views about the world, understanding the reasons for differing opinions , and being able to identify with them

empowered learning – learning dispositions enhanced by conditions and support, conducive to and necessary for optimum learning potential

engaging – creating interest to motivate the learner to participate and achieve

evidence-based practice - improving teaching and learning based on 'what works' and 'what the experts say'; gathering demonstrations of success, analyzing the evidence and then using it to change or tweak practice

excellence – teaching and learning beyond minimal expectations or the specific standards

Experimental Learning Center – the place both physical and virtual where professional development, action research, and experimental programs are being tests, exhibited, and analyzed before going out for widespread adoption in the rest of the school.

expert bar – a service either physical or virtual, in the Learning Commons, where students and adults provide individual or small group advice and informal tutorials on software and hardware

extended learning – learning in depth, for deep understanding rather than surface learning of a body of factual knowledge

filters – blocks to undesirable or inappropriate Internet web sites

flexible scheduling – an open calendar for the Learning Commons that invites clients (teachers or groups of learners) to reserve time to use specific physical facilities and specialists of the Learning Commons

formative assessments – assessments of learning done before and during a learning experience to measure progress toward the learning goals

Google model – a client-side organization where users are provided many tool choices; services they require and help create, with the philosophy that if they build it, they will use it.

group reflection – looking back and assessing the impact of a learning experience done together as teachers and/or learners

Habits of Mind – certain intellectual dispositions and routines systematically applied to learning situations

Hack - To gain access to another person's code or creations without permission with the intent of destroying the intention for which the code and purpose of the program or site is disrupted.

ICT literacy – Instructional Communications Technology; the various tools of technology used to enhance the teaching and learning process

Information circles - small groups studying how to learn in an information rich world.

information coach – one of the roles of a teacher librarian; guiding teachers and learners in how to seek, use, analyze, judge, present, and think about the vast quantities of information available

information literacy – the ability to question, find quality information, consume that information with understanding, analyze and synthesize, draw conclusions, present, communication, and finally reflect on the process and the product

information space – a digital space under control of the user; a personal space such as an iGoogle page or a personal website constructed by the user

inquiry learning – an instructional method where students construct personal meaning by working with diverse information and ideas to solve a problem or inquiry questions; a circular process, (in which teachers are facilitators,) designed to engage students in higher levels of thinking, investigating, testing of ideas and the creation and communication of new knowledge

instructional computing – the computer system in the school and district where the tools, networks, and information to support teaching and learning reside; contrary to the administrative computing, this space is open and available to all teachers and learners

ISTE - International Society for Technology in Education

job-embedded professional development – is learning that occurs as educators engage in their daily work rather than transmission of knowledge and skills to teachers by experts alone; can be formal or informal, e.g., discussion, peer coaching, mentoring, study groups and action research

just in time – the practice of teaching a skill at the time when that skill will be needed to pursue an assignment or project

knowledge building – a constructivist activity, individual or collaborative, where inquiries and research are conducted to build deep personal understanding; understanding is advanced with planned teacher interventions such as question prompts, graphic organizers and conferencing

learner-constructed information systems- client side technology systems created with input from users and designed to meet the users' need and wishes

Learning Commons – the place, either physical or virtual that is the hub of the school, where exemplary teaching and learning are showcased, where all professional development, teaching and learning experimentation and action research happen; and where the various specialists of the school office, (whether virtually or physically).

learning dispositions – learners' attitude and behaviors toward the learning process

learning experience – any activities, taught and coached by teachers or specialists, which engage learners in the pursuit of knowledge and understanding *learning leadership team* – the group of adults and learner representatives working with teachers and learners to improve the quality of teaching and learning in the school

learning literacies leadership team – the group of adults and learner representatives working together to create conditions to improve the skill levels of all learners and across all literacies

learning organization – a school whose teachers and learners are focused on high quality teaching and learning

learning science - an interdisciplinary field that studies teaching and learning to create more effective learning experiences; sciences of learning include cognitive science, educational psychology, computer science, sociology, neuroscience and other fields.

learning specialist – any of the specialists in the school other than the classroom teacher, such as the teacher librarian, teacher technologist, literacy coach, etc.

learning to learn– applying the many skills and behaviors associated with the process of learning itself; utilizing tools and techniques that assist in the learning process; learning how to learn as opposed to just learning content

library – a predecessor of the Learning Commons

Library Media Center – a predecessor of the Learning Commons

library web sites- school specific sites created and maintained by staff and students to facilitate the teaching and learning needs of the school

literacies – skills necessary to function successfully in school and the world at large as a "literate" citizen, lifelong learning skills including reading, writing, listening, communicating, media Literacy, visual literacy, information literacy, ICT literacy, and emerging literacies

literature circles –collaborative study of student chosen reading in temporary groups; learners record their connections as they read, and at set times share.

They may have roles within the study group as long as discussion is kept natural and free flowing

long term sustainability model- ongoing PD, action research, rethinking and redesigning to address school needs

media literacy – critical interpretation and understanding of all types of media, and creation of new media messages, e.g., seeing through the spin, being a healthy skeptic of media, advertising, messages such as political propaganda; creating a podcast to inform

mentor bar – a physical and virtual service provided in the Learning Commons where strategies and advice to support teaching and learning is available to both teachers and learners

metacognition – literally, thinking about one's thinking; the process of examining the strategies one uses to learn and make plans for improvement

Microsoft model – a command and control organization; top down; pyramid organizational structure, with the philosophy that if we build it, they will come

NETS – National Educational Technology Standards for students; a project of the International Society for Technology in Education (ISTE) that defines standards for teachers and students in the area of technology and learning

on demand – just in time, instruction or coaching available when needed

on-demand networks – computer networks accessible across the school campus and in the homes of teachers and learners

on-demand support – available advice and troubleshooting either in person or from a distance for systems, networks, technology and services, e.g,. homework help

online education - the delivery of instruction via the Internet either fully or partially rather than the traditional face to face meeing

Open Commons – The place, both physical and virtual where classes, individuals, small groups, events are scheduled to benefit from the support and expertise of specialists, the resources, and the comfortable learning environment. The Open Commons is not regularly scheduled by any group but is available using its own calendaring system. It is the place where one can observe the highest quality of teaching and learning throughout the school

open source – the altruistic movement by programmers and groups of programmers to make available computer software to the masses either free or inexpensively; e.g., Open Office

organizational Leadership Team - The group of professionals and learner representatives that govern the operation of the entire Learning Commons

peer evaluation - assessing progress of an equal, based on predetermined criteria

perpetual beta – technology, software, teaching and learning strategies, and skills continually evolving rather than being static

PLE - personal learning environment; the act of creating an interface between yourself and the web; the portal to the web itself, building your own personal learning network, and developing your own eportfolio

PLN - personal learning network; the construction of a system by which you attach yourselv to various persons or organizations on the Web in order to receive their email, blog, twitter, or other feeds.

problem solving – employing critical thinking and information literacy skills to reach a solution or understanding, e.g., finding and analyzing various perspectives on an issue to uncover causes and suggest solutions

professional development – an initiative to help both teachers and specialists sharpen their skills and be more effective at their jobs

professional learning communities PLC – groups of teachers engaged in specific discussion, experimentation, development, grant writing, and any other projects to improve teaching and learning throughout the school

rich learning environments – materials, resources, and technology beyond the traditional teacher, textbook, and lecture

Route 21 – the initiative of the Partnership for 21st Century Learning

RSS feed - a method of linking yourself to another website or blog or wiki in order to receive constant notice of anything that changes on the source your are interested in.

safe instructional computing systems - *networks in which learners can flourish without interruption by unwanted guests, advertising and other bothersome messages*

shadow leadership - watermark leadership, in the background; not dictating or looking over the shoulder but always there to support, guide, and assist

social networking - the interaction between or linking of a group of people who share a common interest by way of discussion, sharing, and collaborating

specialists – all adult professionals who consult in the Learning Commons and work with classroom teachers and learners to integrate their specialty into the curriculum of the school through both in class and pull-out programs. e.g., teacher librarians, teacher technologists, literacy coaches, nurses, counselors, art, music, history, physical education teachers; including administrators

summative assessments – assessments conducted at the end of a learning experience

support staff – the support staff of the Learning Commons consists of computer technicians, clericals, and assistants who handle much of the operation of the Open Commons such as circulation, processing of materials and scheduling of the Open Commons

sustainable excellence – adoption of strategies across the school that are likely to continue to make a difference over time as opposed to a short-term initiative

teacher librarian – the professional who is the full time information specialist in the Learning Commons and leads in the collaborative construction of learning experiences, designing collections, information literacy programs, development of the Virtual Learning Commons, development of the Virtual Exemplary Learning Center, leader in action research and professional development, Use of Web 2.0 to enhance learning,and supports for all staff and students; replacing terms librarian, library media specialist, media specialist, etc.

teacher technologist - the professional who leads the instructional computing program of the school and whose time is devoted to the integration of technology to advance teaching and learning. Often known as technology directors, teacher technologists, technology integrationists.

technology leadership team – the group of adults and learner representatives who orchestrate implementation of hardware, software, and the integration of technology into teaching and learning; school leaders for instructional computing

technology director – See teacher technologist

technology specialist – See the term: teacher technologist

tipping point – an event that triggers a major change

transfer – the ability to apply or use knowledge and understanding in new and different situations, with different topics or for different purposes

triangulation of evidence – evidence collected from the organization level, the teaching unit level, and the learner level, used to compare and contrast in order to identify successes and challenges in the educational program of the school

user centric – designed based on the needs, wishes, learning styles, intelligences, and *real life* habits of the users

Virtual Learning Commons – consists of both an Open Commons and Experimental Learning Center, but accessible on line and available 24/7/365

visual literacy – ability to read and interpret pictures, charts, illustrations; e.g., understanding how visuals can be manipulated with technology to affect the impression given

Web 2.0 – Tools and software available on the World Wide Web that are usually collaborative in nature and often free to anyone. E.g. wikis, blogs, nings, and a host of other creative and collaborative tools

Web 3.0 - An emerging format for the web known as the syntactical web.

wireless – access to the Internet from anywhere in the Learning Commons on any preferred computing device without the restriction of a hard connection

Index

21st Century Literacies, 54
21st Century Skills, 128
21st Century Standards, 57

Action research, 175+, 183
Administrative computing, 78+
Administrative leadership, 150,
Administrators, 31, 60, 64, 84, 110, 132, 163+, 166, 169, 219
Assistive technologies, 98

Background knowledge, 175
Big Think, 38+
Brain-based learning, 198

Calendars of the LC, 144
Center for Critical Thinking, 189
Character development in tech space, 86+
Client-side model, 4+
Collaboration, 107+
Collaboration, benefits of, 112+
Collaborative environments, 109
Collaborative Help Center, 93
Collaborative technologies, 97+
Connections to other ideas, 183+
Constructing knowledge, 78
Costa, Arthur, 195
Crevola, Carmel, 185
Critical Literacy, 55
Current Crisis, The, 203

Difference, 163+
Differentiated instruction, 199
Digital citizenship, 88+
Digital Literacy, 55,
Dodge, Bernie, 186
DuFour, Richard, 194

Eaker, Robert, 194
Evidence based practice central, 165, 174
Evolution of Learning, 27
Evolving Literacies, 55

Experimental Learning Center, 14+

Financial efficiency, 146
Five Minds for the Future, 200
Flexible learning spaces, 143
Flip classroom, 28
Fullen, Michael, 185, 209

Gardner, Howard, 200
Google Model, 2
Guided Inquiry, 201

Habits of Mind, 195
Harada, Vi, 225
Heppell, Stephen, 196
Hill, Peter, 185
Homework assistance, 145

Implement Enablers, 116
Indicators of learning, 31, 60, 84, 110, 132, 163+, 169
Information literacy, 55
Instructional computing, 78+
Instructional designs, 36+
International Baccalaureate Schools, 197
Intervention, 163+

Jenkins, Henry, 202

Kallick, Bena, 195
Knowledge building centers, 34+
Knowledge building in the LC, 25+
Krashen, Stephen, 190
Kuhlthau, Carol, 201

Learner level assessment, 168
Learners, 30, 219
Learners, empowerment of, 57, 83+, 110, 130, 140, 169+
Learners – self-directed, 31
Learners win, 5+
Learning and learning to learn, 163
Learning and technology, 94+

Learning Commons organizational structure, 139
Learning Commons Partnership Team, 20, 115, 147
Learning Commons tour, 11
Learning Commons, elements of, 143
Learning Leadership Team, 43+, 149
Learning Literacies Leadership Team, 68, 148
Learning Literacies, 53+, 61
Learning Skills Journey, 61
Learning Tech Central, 82+
Learning to Learn, 207
Learning to learn, 56
Literacies, 67
Literacy and Libraries, 204
Literacy Central, 64

Marzano, Robert, 184
Media Literacy, 55
Microsoft Model, 2
Multi-modal Literacy, 55

Multiple intelligence, 200

Networks and technology, 92+
Networks for evidence based practice, 178
Networks for experimentation, 116
Networks for the PLE, 134
New learning models, 3
November, Alan, 188

On demand user friendly support, 153
Open Commons, 12+
Organization level assessment, 167
Organizational Leadership Team, 147+
Organizational reconstruction, 156+

Parents, 220
Participatory Culture, 202
Partnership teams, 20
Personal digital space, 87
Personal Knowledge Building Environments, 131

Personal Learning Environments (PLE), 125
Personal learning environments, physical, 129
Personal learning network, 86, 128
Personal organization spaces, 31+
Personal technology access, 32
Plagiarism, 176
PLAY: Participatory Learning and You, 210
PLE elements, 129
Portal building, 127
Portfolio, 128
Problem-based learning, 29
Professional development, 146
Professional learning communities, 194
Professions in the LC, 152
Program elements of the LC, 21
Project New Media Literacies, 210
Public face and image, 32

Questioning, 205

Reading capacity, 58
Research process, 62
Rheingold, Howard, 89
Richardson, Will, 192

School improvement, 161
School libraries, history of, 1+
Science Leadership Academy, 87
Self-directed learners, 31
Six Secrets of Change, The, 209
Social interaction, 111
Specialist staff of the LC, 149
Specialists, empowering of, 173
Staffing of the LC, 152
Standards of Professional Learning, 211
Support personnel, 150, 220
Sustainable excellence, 164
Systems and networks for knowledge building, 44+
Systems and technology, 92+
Systems for evidence based practice, 178

Systems for experimentation, 116
Systems for the PLE, 134
Systems that support literacies, 67

Teacher librarian, 150+, 219
Teacher technologist, 151+
Teacher technologists, 219
Teachers, 219
Teachers, empowerment of, 90+, 111, 132,
    141, 171+, 62,
Teaching and technology, 91
Teaching Unit level assessment, 167
Technologies, collaborative, 97+
Technology, 77+
Technology and learning, 94+
Technology assistance, 144+
Technology Leadership Team, 99, 148
Technology systems, 92+
Technology transformed learning
    environments, 29
Think models of instructional design,
    36+
Todd, Ross, 3, 201
Transformation, 263+
Transliteracy, 55
Triangulation of evidence, 167+
Tutorial assistance, 145

Virtual Experimental Learning
    Center, 17+
Virtual learning, 98
Virtual Learning Commons, 15+
Virtual Open Commons, 16+
Visual Literacy, 55

Warlick, David, 191
WebQuests, 186
What Did You Do in School Today?, 208
Whole Child initiative (ASCD), 193
Winners circle, 218

About the Authors

David V. Loertscher is a "virtual" professor of library and information science at San Jose State University in San Jose California but lives in Salt Lake City, Utah. He is a prolific author and speaker internationally, a past president of the American Association of School Librarians, and the current co-editor of the periodical: *Teacher Librarian*. He can be contacted at: reader.david@gmail.com and his website is: http://davidvl.org

Carol Koechlin is an experienced educator who after formal retirement continues to contribute to the field of information literacy and school librarianship writing books, articles for professional journals, facilitating on-line courses, and presenting workshops in Canada and the United States. Her current work is to help schools address the needs of learners by teaching questioning skills and designing 'high think' assignments and projects that ignite student interest and utilize collaborative learning environments. Working with Dr. David Loertscher, and Sandi Zwaan, the trio has developed foundations for the transformation of school libraries and computer labs into a Learning Commons. Schools are invited to view and participate in this work in progress at http://schoollearningcommons.pbworks.com/

Sandi Zwaan has a long career as a teacher, educator, and consultant in the public schools of Ontario, Canada. She lives in Brighton, Ontario.

Esther Rosenfeld is the former editor of *Teacher Librarian: the Journal for School Library Professionals* and is the former Coordinator of Library and Learning Resources for the Toronto District School Board, one of the largest school districts in North America. She has been the lead writer for publications of the Toronto District School Board, the Ontario Ministry of Education, and was co-editor of *Toward a 21st-Century School Library Media Program*, published by Scarecrow Press and Hi Willow Research and Publishing. A past president of the Ontario Library Association and the Ontario School Library Association, Esther is now an educational and school library consultant.